Buffer ETFs

by Stuart Chaussée

for dummies
A Wiley Brand

Buffer ETFs For Dummies®

Published by: **John Wiley & Sons, Inc.,** 111 River Street, Hoboken, NJ 07030-5774, www.wiley.com

For general information on our other products and services, please contact our Customer Care Department within the U.S. at 877-762-2974, outside the U.S. at 317-572-3993, or fax 317-572-4002. For technical support, please visit https://hub.wiley.com/community/support/dummies.

Wiley publishes in a variety of print and electronic formats and by print-on-demand. Some material included with standard print versions of this book may not be included in e-books or in print-on-demand. If this book refers to media that is not included in the version you purchased, you may download this material at http://booksupport.wiley.com. For more information about Wiley products, visit www.wiley.com.

Library of Congress Control Number: 2026943248

ISBN 978-1-394-40808-5 (pbk); ISBN 978-1-394-40810-8 (ebk); ISBN 978-1-394-40809-2 (ebk)

SKY10165583_081426

Contents at a Glance

Table of Contents

Introduction

Investing is often a tradeoff between risk and reward, but what if that tradeoff could be reshaped? What if you could track the return of the S&P 500 but add protection against the first 10 percent loss? In exchange, would you be willing to cap your return at 15 percent over the next 12 months? Buffer ETFs enable you to make tradeoffs like these, serving as an innovative tool designed to help investors participate in market growth while managing downside risk. Whether you're navigating uncertain markets or seeking greater control over outcomes, buffer ETFs offer a compelling middle ground between traditional unhedged equity investing and capital preservation.

Unfortunately, many investors have never heard of these innovative products. As a result, they're not utilizing a powerful investment tool — one that may help them stay more comfortably invested in uncertain markets and potentially provide a level of protection when markets head south.

Don't make the same mistake. To become a savvy investor, you should be familiar with all the tools at your disposal, including buffer ETFs. And if you're unfamiliar with them, you've come to the right place. *Buffer ETFs For Dummies* is your guide to these intriguing defined outcome investments.

About This Book

This book is designed to demystify buffer ETFs, making them more accessible to individual investors and financial professionals. It begins by breaking down what buffer ETFs are, how they're structured, and how they behave in various market scenarios — from bear markets to bull markets and every scenario in between. From there, it provides guidance on how to find and research different buffer ETFs, equipping you with the knowledge and skills to select buffer ETFs that align with your investment objectives and risk tolerance.

Beyond the fundamentals, this book dives into practical portfolio applications to explain how buffer ETFs can be used alone, together, and in combination with other investments and how to use various buffer ETF strategies to tailor your risk and return objectives. It also explores different types of buffer ETFs and covers more advanced topics that can help you refine your approach.

Whether you're an investor seeking a smoother ride through volatile markets or a financial advisor looking to expand your toolkit with targeted outcome solutions for your clients, this book provides a clear path to understanding buffer ETFs and using them to help achieve your investment objectives.

Foolish Assumptions

As you'll soon discover when you start reading this book, I discourage people from making assumptions about anything related to investing their money, such as assuming that a 60/40 stock/bond portfolio will protect their investment capital in every market scenario. However, to more effectively target the content of this book to your needs, I made the following foolish assumptions about you:

- You're an investor, or you're a financial professional who advises investors or manages their portfolios.
- You have some basic knowledge about investing. For example, you know the difference between stocks and bonds, and you can tell a bear market from a bull market.
- You have some skin in the game (investment capital).
- You value clarity and predictability. You'd rather hit singles and doubles than swing for the fences and strike out a lot.
- You may be generally dissatisfied with a traditional asset allocation, such as the classic 60/40 portfolio.
- You're willing to consider adding an alternative investment to your total portfolio mix to potentially improve your overall performance over the long term.

Icons Used in This Book

Throughout this book, icons in the margins highlight certain types of valuable information that call out for some special attention. Here are the icons you'll encounter and a brief description of each.

REMEMBER

Ideally, you'll remember everything you read in this book, but that's a big ask, so at least remember the important points flagged with this icon.

TIP

The Tip icon flags faster, cheaper, or more efficient ways to perform a task or achieve an objective.

WARNING

"Pump the brakes!" Before you take another step, read these warnings. I provide this cautionary content to help you avoid the common pitfalls that are otherwise likely to set you back on your path to successful investing.

TECHNICAL STUFF

This icon flags any content that's likely to make the average reader's eyes glaze over. If you're fascinated by high-level financial topics, you might find this content interesting. Otherwise, you can safely skip it.

Where to Go from Here

As with all *For Dummies* guides, you can read this book from cover to cover or skip around to the topics you find most interesting or applicable to your situation. If you choose to skip around, use the table of contents at the front of the book or the extensive index at the back of the book as your guide.

To make this book easier to navigate, I divided it into the following six parts:

- **Part 1: Getting Started with Buffer ETFs** brings you up to speed on the basics — what buffer ETFs are, how they work, and whether they're right for you.
- **Part 2: Dipping a Toe into Buffer ETF Investing** covers the fundamentals of investing in buffer ETFs. It explains how to find and research buffer ETFs, choose a level of downside protection that's right for you, and build a buffer ETF portfolio that targets your objectives.
- **Part 3: Investing in Buffer ETFs during Intra-Outcome Periods** addresses variations on the conventional approach to investing in buffer ETFs — buying them at the beginning of their outcome period and holding them for the duration of that period. Here, you discover how to trade buffer ETFs more actively and opportunistically to potentially improve your return or protect your capital beyond the initial buffer.
- **Part 4: Exploring More Buffer ETF Offerings** introduces you to a host of non-conventional buffer ETFs, including step-up strategy, laddered, accelerated, uncapped, and floor ETFs — variations on the standard buffer ETF theme.

- **Part 5: Diving into Advanced Buffer ETF Concepts** enhances your understanding of buffer ETFs by taking a deeper dive into more advanced topics. Here, you get the inside scoop on upside caps, explore different outcome periods and how they impact performance, gain insight into how buffer ETFs reset at the end of their outcome period, and look into the possibility of swapping your bonds for buffer ETFs.
- **Part 6: The Part of Tens** shares ten insights from leaders in the buffer ETF industry and answers ten common questions about buffer ETFs.

Browse through the part titles and chapter titles or simply flip through the book to find something that catches your eye. Feel free to explore the pages and dip into what seems most relevant to you at the moment. You don't need to read the book cover to cover, although you may find yourself compelled to do so as the many aspects of investing in buffer ETFs combine to form a comprehensive guide.

Beyond the Book

As if this book wasn't already packed with a ton of great information on investing in buffer ETFs, you can access the book's Cheat Sheet at `www.dummies.com`. Once on the Dummies site, search for this book's title to find the Cheat Sheet. This Cheat Sheet provides quick and handy information and guidance you can use on the go, including the following:

- An illustrated definition of a *buffer ETF*
- Links to 10 buffer ETF issuer websites
- One big pitfall to avoid and two key points to keep in mind as you start to invest in buffer ETFs
- Five tips for getting the most out of buffer ETFs
- Seven buffer ETF pitfalls along with guidance on how to avoid them

Disclaimer

This publication contains the opinions of its author and is designed to provide useful content in regard to the subject matter covered. However, all content is offered with the understanding that neither the author nor the publisher is engaged in rendering investment, tax, estate planning, or other professional services. If investment or other advice is required, the services of a competent professional should be sought. The author and publisher specifically disclaim any responsibility for liability, loss, or risk, personal or otherwise, that is incurred as a consequence, directly or indirectly, of the use and application of any of the contents of this book.

Notwithstanding anything to the contrary set forth herein, the author, his officers and employees, affiliates, successors and assigns shall not, directly or indirectly, be liable, in any way, to the reader or any other person for any reliance upon the information contained herein, or inaccuracies or errors in, or omissions from the book, including but not limited to financial or investment data.

1

Getting Started with Buffer ETFs

IN THIS PART . . .

Wrap your brain around the buffer ETF concept.

Gain insight into how buffer ETFs function.

Weigh the pros and cons of buffer ETFs.

Determine whether buffer ETFs are a good fit for your investment objectives and risk profile.

IN THIS CHAPTER

» Knowing what a buffer ETF is

» Appreciating what it can do

» Exploring buffer ETF types

» Building a portfolio (the basics)

» Navigating intra-outcome periods

Chapter 1
Brushing Up on Buffer ETF Fundamentals

The longest journey starts with the first step. When it comes to investing in *buffer exchange-traded funds* (buffer ETFs), the first step involves wrapping your brain around the concept, which starts with understanding what they are, what they can and can't do, and how you can use them to build or enhance an investment portfolio.

This chapter covers all that and more while introducing you to key concepts and essential steps covered in greater detail in subsequent chapters.

What Is a Buffer ETF?

In short, a *buffer ETF* is an investment vehicle that enables you to participate in market gains up to a predetermined cap while also setting a defined level of downside protection (the "buffer"), as shown in Figure 1-1. (An *exchange-traded fund*

[ETF] is a basket of securities that trades like a stock; every ETF has its own ticker symbol.) Every buffer ETF is defined by the following five characteristics:

- **Reference asset:** The asset the buffer ETF is designed to track during its defined outcome period, such as SPDR S&P 500 ETF Trust (SPY), Invesco QQQ Trust (QQQ), or iShares Russell 2000 ETF (IWM).
- **Downside buffer:** The initial amount of reference asset loss the fund seeks to protect against over the full outcome period. Typically, the buffer protects against the first loss of 9, 10, 15, or 20 percent, but some funds have deeper buffers offering up to 100 percent protection.
- **Upside cap:** The maximum return the fund can earn over the full outcome period. Caps vary depending on the fund, the buffer level, the underlying reference asset, market conditions (volatility and interest rates), and other factors. Some buffer ETF issuers publish the estimated upside cap levels on their websites beginning one week prior to the start of the new outcome period. The final cap for the new outcome period is determined at the close of trading on the reset date (the last trading day of the outcome period).
- **Outcome period:** The duration the upside cap and downside buffer are in effect, typically 3, 6, or 12 months. During the outcome period, the remaining cap and buffer fluctuate; for example, if the buffer starts at 15 percent, and the reference asset loses 5 percent three months into the fund's 12-month outcome period, the remaining buffer likely will be less than 15 percent, depending on how closely the buffer ETF tracks the reference asset. The cap and buffer reset at the start of each outcome period with fresh downside protection and a new upside cap.
- **ETF wrapper:** The ETF wrapper facilitates the buying and selling process and makes buffer ETFs highly liquid and tax-efficient, meaning they typically contain gains and losses within the fund without creating a taxable event for shareholders.

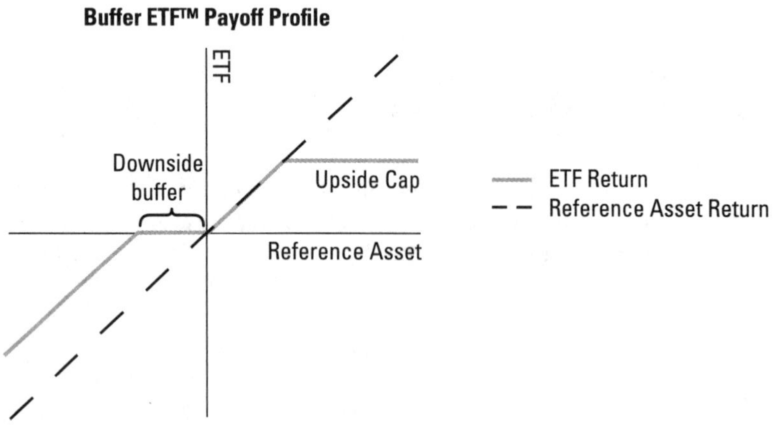

FIGURE 1-1: Buffer ETF payoff profile.

Courtesy of Innovator

Buffer ETFs, often referred to as defined outcome ETFs, are designed to provide more predictable, predetermined outcomes compared to the underlying reference asset they track. You may also see them referred to as *target outcome ETFs* or *buffered ETFs*.

INCREASINGLY POPULAR

Buffer ETFs are one of the fastest-growing segments of the ETF marketplace. According to *Morningstar*, assets have grown from $200 million in 2018 to over $80 billion in 2026, with more than 400 buffer ETFs trading on U.S. markets. Their growing popularity isn't surprising. After all, they're getting a lot of positive press. Here's a small sample:

> ". . . buffer ETFs draw billions amid jitters over market swings." — *The Wall Street Journal*
>
> "These ETFs promise protection in a down market. It's working." — *Barron's*
>
> "If you need downside protection, Buffer ETFs are having a moment." — *TheStreet*
>
> "Uncertain times drive record flow week for Innovator's defined outcome ETFs." — *Pension & Investments*
>
> "Buffered ETFs make gains in Retirement Portfolios." — *Financial Times*
>
> "Buffer ETFs add 'guard rails' to uneasy equity markets." — *Investment News*
>
> "Buffer ETFs can limit losses in uncertain times." — *Kiplinger*
>
> "Volatile markets increase appeal of ETFs with a buffer." — *Financial Times*
>
> "Buffered ETFs Grow as Investors Shun Risk." — ETF.com
>
> "The Balancing Act: Buffer ETFs offer both Downside Protection and Growth Potential." — Nasdaq.com

Their appeal is easy to understand — investors love to participate in the upside of the stock market, but they don't like the prospect of losing money. Buffer ETFs offer a potential solution by providing a defined level of downside protection while allowing investors to participate in stock market gains up to a predetermined cap.

TECHNICAL STUFF

Buffer ETFs don't actually own stocks. They use options to track the performance of a reference asset, such as SPDR S&P 500 ETF Trust (SPY), Invesco QQQ Trust (QQQ), or iShares Russell 2000 ETF (IWM). Historically, defined outcome investments have been available only through certain banks and insurance companies in the form of annuities and structured products. Now, you can invest using similar strategies but with the benefits of an ETF wrapper and without some of the drawbacks of structured products and annuities, such as illiquidity, lock-up periods, and surrender charges.

Understanding What Buffer ETFs Can and Can't Do

On their surface, buffer ETFs appear to be the perfect remedy for stock market volatility and investor jitters. However, everything comes with a price. With buffer ETFs, the price you pay for downside protection is your limited upside gain potential, which is determined by the upside cap. However, other factors need to be considered, as well. In the spirit of full transparency, the following sections reveal the advantages and limitations of buffer ETFs.

REMEMBER

All managed funds, including ETFs, charge a management fee. As you shop for a buffer ETF, be sure to compare fees. They will have an impact on your net return. See Chapter 5 for more about management fees and other expenses.

What they can do

Here's what buffer ETFs can do to benefit you as an investor:

- **Provide downside protection:** They can absorb the initial losses of the reference asset they track, typically the first 10 or 15 percent loss on a reference asset over the defined outcome period. For example, if your ETF has a 15 percent buffer and the reference asset it tracks drops 20 percent, you lose 5 percent of your investment, before fees.
- **Reduce short-term volatility:** Buffer ETFs are less susceptible to the daily rise and fall of the reference asset, resulting in a smoother ride through market corrections and less worry for risk-averse investors. Typically, the deeper the buffer, the smoother the ride.

- **Enable you to participate in the upside of the reference asset, to a cap:** In contrast to a fully hedged approach that removes upside potential, you can still reap the benefits of the gains in the reference asset up to the predetermined cap.
- **Feature transparency and rules-based performance:** You can check the key outcome parameters before you invest. Each buffer ETF issuer's website shows the buffer, upside cap, downside before buffer, remaining days in the outcome period, and the reference asset the buffer ETF tracks. If you do your homework, you know what you're getting into.
- **Provide liquidity:** You can trade buffer ETFs throughout the day from a brokerage account — just like other ETFs or individual stocks — and at any time during the outcome period.

  WARNING

  Although you *can* trade buffer ETFs like stocks and other ETFs, that doesn't mean you *should*. The remaining buffer and cap change over the course of the outcome period and even over the course of the trading day, so if you're trading during the intra-outcome period (any day other than the reset date), you may not get the exact buffer and cap you expect when you place your order. See the later section, "Trading Buffer ETFs during Their Intra-Outcome Periods," for details.
- **Facilitate tax efficiency:** With buffer ETFs, you can generally defer taxes until you cash out, avoiding nasty surprises from taxable year-end distributions typically seen when investing in actively managed mutual funds. If you sell your shares, any realized gains or losses are simply reported on a 1099 from your custodian.

What they can't do

Buffer ETFs are impressive, but they're not a perfect solution for all investors, in all situations. Here are some of the key limitations you need to be aware of — what buffer ETFs *can't* do:

- **Provide more total downside protection than published at the outset of the outcome period:** Buffer ETFs typically protect only against initial losses of the reference asset they are designed to track, say the first 10 or 15 percent loss. You, as a shareholder, absorb any losses beyond the protection level.

  REMEMBER

  Some buffer ETFs are structured to have shareholders absorb initial losses, say the first 5 percent loss, but provide deeper protection (for example, –5 percent to –30 percent). And some buffer ETFs provide total downside protection. (See the next section, "Becoming Familiar with Different Variations of Buffer ETFs," for details.)

- **Provide the published downside protection if you sell early:** Selling before the end of the outcome period may negate the buffer or forfeit a portion of the upside. Their performance is most predictable when purchased at the start of the outcome period and held to the next reset date.
- **Allow unlimited upside potential:** In a strong bull market, the reference asset the buffer ETF tracks may rise significantly higher than the cap, so you miss out on any gains that exceed the cap during the outcome period. (Note, uncapped buffer ETFs allow for unlimited upside potential beyond the "spread." See Chapter 14 for detailed coverage.)
- **Guarantee a buffer/cap if bought during the intra-outcome period:** The remaining buffer and cap change over the course of the outcome period, so if you buy during the intra-outcome period, you may not get the full downside protection or the maximum return potential published at the start of the outcome period.
- **Compete with comparable long-term stock index ETF returns:** Buffer ETFs aren't built to maximize returns but to reduce exposure to risk while allowing for limited participation in the upside of the reference asset. As a result, they tend to underperform the reference asset over the long run.

Becoming Familiar with Different Variations of Buffer ETFs

Not all buffer ETFs are the same. They vary not only according to their outcome periods, buffers, caps, and reference assets, but also in terms of their objectives. As you research buffer ETFs, you're likely to encounter the following classifications:

- **Buffer ETFs** use options to provide a specified range of investment returns over a set outcome period (usually one year), protecting against a specific percentage of initial losses (for example, 15 percent) while capping potential gains.
- **Buffer step-up strategy ETFs** reevaluate the buffer and cap on a regular basis, looking for opportunities to increase the upside cap and adjust the level of protection. If a step-up threshold is met, the fund rolls into a new outcome period with a fresh buffer and a new, higher cap. (You can do this yourself by actively trading conventional buffer ETFs, but buffer step-up strategy ETFs take the monitoring and active management off your plate.)

- **Laddered buffer ETFs** hold multiple underlying buffer ETFs with different reset months, so you always have some holdings early, in the middle of, and near the end of an outcome period. This strategy helps to smooth out the timing risk and diversify your holdings. Note, laddered buffer ETF strategies are most popular in the investment advisory community. (You can implement a laddered strategy yourself by actively managing a portfolio of conventional buffer ETFs, but a laddered buffer ETF does the work for you.)
- **Accelerated buffer ETFs** seek to provide two or three times the upside of the reference asset, to a cap. These ETFs are generally a good option when investing in a low-return market, when you expect the underlying reference asset to deliver positive, but only single-digit returns.
- **Uncapped buffer ETFs** blend the best of both worlds — downside protection with unlimited growth potential. What's the catch? Uncapped buffer ETFs have a spread, so you participate in upside gains only if the reference asset rises above the spread. For example, if you own an uncapped buffer ETF with a net spread of 4 percent, and the reference asset produces a 10 percent return, you earn 6 percent. If the reference asset rises less than 4 percent, you earn nothing. So, you give up initial gains but have unlimited upside afterwards.
- **Dual-directional buffer ETFs** are designed to generate positive returns in both up and down markets while also providing downside protection. You win if the reference asset rises, win if it declines, and lose only if the reference asset experiences a loss that exceeds the buffer.
- **Floor products** protect you from losses beyond a predetermined level. For example, if the floor is –5 percent, you absorb the first 5 percent loss (plus fees) of your initial investment, but have protection below –5 percent.
- **Protected bitcoin ETFs** allow investors to participate in bitcoin's upside price potential, to a cap, while providing a predetermined percentage of downside protection. Note, many protected bitcoin strategies are designed to have shareholders absorb initial losses, but provide deeper protection due to the volatile nature of this asset class.
- **Gold strategy buffer ETFs** allow investors to participate in the upside of the price of gold, to a cap, while providing a predetermined percentage of downside protection.
- **Buffer income ETFs** are designed to generate income over the outcome period, typically with monthly distributions, while providing downside protection against initial losses in the reference asset. These products are designed for risk-averse investors who want their investments to generate a predictable income stream.

» **Barrier income ETFs** generate a predefined rate of income (paid quarterly) as long as the value of the reference asset doesn't fall below a certain level (the barrier). Although these ETFs may offer higher yields than others, if a barrier is breached at the end of the outcome period, it could result in no protection whatsoever, so there can be a greater risk of loss.

See Part 4 for details about each of these buffer ETF types.

Getting Up To Speed on Buffer ETF Investing Basics

Investing in buffer ETFs is easy because you can buy and sell them on any trading platform. Investing in them intelligently, however, requires some know-how. In this section, I bring you up to speed on the basics of finding and researching buffer ETFs, developing an investment strategy, and building a portfolio. (See Part 3 for more detailed coverage.)

Finding and researching buffer ETFs

Buffer ETFs trade like traditional ETFs. Each has its own ticker symbol, and you can buy and sell them through any trading platform, such as E*TRADE, Fidelity, or Schwab. However, they may not be easy to find and research on these platforms. As of this writing, ETF screeners typically don't allow users to pull up a list of buffer ETFs exclusively, and they don't highlight key information about these products, such as the cap and buffer and how many days remain in the outcome period.

REMEMBER

To find and research buffer ETFs, use tools on the issuer's website. For example, if you go to Innovator's website at `www.innovatoretfs.com` and select ETFs from the menu near the top, then select Product Table, you'll see a complete list of Innovator's ETFs (a partial list is shown in Figure 1-2). You can also create an account with an issuer to access more advanced tools.

TIP

Poke around on issuer websites to see whether they provide additional tools for finding and researching their products. For example, Innovator's ETF Finder enables you to search for products by investment goal and reference asset, and then use sliders to specify an acceptable range for the buffer, cap, and outcome period.

All | **Buffer** | Dual Directional | Income | Accelerated | Floor | Resetting | My List | **Advanced Filter**

Reference Asset:
- [x] U.S. Large Cap Equity ETF
- [ ] Growth-100 ETF
- [ ] U.S. Small Cap Equity ETF
- [ ] Int'l. Developed Equity ETF
- [ ] Emerging Market Equity ETF
- [ ] Treasury Fixed Income ETF
- [ ] Bitcoin Index

Type:
- [ ] Barrier Income
- [ ] Buffer Income
- [x] Buffer
- [ ] 2X Accelerated
- [ ] 3X Accelerated
- [ ] Floor
- [ ] Dual Directional

Buffer:
- [ ] 5%
- [ ] 9%
- [ ] 10%
- [x] 15%
- [ ] 20%
- [ ] 30%
- [ ] 100%

Barrier:
- [ ] 20%
- [ ] 30%

Rebalance Frequency:
- [ ] 3 months
- [ ] 6 months
- [ ] 12 months
- [ ] 24 months

Series:
- [ ] January
- [ ] February
- [ ] March
- [ ] April
- [ ] May
- [ ] June
- [ ] July
- [ ] August
- [ ] September
- [ ] October
- [ ] November
- [ ] December

Reset All

As of 1/29/2026 9:39:49 AM CT

Download CSV

NAME	SERIES	REFERENCE ASSET	FUND PRICE	FUND RETURN	REF. ASSET RETURN	RETURN DIFF	REF. ASSET RETURN TO CAP	REMAINING CAP	REMAINING BUFFER	DOWNSIDE BEFORE BUFFER	REMAINING OUTCOME PERIOD
U.S. Equity Power Buffer ETF	January	U.S. Large Cap Equity ETF	$47.30	0.66%	1.27%	-0.60%	10.89%	11.50%	15.34%	-0.72%	336 days
U.S. Equity Power Buffer ETF	December	U.S. Large Cap Equity ETF	$43.63	1.15%	1.05%	0.10%	11.96%	11.72%	14.61%	-1.27%	305 days
U.S. Equity Power Buffer ETF	November	U.S. Large Cap Equity ETF	$42.08	1.54%	1.25%	0.29%	11.85%	11.34%	14.34%	-1.71%	275 days
U.S. Equity Power Buffer ETF	October	U.S. Large Cap Equity ETF	$44.17	2.55%	3.66%	-1.11%	7.86%	8.77%	15.25%	-2.75%	244 days
U.S. Equity Power Buffer ETF	September	U.S. Large Cap Equity ETF	$43.98	4.22%	7.06%	-2.84%	4.36%	6.87%	16.23%	-4.38%	214 days
U.S. Equity Power Buffer ETF	August	U.S. Large Cap Equity ETF	$43.55	5.60%	9.25%	-3.65%	2.74%	5.90%	16.50%	-5.70%	183 days
U.S. Equity Power Buffer ETF	July	U.S. Large Cap Equity ETF	$46.72	6.65%	11.77%	-5.12%	0.29%	4.64%	17.26%	-6.69%	152 days
U.S. Equity Power Buffer ETF	June	U.S. Large Cap Equity ETF	$42.12	8.63%	17.17%	-8.54%	-3.91%	3.11%	18.98%	-8.47%	122 days
U.S. Equity Power Buffer ETF	May	U.S. Large Cap Equity ETF	$39.79	11.10%	24.53%	-13.43%	-8.56%	1.89%	21.15%	-10.59%	91 days
U.S. Equity Power Buffer ETF	April	U.S. Large Cap Equity ETF	$39.31	10.30%	23.45%	-13.15%	-8.96%	1.23%	21.15%	-10.00%	61 days
U.S. Equity Power Buffer ETF	March	U.S. Large Cap Equity ETF	$45.26	10.34%	16.22%	-5.89%	-3.52%	0.90%	16.77%	-10.10%	30 days
U.S. Equity Power Buffer ETF	February	U.S. Large Cap Equity ETF	$41.15	10.93%	14.75%	-3.81%	-2.57%	0.00%	15.28%	-10.65%	2 days

Educational content provided by Innovator

FIGURE 1-2: Innovator's ETF product table.

Courtesy of Innovator

Above the comprehensive list of ETFs are checkbox options that enable you to filter the list based on Reference Asset, Type, Buffer, Rebalance Frequency, and Series (the month the buffer and cap reset).

The list contains key details about each buffer ETF that matches your search criteria, including the fund's price, the fund's return since its most recent reset date versus that of its reference asset, the cap and what remains of it, the remaining buffer, and the downside-before-buffer risk (the percentage loss you're exposed to before the buffer provides any protection). These details are mostly relevant only if you're trading buffer ETFs during the intra-outcome period (see the later section "Trading Buffer ETFs during Their Intra-Outcome Periods" for details).

Select a buffer ETF from the list to view its summary, as shown in Figure 1-3. Here, you'll see the series, outcome period, rebalance frequency, starting cap, starting buffer, and exposure (reference asset). These are the details you want to be looking at if you're planning to invest in the fund at the start of the outcome period and hold it for the duration of the period or longer.

REMEMBER

To take full advantage of the fund's published buffer and cap, buy the fund at the beginning of the outcome period and hold it to the next reset date or longer. Place your order in the closing hours of the market, on the trading day before the new outcome period's start date.

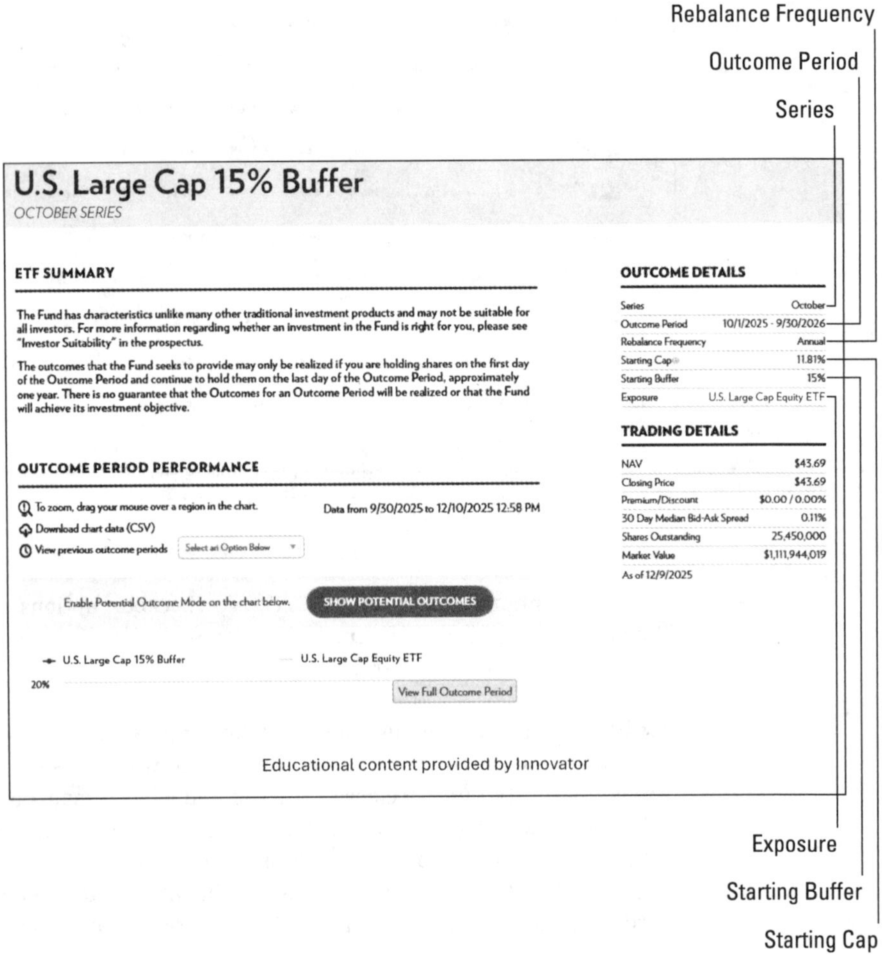

Courtesy of Innovator

FIGURE 1-3: A buffer ETF summary sheet.

WARNING

Buying during the intra-outcome period can be risky for the following reasons:

- If the reference asset has fallen, the buffer might be partially or fully depleted already, potentially increasing your exposure to further downside risk.
- If the reference asset has risen, the cap may be reduced (possibly down to zero), and you may be exposed to considerable downside-before-buffer risk (how much you could lose before the buffer starts to provide protection).

Trading a buffer ETF during its intra-outcome period can be advantageous, assuming you know what you're doing. See the later section "Opportunistic strategy" for details. See Part 3 for more in-depth guidance.

Placing your order

When you find a buffer ETF you want to purchase, you can place your order on any trading platform, as shown in Figure 1-4. You simply specify the ticker symbol of the buffer ETF you want to buy, the number of shares, and the type of order, such as Market (your order executes immediately at the best available price) or Limit (you specify the price you're willing to pay).

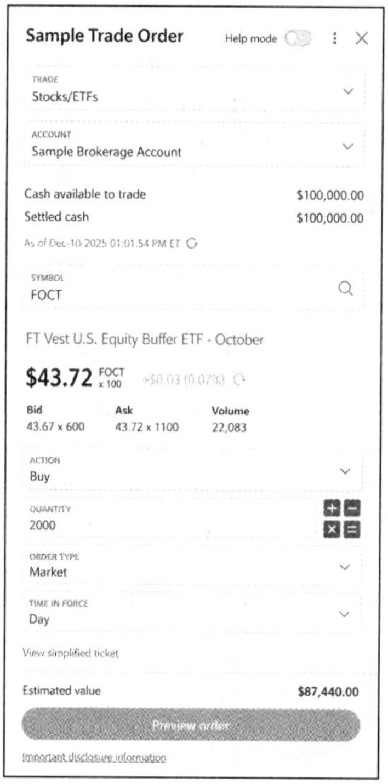

FIGURE 1-4: You can place your order on any trading platform.

WARNING

Hold off on placing an order for any buffer ETF until you feel confident in your understanding of how they work and your ability to find and research buffer ETFs, and you have a clear investment goal and a strategy in place for achieving it.

Sampling common investment strategies

You can get creative with buffer ETFs by combining different funds and staggering your buys and sells strategically to maximize your potential returns or protection. In this section, I introduce you to three common strategies. (See Chapter 4 for details about these strategies, along with examples.)

Static strategy

Buy a single buffer ETF at the start of its outcome period and hold it through the entire outcome period to realize the defined outcome. The static strategy has two key advantages:

- **Predictability:** You benefit from the full downside protection and are aware in advance of the upside cap on your return.
- **Simplicity:** You buy at the beginning of the outcome period and hold it to the end or longer. No active monitoring or management is required.

For example, you purchase FT Vest U.S. Equity Buffer — December (FDEC) on its reset date, December 23, 2024, with a 10 percent buffer and a starting cap of 14.76 percent. One year later, the reference asset, SPDR S&P 500 ETF Trust (SPY), finishes the outcome period up 15.13 percent. FDEC delivers its defined outcome, providing a total return of 13.99 percent (net of fees).

Laddered strategy

A laddered strategy is implemented by purchasing multiple buffer ETFs that have different reset dates. For example, you allocate 25 percent of your portfolio to GJAN (FT Vest U.S. Equity Moderate Buffer ETF — January), 25 percent to GAPR (FT Vest U.S. Equity Moderate Buffer ETF — April), 25 percent to GJUL (FT Vest U.S. Equity Moderate Buffer ETF — July), and 25 percent to GOCT (FT Vest U.S. Equity Moderate Buffer ETF — October). This strategy has three key advantages:

- **Less work:** You don't need to continuously research and evaluate monthly buffer ETFs.
- **Low volatility:** Each fund is at a different point in its outcome period, which allows the average buffer and cap across your portfolio to remain relatively steady as the price of the reference asset changes.

- **Diversified exposure:** By spreading out your total investment over time, you avoid being locked into a single 12-month period, and you're not depending on one specific market entry point.

REMEMBER

You can place your orders for the different funds all on the same day (if you like the outcome parameters for each fund), or you can place your order for each fund on its reset date (an hour or two prior to the close of trading). Take the second approach if your objective is to get the full starting buffer and cap for each of the funds.

Opportunistic strategy

The opportunistic strategy involves monitoring your buffer ETFs for opportunities to improve your positions (obtain more downside protection or a higher cap). You purchase a buffer ETF with your desired buffer level and cap. If performance exceeds predetermined positive or negative thresholds, you rotate — "step up" or "step down" — into a buffer ETF that is closest to the start of its next outcome period, providing a new buffer and upside cap.

REMEMBER

Step up means to enter a fund with a higher remaining cap when the reference asset has risen, you expect it to rise even higher, and little to no cap remains in the existing fund. *Step down* means to enter a fund with more downside protection after the reference asset has dropped. You fear it may decline further, and little or no buffer remains in the existing fund.

The opportunistic strategy involves more monitoring and active management but offers the following potential benefits:

- **Less risk:** You can jump ship before the buffer is depleted.
- **Higher return:** You can step up to a fund with a higher remaining cap when the fund you currently hold has mostly maxed out its upside potential.

Building a portfolio

Your investment portfolio is like a canvas on which you paint your financial future. It can include stocks, bonds, mutual funds, ETFs, cash, gold, bitcoin, real estate, and more. How creative and diverse you want it to be is up to you. You can place all your eggs in one basket or distribute them widely. You can invest entirely in one or more buffer ETFs or use them for only a portion of your investment capital.

INVESTING STRATEGICALLY

During an interview I conducted with Johan Grahn, former Head ETF Strategist at Allianz Investment Management LLC, I asked, "Have you found that advisors are using your products with tactical strategies and making changes during the intra-outcome period — locking in profits, creating a new buffer — or are they passively invested?" Here's what he had to say:

> "The majority of advisors are thinking about this as an allocation. A strategic allocation to buffered ETFs provides diversification and portfolio-level downside protection. But at the same time, there might be some active management of that allocation so they can rotate in and out of different buffered ETFs depending on where they're trading in relation to the caps and what the market's doing. So, perhaps a passive allocation, but with some active management inside of it. So, that's one type of investor."
>
> "The other type of investor who wants to be more tactical and perhaps try to beat a benchmark, say a 60/40 benchmark [60 percent stocks/40 percent bonds], for example, that would imply they have a market opinion and want to implement that either by overweighting or underweighting equities. So, one of the really cool things with buffered ETFs is that if 'you're overweight equities because you have a positive view on the economy, 'let's say, but instead of buying just more equities at the expense of fixed income or cash (where you will immediately be judged if the market declines and you underperform) — instead, you could buy buffered ETFs."

If you're an investor who doesn't want to spend much time monitoring the markets, you can take a simple approach by investing in one or two buffer ETFs and holding them for the long term.

For example, suppose you have $1 million you'd like to invest in buffer ETFs. You could build a portfolio using two funds from Innovator — U.S. Equity Buffer ETF — January Series (ticker symbol BJAN) and U.S. Equity Buffer ETF — April Series (ticker symbol BAPR). Both ETFs have a downside buffer of 9 percent at the start of each 12-month outcome period.

You check Innovator's website a week before the reset date, when the issuer gives an estimate as to the upcoming caps for the ETFs that will soon reset. The gross cap for the new outcome period is estimated at 16 percent for BJAN, and you're good with that. You invest half your portfolio ($500,000) in BJAN on December 31, 2025 (in the closing hours of trading the day before the new outcome period begins). The final cap came in at 16.4 percent (before fees).

You decide to wait a few months to allocate the remainder of your cash and purchase BAPR on its reset date. A week before the reset date, you check Innovator's website, and it indicates the gross cap for the new outcome period is estimated at 18 percent, and that's attractive to you. You invest the remainder of your cash ($500,000) in BAPR on March 31, 2026 (in the closing hours of trading the day before the new outcome period begins). The final cap came in at 18.4 percent (before fees).

You could stagger your purchases over several months or more and build a laddered portfolio. However, if the upside cap is attractive when you have cash available to invest, you have little reason to delay a purchase, unless you believe markets are very extended, overvalued, and due for a sizeable correction.

REMEMBER

If you believe current market prices are compelling, you may choose to allocate your entire portfolio all at once. There's nothing wrong with this approach, assuming the downside protection and upside cap levels meet your investment objectives.

WARNING

Never purchase a buffer ETF without knowing the current potential outcome parameters — the buffer, cap, downside-before-buffer risk (if any), and the days remaining in the outcome period. This warning cannot be overstated. Most issuers update these parameters daily, and they can change throughout the trading day, so always check them before making a purchase. See "Trading Buffer ETFs during Their Intra-Outcome Periods" later in this chapter for details.

REMEMBER

BUYING INTO BUFFER ETFS

I started tracking buffer ETFs in 2020 because I thought they could be very attractive for my clients. Most of my clients are either nearing retirement or retired. Buffer ETFs give my clients plenty of downside protection while enabling them to participate in stock market gains, to a cap. The ETFs are liquid with no lock-up periods or surrender charges. The buffer ETF concept was indeed a very innovative idea.

I did a lot of research prior to investing and spent considerable time getting comfortable with buffer ETFs and finding an opportune time to invest. I interviewed strategists at leading buffer ETF firms, along with sub-advisors of the ETFs. I wanted to talk to the individuals who actually managed the option strategies within the ETFs. The more I learned, the more comfortable I felt about investing for my clients.

(continued)

(continued)

During the market sell-off in 2022, when both stocks and bonds were hit hard, I was focused on controlling risk for my clients. I had a lot of cash on hand in the fall of 2022, and I was considering where to reinvest. Valuations were decent, but stocks weren't cheap, and investors were pessimistic given how poorly the market had performed that year. I viewed the negative sentiment as healthy and thought it could help stocks surprise to the upside in 2023. Still, I wasn't willing to make an unhedged "bet" on the market — I wanted some protection.

I had been checking the upside cap levels of Innovator's buffer ETF offerings and was particularly intrigued by its 15 percent Power Buffer series as November approached. The S&P 500 was already down nearly 20 percent from its peak, so adding another 15 percent layer of protection was very appealing to me. At that point, the additional "buffer" would basically protect my clients from a very deep peak-to-valley decline in the market.

The 20.5 percent upside cap for Innovator's U.S. Equity Power Buffer ETF — November (PNOV is the trading symbol) on its reset date, October 31, 2022, was nearly the highest I had ever seen for a 15 percent buffer ETF. PNOV offered 15 percent downside protection, and if the reference asset, SPDR S&P 500 ETF Trust (SPY), rebounded in 2023, my clients had the potential to make approximately 20 percent during the 12-month outcome period. And, if SPY had another bad year, my clients had plenty of protection in place. What's not to like? I thought it was a tremendous risk versus reward opportunity.

My first purchase of PNOV on October 31, 2022, and another purchase of Innovator's U.S. Equity Power Buffer ETF — September (PSEP), during its intra-outcome period, represented a substantial percentage of my assets under management. I had no concern about entering sizeable orders in these ETFs due to the highly liquid underlying exposure in SPY. The bid-ask spreads were tight, and execution on both trades through the custodian's block trading desk was seamless.

Both PNOV and PSEP have provided meaningful double-digit gains since late 2022, but investing directly in a stock market index (for example, S&P 500, Nasdaq-100) would have resulted in even better performance over the same period, but obviously without any downside protection.

Comparing buffer ETFs to the returns of a stock market index is really "apples-to-oranges." One has a level of downside protection, and the other doesn't. In general, a conventional buffer ETF tends to lag its reference asset at least slightly in a rising market, due to fees, but it typically holds up better and outperforms in a declining market.

Trading Buffer ETFs during Their Intra-Outcome Periods

As explained earlier, in the section "Opportunistic strategy," buying and selling buffer ETFs during their intra-outcome period can be advantageous, but you need to know what you're doing. Buying when the buffer or cap is nearly exhausted is an easy yet serious mistake to make, so always check key intra-outcome parameters on the issuer's website, as shown in Figure 1-5, before buying or selling shares. Key intra-outcome parameters include the following (parameters may go by different names depending on the ETF issuer):

- **Reference asset:** The underlying asset the fund tracks.
- **Fund return:** The percentage the fund has gained or lost since the most recent reset date.
- **Reference asset return:** The percentage the underlying asset has gained or lost since the most recent reset date.
- **Return difference:** The percentage difference in performance between the underlying reference asset and the buffer ETF since the most recent reset date.
- **Reference asset return to cap:** How much the reference asset would have to increase for the buffer ETF to reach its upside cap.
- **Remaining cap:** The maximum percentage the fund's value can increase from now until the end of the outcome period.
- **Downside before buffer:** How much the fund's value could decrease before buffer protection kicks in. If the fund has increased in value since its most recent reset date, it must drop nearly the same amount before it reaches a level at which the buffer protects against a loss. So, suppose a fund's value rose 10 percent since the start of the current outcome period, and you buy it midperiod; you could lose 10 percent of your investment before you'd get any downside protection.
- **Remaining outcome period:** The number of days before the next reset date.

NAME	SERIES	REF. ASSET	FUND RETURN	ASSET RETURN	RETURN DIFF	ASSET RETURN TO CAP	REM. CAP	REM. BUFFER	DOWN BEFORE BUFFER	REM. OUT-PERIOD
U.S. Large Cap 9% Buffer ETF	April	U.S. Large Cap Equity ETF	5.47%	8.82%	-3.35%	8.88%	11.55%	10.40%	-5.98%	348
U.S. Large Cap 15% Buffer ETF	April	U.S. Large Cap Equity ETF	3.87%	8.82%	-4.95%	4.74%	8.94%	17.37%	-4.52%	348
U.S. Large Cap 9% Buffer ETF	March	U.S. Large Cap Equity ETF	2.44%	3.17%	-0.72%	13.38%	13.39%	8.62%	-3.18%	317
U.S. Large Cap 15% Buffer ETF	March	U.S. Large Cap Equity ETF	1.95%	3.17%	-1.22%	9.33%	9.84%	14.90%	-2.71%	317
U.S. Large Cap 9% Buffer ETF	February	U.S. Large Cap Equity ETF	2.04%	2.28%	-0.24%	14.01%	13.48%	8.23%	-2.79%	289
U.S. Large Cap 15% Buffer ETF	February	U.S. Large Cap Equity ETF	1.71%	2.28%	-0.57%	9.92%	9.73%	14.42%	-2.48%	289
U.S. Large Cap 9% Buffer ETF	January	U.S. Large Cap Equity ETF	3.14%	3.78%	-0.64%	12.21%	12.12%	8.48%	-3.84%	258
U.S. Large Cap 15% Buffer ETF	January	U.S. Large Cap Equity ETF	2.57%	3.78%	-1.22%	8.20%	8.69%	14.80%	-3.30%	258
U.S. Large Cap 9% Buffer ETF	December	U.S. Large Cap Equity ETF	3.60%	3.56%	0.04%	13.38%	12.55%	7.86%	-4.26%	227
U.S. Large Cap 15% Buffer ETF	December	U.S. Large Cap Equity ETF	3.24%	3.56%	-0.32%	9.25%	8.80%	13.99%	-3.93%	227
U.S. Large Cap 9% Buffer ETF	November	U.S. Large Cap Equity ETF	3.86%	3.76%	0.10%	13.34%	12.43%	7.79%	-4.51%	197
U.S. Large Cap 15% Buffer ETF	November	U.S. Large Cap Equity ETF	3.49%	3.76%	-0.27%	9.14%	8.64%	13.92%	-4.16%	197

As of 4/17/26

Educational content provided by Innovator

FIGURE 1-5: Key intra-outcome parameters for a partial list of Innovator buffer ETFs as of April 17, 2026.

Courtesy of Innovator

IN THIS CHAPTER

» Peeking behind the curtain

» Seeing how buffer ETFs behave in different markets

» Knowing what to expect when markets rise and fall

Chapter 2
Understanding How Buffer ETFs Work

You don't need to know how an internal combustion engine works to drive a car. Likewise, you don't need to know how a buffer ETF works to invest in one. However, knowing a little bit about how they perform their magic and how you can expect them to behave in different market conditions can make you a more confident and competent investor.

In this chapter, I take you behind the scenes with these innovative investment products and start to shape your expectations about their performance in different market scenarios.

REMEMBER

The two key benefits of buffer ETFs are that they provide downside protection while allowing for upside participation in the stock market, up to a cap. Some investors have described them as "ETFs with airbags."

Reaping the Benefits of Options Trading without Having to Do It

An *option* is a contract that gives the buyer the right but not the obligation to buy or sell a stock at a specific price (*strike price*) by a specific date. Options come in two types:

- **Call option** gives you the right to buy a stock at the strike price before the option expires. For example, you buy a call with a strike price of $100, expecting the stock's price to increase. The stock's price shoots up to $130, and you exercise your option to buy, getting a $130 a share stock for $100 a share (minus the premium you paid for the option). If the share price drops, you simply choose not to exercise your option to buy (you lose only the premium you paid for the option).
- **Put option** gives you the right to sell a stock at the strike price before the option expires. For example, you buy a put with a $50 strike price, expecting the share price to drop. The price drops to $35, and you sell your shares for $50, earning $15 per share (minus the premium you paid for the option). If the share price increases after you buy the put, you simply choose not to exercise your option to sell the shares (you lose only the premium you paid for the option).

Options trading offers several potential benefits, including the ability to use leverage, utilize various trading strategies in different market conditions, and hedge against potential losses. Some options enable you to mitigate the risks of investing and potentially profit whether the market rises or falls. In the context of buffer ETFs, they're typically used to provide exposure to the reference asset and define the fund's buffer and cap.

TECHNICAL STUFF

How much does an option cost? The premium changes constantly based on the stock's price, market conditions, and other factors. You pay a certain amount per share to control a specific number of shares, typically 100. So, if the option is priced at $2.50 per share, the premium would be $2.50 × 100 = $250. Of course, when you're investing in buffer ETFs, you don't need to be concerned with the cost of options; they're included as part of the fund's expense ratio.

Buffer ETFs are created with a package of FLexible EXchange (FLEX) options — a type of option that allows customized strike prices, underlying reference assets, and expiration dates. Specifically, buffer ETFs consist of a basket of FLEX options with strike prices expiring on a designated date, forming an outcome period. The options work together to generate the reference asset exposure, buffer, and upside cap.

Most buffer ETFs use a deep-in-the-money call option to track the return of a reference asset (for example, SPDR S&P 500 ETF Trust). Some may instead use futures or direct holdings. For example, BlackRock tracks the reference asset in its buffer ETFs by purchasing iShares Core S&P 500 ETF (IVV), but this approach is less common.

While a fund's options are all established at the same time, visualizing them as different layers can be helpful. For example, consider a buffer ETF with 15 percent downside protection. The following three layers contribute to the construction of the defined outcome:

Layer 1 (A) — Reference asset participation: The first layer involves buying a call option on the reference asset, which provides synthetic 1:1 exposure to the reference asset (see Figure 2-1). A *synthetic investment* is designed to replicate the return of a selected asset — for example, the SPDR S&P 500 ETF Trust (SPY) or Invesco QQQ Trust (QQQ) — without owning the underlying asset.

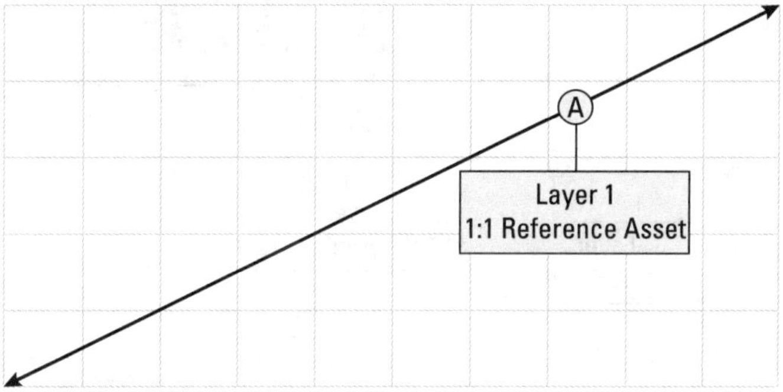

FIGURE 2-1: Layer 1 provides exposure to the reference asset.

Courtesy of Innovator

Layer 2 (B, C) — Downside buffer: The second layer incorporates a put spread. Together, the long put (C) and short put (B) produce the downside buffer of 15 percent (see Figure 2-2). A *put spread* is an investment strategy that involves buying one put option and selling another put option on the same underlying asset with the same expiration date but with different strike prices. Buying a put at a higher strike price (*long put*) provides downside protection because its value increases if the reference asset falls. Selling a put at a lower strike price (*short put*) offsets part of the cost of the long put and creates protection down to the lower strike price. This combination provides protection between the two strike prices but not below the lower strike price, and this is what defines the downside buffer.

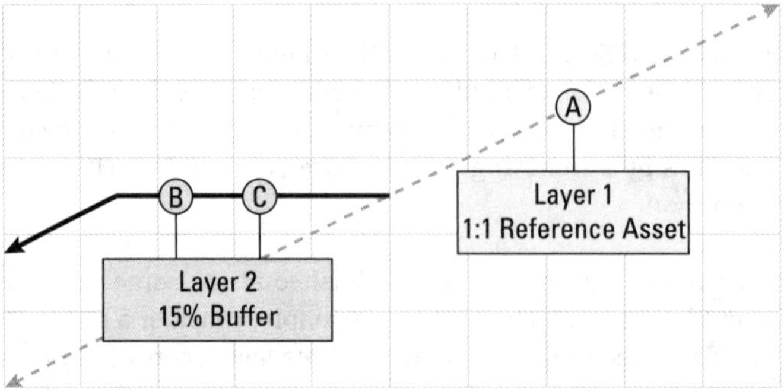

FIGURE 2-2: Layer 2 establishes the downside buffer.

Courtesy of Innovator

Layer 3 (D) — Upside cap: The third layer involves selling a call option to generate enough premium to cover the cost of the put spread, or buffer. The sale of this call option creates the upside cap (see Figure 2-3).

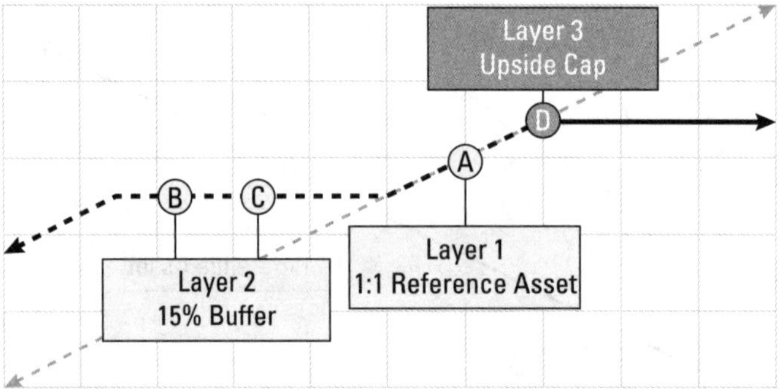

FIGURE 2-3: Layer 3 establishes the upside cap.

Courtesy of Innovator

The result is a reshaped return profile that protects against the first 15 percent loss and allows participation in the reference asset up to the cap (see Figure 2-4).

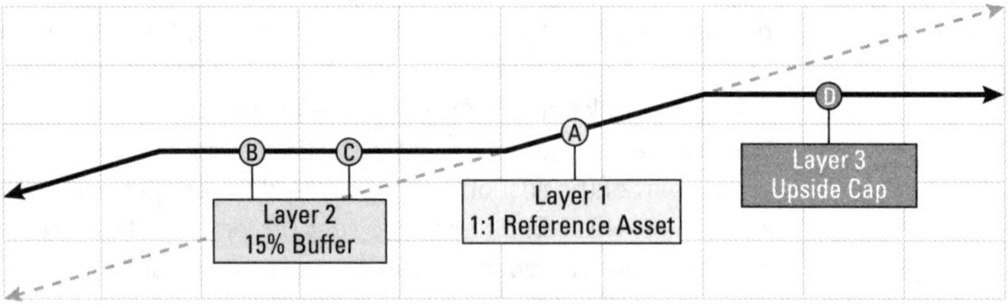

FIGURE 2-4: The option layers work together to construct the defined outcome.

Courtesy of Innovator

PROOF OF CONCEPT

The real test of whether a system delivers the desired outcome is the proof of concept. During an interview I conducted with Johan Grahn, former Head ETF Strategist at Allianz Investment Management LLC, he shared the following two proofs of concept:

> "In 2022, the market was down just about 20 percent, and AllianzIM's 20 percent buffer ETF didn't lose any money — the return was basically flat (gross of fees). We couldn't have dreamt up a better proof point! It really demonstrated that these products work."

> "2023 served as the second-best proof point because the market rallied. So now an investor who had 'hypothetically' invested $1 million in a 20-percent buffer ETF throughout 2022 would still have that $1 million (less fees). As the markets rallied by over 25 percent in 2023, he then would have participated up to a cap that was set at approximately 15 percent. He would have had $1.15 million at the end of the year. If he had been invested in the S&P 500 over that same period, he would have only about $1 million (due to the loss of 20 percent in 2022 and the gain of 25 percent in 2023)."

He went on to explain:

> "These two proof points really demonstrate the diversification benefit and the 'win more by losing less' concept. The numbers really played out favorably for these types of products, not because of what they helped drive in terms of assets under management (AUM) growth, but because they demonstrated how buffer ETFs work, and that they did indeed work, as intended and as advertised."

Appreciating the Benefits of a Defined Outcome

Most investments these days are somewhat of a crap shoot, especially for investors who aren't skilled and don't have the time to perform the research necessary to make well-informed investment decisions. Even if you do your homework, unexpected events can have a devastating impact on your returns.

Defined outcome investments, such as buffer ETFs, take some of the unpredictability out of the equation to deliver the following benefits:

- You have a clearer idea of what you stand to gain or lose before you invest.
- Your investment capital is less exposed to market-timing risk, because your return is determined more by the defined outcome parameters than your entry date.
- The ETF wrapper facilitates diversification, and the buffer helps protect against poor timing and bad investment decisions.
- You remain invested in the market for the long haul. And, you're not sitting on the sidelines in cash waiting for a good opportunity to enter the market.

With a buffer ETF, you know your return potential over its defined outcome period, even if the reference asset doesn't perform according to your expectations. Figure 2-5 illustrates how a buffer ETF with 15 percent downside protection and a 15 percent cap would perform in the following four market scenarios:

- **Major sell-off:** During a major sell-off, as happened during the COVID-19 pandemic, the reference asset loses 30 percent of its value, while the fund loses only 15 percent (because the first 15 percent loss was buffered).
- **Normal market correction:** During a market correction, the reference asset loses 10 percent of its value, while the buffer ETF loses nothing, thanks to its buffer.
- **Normal growth:** During a period of normal growth, performance for the fund and the reference asset, over the full outcome period, is pretty much the same. The only difference will likely be the *fee drag* (net performance after the expense ratio is deducted).
- **High growth:** During a period of high growth, the reference asset outperforms the buffer ETF because the reference asset's upside is uncapped. Figure 2-5 shows what would happen if the reference asset delivered a 30 percent return; the buffer ETF's return would be limited to its predetermined cap of 15 percent.

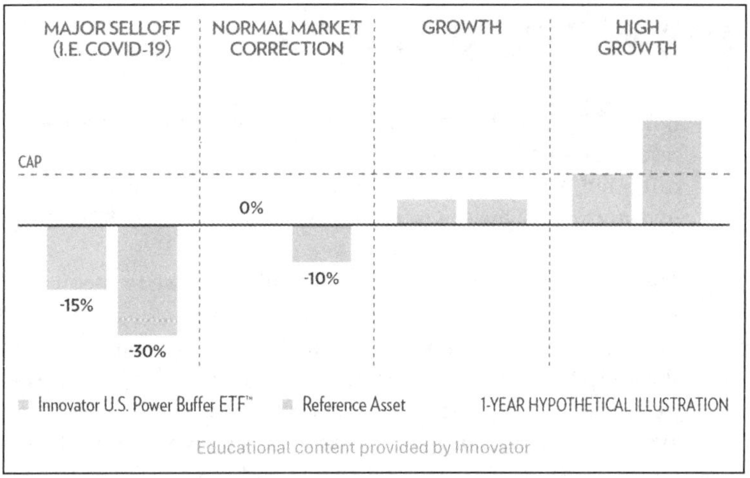

FIGURE 2-5: Buffer ETFs allow investors to know their potential outcomes relative to the reference asset over the full outcome period.

Courtesy of Innovator

PROTECTION AGAINST POOR INVESTMENT DECISIONS

I asked Johan Grahn, former Head ETF Strategist at Allianz Investment Management LLC, the following question: "Was 2022 a turning point for Defined Outcome ETFs? Investors were losing money in both stocks and bonds, which typically are somewhat uncorrelated, but that wasn't the case in 2022. Do you believe that when markets are difficult, and investors are losing money, that's when they start to look for a better solution?" Here's his response:

> "I say human nature guides you, and you feel pain points five times more heavily than the positive points. So, when bad events happen, your brain automatically kicks into survival mode, and you try to do something about it because it doesn't feel right. And when things don't feel right, you want to take action. And, a lot of times in the investing world, you take the wrong action, and you make a bad decision."
>
> "Did more eyeballs turn to these strategies in a year like 2022? Yes, there's no doubt. They turn to anything that looks like a "risk-off" asset, but one of the benefits of the defined outcome space is that it helps mitigate poor decision-making that, frankly, is somewhat pervasive. If you are invested in these types of products, then you won't feel as much pain, and you will be less inclined to make poor decisions when the sky is falling, so to speak."

Knowing What to Expect

Buffer ETFs don't remove all the volatility from the markets. As the price of the reference asset rises and falls, so too does the fund's share price. However, typically, buffer ETF shareholders will experience less volatility than an unhedged investor who owns the reference asset (for example, SPY, QQQ, IWM) outright.

REMEMBER

The *beta* (measure of the asset's volatility relative to the market itself) of a buffer ETF decreases with more protection. For example, a buffer ETF with 10 percent protection may typically, but not always, mirror the performance (up or down) of the underlying asset by approximately 75 percent, so its beta is 0.75 (as compared to the underlying asset's beta of 1.0). Deeper buffer ETFs will generally have an even lower beta throughout much of the outcome period. The lower beta (reduced volatility) allows for a smoother ride for buffer ETF owners.

If you look at a graph of the two — the reference asset price and the fund price — alongside each other over time, you notice the peaks and valleys are a little less dramatic for the buffer ETF. At the end of the outcome period, the buffer ETF outperforms the reference asset in a down market and underperforms it over a high-growth period, as explained in the following sections.

Negative reference asset return

Consider how a buffer ETF with 15 percent downside protection would behave when the reference asset — in this hypothetical case, the SPDR S&P 500 ETF Trust (SPY) — produces a negative return (see Figure 2-6).

In this scenario, as the reference asset traded lower, the ETF traded in the buffer zone. At the end of the outcome period, when the reference asset was down 13 percent, the buffer ETF was protected against the loss and finished the period flat (before fees). Also, notice that the value of the buffer ETF is less susceptible to the upward and downward swings of the reference asset.

Positive reference asset return

Figure 2-7 shows what you can expect when the reference asset produces a positive return. Again, the reference asset in this hypothetical case is the SPDR S&P 500 ETF Trust (SPY). The fund has a 9 percent buffer and a 15 percent cap. Over the course of the outcome period, the ETF climbed toward its cap while exhibiting less volatility than the reference asset.

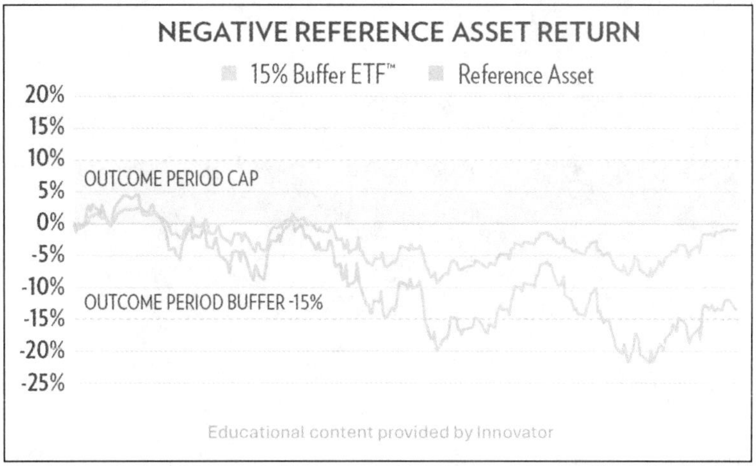

FIGURE 2-6: In a down market, the buffer ETF provides downside protection.

Courtesy of Innovator

In the outcome period, as the reference asset traded higher, the ETF trended higher toward the cap. At the end of the outcome period, when the reference asset was up 17 percent, the ETF finished at its 15 percent cap.

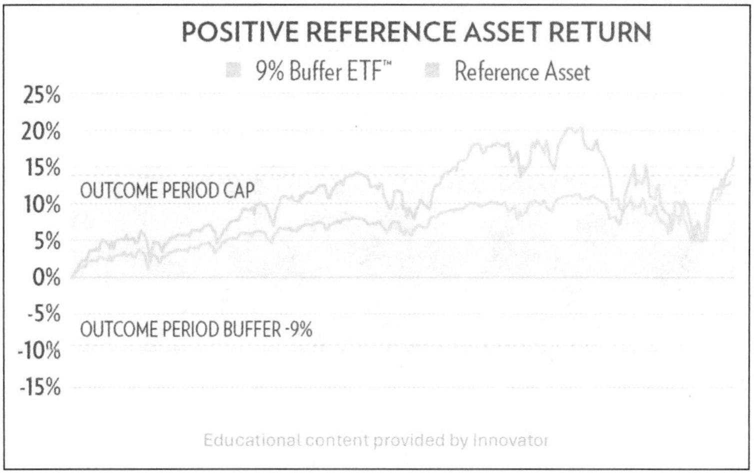

FIGURE 2-7: In an up market, the buffer ETF produces a positive return, up to a cap.

Courtesy of Innovator

IN THIS CHAPTER

» Considering the pros and cons of buffer ETFs

» Understanding why losing less matters

» Calming your fears about investing

Chapter 3
Deciding Whether Buffer ETFs Are Right for You

Deciding whether any investment is right for you can be a challenge. You need to evaluate your investment objectives, risk tolerance, time horizon, the amount of time and effort you're willing and able to spend monitoring and managing your portfolio, and more. In this chapter, I lead you through the process of determining whether buffer ETFs are a good fit for you by highlighting key considerations.

Taking a Look at Your Financial Profile

Your financial profile includes your goals and timeline for achieving them, your cash flow (income and expenses), your net worth (assets minus liabilities), your tax situation, and other factors. This section focuses on three key components of your financial profile that can help you determine whether buffer ETFs are right for you, as well as your financial goals, timeline, and need for liquidity.

REMEMBER

Your financial profile has less to do with *whether* buffer ETFs are right for you than with *how* you use them as tools to help achieve your financial and life goals. The variety of buffer ETFs available and how they function enable you to use them strategically to help meet your objectives.

Evaluating your financial goals and timelines

Buffer ETFs are best suited for achieving specific investment objectives, such as the following:

- Saving for a major purchase or expense, such as a car, home, renovation, wedding, or dream vacation.
- Preserving capital before retirement or college; for example, a buffer ETF could be used to reduce stock market volatility and potential losses in the final years of an account earmarked to cover college costs.
- Transitioning a portfolio as you near retirement, when preservation of capital with moderate growth typically becomes paramount.

TIP

Investing in buffer ETFs can be a useful way to transition from a high-growth strategy to a capital-preservation or moderate-growth strategy.

In contrast, buffer ETFs are less suitable for goals that are best achieved through a long-term, multi-decade, high-growth strategy; for example, when you're in the early stages of saving for retirement or for a young child's future. In situations such as these, you typically get a higher return by investing in securities that have no upside cap (depending, of course, on how you choose to invest).

Accounting for your liquidity needs

Liquidity is a measure of how quickly, easily, and affordably you can turn an asset into cash. A home, for example, is not a very liquid asset, because it takes time to list and sell it, and if you need to sell it in a hurry, you may have to accept less for it than it's worth. A buffer ETF is very liquid, because you can sell your shares throughout any trading day; however, if you sell before the end of the outcome period, you can lose some or all of the downside protection, and you may not receive the full benefit of your investment's upside potential.

REMEMBER

A good rule of thumb is to invest in a buffer ETF only if you know you're not going to need the money until the end of its outcome period. Keep in mind that some ETFs have shorter outcome periods than others. If you know you're going to need the money three months from now, a 3-month buffer ETF could be the appropriate choice.

Considering potential tax advantages

Buffer ETFs are suitable for both taxable and tax-deferred accounts, such as individual retirement accounts (IRAs) and 401(k)s. They're considered "tax-efficient," meaning they typically don't distribute taxable income or capital gains to investors during the holding period. Capital gains and losses are generally contained within the fund until you sell your shares, enabling you to essentially defer taxes until you sell.

TIP

Consider holding buffer ETFs for more than one year, so any gains are taxed as long-term capital gains, which are typically taxed at a lower rate than short-term capital gains. For most investors, long-term capital gains rates are 0, 15, or 20 percent, at the federal level, depending on their income levels. Higher earners may be required to pay an additional 3.8 percent in net investment income tax, so the maximum rate for long-term capital gains is 23.8 percent. Short-term capital gains are taxed as ordinary income, up to 37 percent. And, of course, there are state and local taxes to consider, too.

Weighing the Advantages and Disadvantages of Buffer ETFs

Decision-making generally boils down to performing a cost-benefit analysis. You weigh the pros against the cons, the benefits against the drawbacks, and let the scales tell you which option is most attractive. In this section, I break down the pros and cons of investing in buffer ETFs, explain why losing less matters, and reveal cost considerations, so you can perform your own cost-benefit analysis.

Considering the pros

Buffer ETFs offer a long list of benefits:

- Provide downside protection while enabling upside participation in a reference asset (for example, SPDR S&P 500 ETF Trust) to a cap.
- Track a reference asset with less volatility and risk than the underlying asset itself.
- Choose your level of downside protection according to your risk profile. You can find buffer ETFs that are appropriate for conservative, moderate, or more aggressive investors.
- Trade like stocks and traditional ETFs with daily liquidity and transparency.

- **»** Carry no credit risk. With many structured products, you depend on the issuer to pay what's promised. If the issuer defaults, you could lose money. Buffer ETFs are not debt instruments, so the failure of the ETF issuer should not cause a loss of assets.
- **»** Have no lock-up periods or surrender charges. Some defined-outcome products, such as annuities, require that you hold them for perhaps many years before you can access the funds without a penalty or surrender charge. Buffer ETFs have no such requirements.

WARNING

Although buffer ETFs have no lock-up periods or surrender charges, selling your shares before the end of the outcome period (reset date) may negate or reduce the downside buffer and/or the upside potential of your holdings.

- **»** Reset automatically at the end of the outcome period with a fresh buffer and new cap.
- **»** Are tax-efficient. See "Considering potential tax advantages" earlier in this chapter for details.
- **»** Are suitable for both taxable and tax-deferred accounts, such as IRAs and 401(k)s.
- **»** Appeal to conservative and moderate risk investors who are looking for stable growth with less volatility and a defined level of downside protection.
- **»** Allow risk-averse investors the opportunity to participate in the potential upside of the stock market with less worry.
- **»** Allow investors who are retired or nearing retirement the ability to participate in the stock market and potentially increase the value of their investment portfolios while providing some degree of protection for their nest egg.
- **»** Provide investors who are concerned about a market correction or *bear market* (a drop in value of 20 percent or more) with a safety net that gives them the confidence to remain invested in the stock market and continue to participate in its potential upside.
- **»** Offer a viable alternative to a traditional 60/40 stock/bond portfolio allocation, with the possibility of higher growth.
- **»** Reduce the likelihood of large negative returns in a portfolio. For many conservative and moderate risk investors, reducing the risk of a large loss is much more important than potentially missing out on high returns.
- **»** Offer an attractive, risk-managed, core portfolio holding for long-term investors.

REMEMBER

A primary reason to accept a cap in exchange for downside protection is that you can greatly reduce the likelihood of large negative returns in your portfolio.

BEAR MARKET FACTS AND STATS

A bear market often coincides with a weakening economy, massive liquidation of securities, and widespread investor fear and pessimism. The shortest bear markets have lasted about three months (1987 and 1990). The longest bear market lasted three years, from 1946 to 1949. Taking the past 12 bear markets into consideration, the average length of a bear market is about 14 months.

The shallowest bear market loss took place in 1990, when the S&P 500 lost around 20 percent. The deepest bear market loss happened during the Financial Crisis of 2007–2008, when the S&P 500 lost approximately 57 percent of its value in about 27 months. On average, in past bear markets, stocks have declined approximately 34 percent.

Accounting for the cons

Buffer ETFs aren't a perfect solution for every investor in every stock market environment. Their disadvantages are at the extremes. If you buy a buffer ETF that offers 15 percent downside protection, but the reference asset tumbles 25 percent over the outcome period, you'll lose the difference — 10 percent (plus fees). And, if the reference asset soars coming out of a bear market, but your upside is capped, you could miss out on high returns.

REMEMBER

I think the worst time to invest in buffer ETFs is when the stock market is already deep in bear market territory. If stock valuations are attractive, and the reference asset is already trading down 20 percent or more from its peak, you probably don't want to be invested in an asset with an upside cap. Stocks can skyrocket coming out of a bear market, and you don't want your return capped when they do. Keep in mind, however, that some providers offer *uncapped* buffer ETFs, which can be an attractive solution when stocks are depressed and trading at attractive valuations during bear markets. See Chapter 14 for details.

Winning by losing less

You've probably heard the adage, "The best defense is a good offense." Buffer ETFs turn that advice on its head, proving that, in a declining market, the best offense is a good defense.

In a bear market, losing less with a built-in buffer can be powerful. Without a buffer, if your portfolio declines, it subsequently needs to gain more (as a percentage) than it lost to get back to even. For example, if your million-dollar investment suffers a 20 percent loss ($200,000), the remaining $800,000 would need to gain 25 percent to get back to $1 million (see Table 3-1).

TABLE 3-1 The More You Lose, the Harder It Is to Catch Up

	If your portfolio loses. . .					
	5%	10%	20%	30%	40%	50%
. . . with a buffer of. . .	. . .it would need to gain the following to break even:					
0% (no buffer)	5%	11%	25%	43%	67%	100%
9%	0%	1%	12%	27%	45%	69%
15%	0%	0%	5%	18%	33%	54%
30% (–5% to –35%)	5%	5%	5%	5%	11%	25%

REMEMBER

If history is a guide, buffer ETFs that offer 15 to 20 percent downside protection should provide a sufficient level of protection to help mitigate losses in most market environments.

Steep market declines are infrequent. During the past 68 years (1957-2025), the S&P 500 lost more than 20 percent only three times (1974, 2002, 2008). It lost more than 15 percent but less than 20 percent only twice (1973, 2022). Table 3-2 provides a comprehensive rundown of S&P 500 losses over the past 68 years.

TABLE 3-2 S&P 500 Losses over the Past 68 Years

Year	Loss	Year	Loss	Year	Loss
1957	14.31%	1977	11.50%	2008	39.49%
1960	2.97%	1981	9.73%	2011	0.003%
1962	11.81%	1990	6.56%	2015	0.73%
1966	13.09%	1994	1.54%	2018	6.24%
1969	11.36%	2000	10.14%	2022	19.44%
1973	17.37%	2001	13.04%		
1974	29.72%	2002	23.37%		

Buffer ETFs are offered for every month of the year, so investors should consider all historical rolling one-year period returns — not just calendar-year returns. (A *rolling one-year period* is any 12-month period, not exclusive to January–December.) *Morningstar* data from 1952 to 2025 reveals the following:

- 74 percent of rolling one-year periods were positive.
- 89 percent of rolling one-year period returns were better than –12 percent.
- 96 percent of rolling one-year period returns were better than –20 percent.
- The average return during negative periods was –11.8 percent, and the average return during positive periods was 16 percent.

Weighing the cost of downside protection

Investing in buffer ETFs comes at a cost, mostly an opportunity cost. You're paying for downside protection by limiting your upside potential with a cap on gains. The key questions to answer are:

- Do you want downside protection?
- Is it worth the cost?

REMEMBER

Think of the buffer as an insurance policy against a potential drop in the market. The opportunity cost is the premium you pay for the insurance. The premium varies depending on market volatility and interest rates, which affect the upside cap levels.

Ask yourself, "Is the cost of having downside protection for my investment portfolio worth it?" The answer to this question boils down to the following two factors:

- **Your risk tolerance:** If you have a low to moderate risk tolerance, you'll probably be willing to pay for some downside protection.
- **Market conditions:** If markets are up and valuations are historically high, your portfolio could benefit from some level of downside protection. In contrast, if the market is deep in bear territory and valuations are attractive, you may not want to cap your return in exchange for downside protection.

Consider the following scenarios to help you gauge whether the cost of downside protection is worth it:

- In normal market environments, I think the cost of protection is reasonable. For example, suppose you purchase a 15 percent buffer ETF series that offers upside participation in the S&P 500 over the next 12 months, to a cap of 14 percent. You're forfeiting any gain above 14 percent over the outcome period — that's the premium you're paying for downside protection. But wouldn't you typically be happy with a 14 percent annual return? In exchange, you're protected against the first 15 percent loss (before fees) over the outcome period. In any market, other than a bear market, that would likely be enough protection to shield a portfolio from loss with enough upside potential to keep most investors satisfied.

- If the upside cap is attractive, which to me would be a cap that's at least as high as the average annual historical return of the stock market (10.5 percent), then the protection is likely worth the cost. A 15 percent buffer provides a lot of protection in nearly any market environment. If the potential upside is at least 10.5 percent net of fees over a 12-month outcome period, then I think it's worth considering a purchase.
- If valuations are high, or even in the normal historical range — a price-to-earnings (P/E) ratio of 16× or higher for the S&P 500 — I'd argue the protection is likely worth the cost.
- In the throes of a bear market, when stocks are already trading down 20 percent or more, downside protection may not be worth the cost of a cap on return potential. The opportunity cost (capped upside) could potentially be too expensive if the reference asset could surge coming out of a steep decline.

REMEMBER

Most of the investors I've talked to are very interested in the portfolio protection that buffer ETFs provide, assuming the upside caps are equal to or higher than the average annual historical return of the reference asset. Thankfully, in recent years, most buffer ETFs have offered upside caps of 12 to 14 percent or more, with moderate downside protection of 15 percent. This is an attractive risk/reward profile for most investors.

Considering Your Financial Situation and Temperament

Your decision to purchase portfolio protection through buffer ETFs should depend on your current outlook for the reference asset the ETF tracks and, more importantly, your tolerance for risk. If you're a conservative or moderate risk investor, you may always want some level of downside protection in your portfolio. If you're an aggressive investor who can withstand a 30 percent decline (or more) in the value of your stock portfolio during a bear market, and you can afford to wait potentially many years for a recovery, then you may decide that you never want any protection because you don't want to cap your upside return potential.

You're likely to be a good candidate for investing in buffer ETFs if you match one or more of the following profiles:

- **You're a conservative or moderate risk investor.** You're not interested in speculating in the stock market. You're looking for stable growth with reduced volatility and decreased risk.
- **You're a defensive-minded investor.** You're more concerned about striking out (losing money) than hitting a home run.
- **You're retired or nearing retirement.** You'd like to grow your nest egg, if possible, but you may not have the time or temperament to wait for the market to recover after suffering a big loss.
- **You're relying on your retirement savings to help cover expenses.** You can't afford the negative effects of a deep market decline and how that would affect your lifestyle in retirement.
- **You want to protect your gains while remaining invested.** You're not so afraid of a market crash or bear market that you want to sell your stock holdings and sit in cash on the sidelines, but you still don't want to lose a significant portion of your portfolio in the event of a steep market decline.
- **You're wary of high stock market valuations.** You think stocks are overpriced and you're afraid of a market decline, but you still want to remain invested, with a defined level of downside protection.
- **You're sitting on cash you'd like to invest, but not without some downside protection.** You have cash that you'd like to put to work. Buffer ETFs offer a simple way to allocate money into the stock market without full downside exposure to losses. They can make investing in the stock market less stressful with reduced risk.
- **You'd like an alternative to bonds with the potential for higher returns.** Buffer ETFs may be helpful for complementing or replacing bonds, increasing the potential for higher returns.
- **You own annuities or structured notes, but you prefer a more liquid investment vehicle without penalties.** Unlike annuities and structured notes, you can sell buffer ETFs at any time without a penalty. (However, selling prior to the end of an outcome period can result in forfeiting some or all of the downside protection and upside gain potential.)

REMEMBER

Bottom line, if the thought of losing 30 percent or more in your stock portfolio during the next bear market will keep you awake at night, then please consider the advantages of investing in buffer ETFs.

AGE CONSIDERATIONS

I asked Karan Sood, CEO of Vest Financial LLC, "Are advisors purchasing Buffer ETFs for pre-retirees and retirees, or for younger clients?" His response:

> "It is my general sense, from speaking with many advisors over the years, that heavier usage has been among clients who are in or near retirement, and tactical usage is more characteristic of younger clients. Of course, every practice is different. Every investor's circumstances and risk appetite are different."

2

Dipping a Toe into Buffer ETF Investing

IN THIS PART . . .

Explore three common buffer ETF investment strategies.

Find buffer ETFs to invest in and compare available options.

Strike the right balance between downside protection and upside potential.

Structure your investment portfolio around buffer ETFs.

IN THIS CHAPTER

» Buying and holding

» Staggering your buys

» Seizing opportunities to improve your position

» Deciding whether to go all-in

» Responding to changing markets

Chapter 4

Looking at Common Ways to Invest in Buffer ETFs

Buffer ETFs are designed with unique structures and features that make them versatile tools for investors, allowing them to support a variety of ways to pursue a range of investment goals and outcomes. In this chapter, I explain several techniques for investing with buffer ETFs, which may inspire you to come up with your own creative approach.

Considering Three Common Strategies

In this section, I describe three common approaches to investing in buffer ETFs and highlight the pros and cons of each.

Static strategy

The static strategy involves buying a single buffer ETF at the start of its outcome period and holding it through the entire outcome period (and perhaps longer) to realize the defined outcome. For example, you purchase FFEB (FT Vest U.S. Equity Buffer ETF — February) at the beginning of its outcome period on February 20, 2024, with a starting gross cap of 16.82 percent and a 10 percent buffer. One year later, the reference asset, the SPDR S&P 500 ETF Trust (SPY), finishes the outcome period up 20.11 percent. FFEB delivers its defined outcome, providing a total return of 16.02 percent (net of fees).

This approach offers the following potential benefits:

- **Predictability:** You know the full starting outcome parameters before you invest, so you know about how much you stand to lose if the reference asset drops below your buffer and the maximum return on your investment if the reference asset rises.
- **Simplicity:** The strategy could be considered a "set it and forget it" passive approach.
- **Protection against emotional investing:** By taking a hands-off approach, you don't buy and sell in response to market swings. In addition, you don't place yourself at potential risk of losing some downside protection or potential upside gain by buying or selling during the intra-outcome period.

The static strategy does have some potential drawbacks, such as the following:

- **Potential loss:** If the fund's value is below the buffer at the end of the outcome period, you absorb the loss that's in excess of the buffer. For example, if you buy a fund with a 10 percent buffer, and the fund is down 25 percent at the end of the outcome period, you lose 15 percent (before fees).
- **Opportunity cost:** If the reference asset finishes the outcome period above the cap, you miss out on any gains that exceed the cap.
- **Unrealized gains evaporate:** If you take a passive, hands-off approach, you could lose all of your unrealized gains that show before the end of the outcome period. Remember, the unrealized gains in your buffer ETF are unprotected until the next reset date. For example, if your ETF shows an unrealized gain of 10 percent six months into the 12-month outcome period, but the reference asset tumbles in the subsequent months and finishes negative on the reset date, you will have forfeited all your gains. With a more

active, hands-on approach, you could have protected your profits early by selling your ETF, and reset your protection level in a different buffer ETF, with new upside potential too. (See Part 3 for more about buying and selling buffer ETFs during the intra-outcome period.)

Laddered strategy

The *laddered strategy* consists of investing a portion of your portfolio into multiple ETFs that have different reset dates. For example, you allocate 25 percent of your portfolio to GJAN (FT Vest U.S. Equity Moderate Buffer ETF — January), 25 percent to GAPR (FT Vest U.S. Equity Moderate Buffer ETF — April), 25 percent to GJUL (FT Vest U.S. Equity Moderate Buffer ETF — July), and 25 percent to GOCT (FT Vest U.S. Equity Moderate Buffer ETF — October). This strategy has three key advantages:

- **Less work than actively managing your investments:** You don't need to continuously research and evaluate monthly buffer ETFs.
- **Potential for less volatility:** Each fund is at a different point in its outcome period, which allows the average buffer and cap across your portfolio to remain balanced and varied as the price of the reference asset changes.
- **Diversified exposure:** By spreading out your total investment over time, you avoid being limited to the return of the reference asset over a single 12-month period, and you're not relying on the timing of one single market entry point.

A laddered strategy has some potential drawbacks, such as the following:

- **Possible dilution of downside protection:** During a sharp market decline, the protection will vary for each ETF. Some "rungs" of the ladder may have partially or fully depleted buffers.
- **Greater complexity:** You have multiple outcome periods, buffers, and caps to keep track of, which requires ongoing rebalancing and investment decisions.
- **Less predictability:** With multiple outcome periods, buffers, and caps, your return at the end of any given period is less predictable than if you were invested in a single buffer ETF.

TIP

You can benefit from a laddered strategy and avoid many of its drawbacks by investing in a laddered buffer ETF, which takes the complexity of executing this strategy off your plate. See Chapter 12 for details.

Opportunistic strategy

The *opportunistic strategy* involves purchasing a buffer ETF with your desired buffer level and cap, and then stepping up or stepping down into a fund with more downside protection or upside potential if your fund's remaining buffer or cap is nearly exhausted.

REMEMBER

Step up means to enter a fund with a higher remaining cap after the reference asset has risen. You expect the reference asset to continue to rise, but only a portion of the cap remains in the existing fund. *Step down* means to enter a fund with more downside protection after the reference asset has dropped. You fear the reference asset may decline further, but only a portion of the buffer remains in the existing fund.

The opportunistic strategy offers the following potential benefits:

- **Less risk:** You can jump ship before the buffer is depleted.
- **Higher return:** You can step up to a fund with a higher remaining cap when the fund you currently hold has perhaps maxed out most of its upside potential.

Stepping up into a higher cap when possible and stepping down to a more protective fund as the buffer erodes certainly seems appealing, but it does have several potential drawbacks, including these:

- **Greater complexity and more work:** Rotating into ETFs with new buffers and caps involves more active management of your portfolio and introduces greater complexity into the process.
- **Reduced tax efficiency:** Every time you sell one fund to buy another, you're creating a taxable event and reducing the tax efficiency built into ETFs. Of course, if the buffer ETF is held in a tax-deferred account such as a traditional or Roth IRA, this is moot.
- **Market timing risk and potential regret:** By stepping up or down, you are introducing an element of market timing into your portfolio. With the benefit of hindsight, after stepping up or down, you may look back some months later and realize you would have performed better had you done nothing — made no portfolio changes. This is always a risk when considering any portfolio adjustment, including stepping up or down in buffer ETFs.

Deciding How Much of Your Portfolio to Invest in Buffer ETFs

Part of any approach to investing in buffer ETFs involves deciding how much of your portfolio to allocate to these investments. Traditionally, investors and their advisors have attempted to diversify their holdings to some degree — for example, 60 percent in stocks, 30 percent in bonds, and 10 percent in cash equivalent investments. Or, if income is the goal, spreading investment capital across dividend stocks, bonds, real-estate investment trusts (REITs), and income-focused ETFs or mutual funds has been a common approach.

Buffer ETFs provide additional tools for diversifying your portfolio — you just need to decide how much of your portfolio you want to allocate to them. Do you want to use them as a slice of your portfolio, a core holding, or your sole holding? Here are some important considerations to help you make a well-informed decision:

- If preserving your investment capital is most important, consider using buffer ETFs as a core holding. If you allocate only a small slice of your portfolio, only that portion of your portfolio has downside protection.
- If long-term compounding high growth is your goal, invest only a slice of your portfolio, if any of it, into buffer ETFs.
- If behavior control matters most (keeping you from making rash investment decisions in response to market volatility), use buffer ETFs as a core holding. They can compel you to take a more disciplined approach to investing.

SLICE OR CORE HOLDING?

I asked Bruce Bond, co-founder and CEO of Innovator Capital Management LLC, "Are advisors using buffer ETFs as core holdings now or as a slice of their overall asset allocation for clients?" His response:

> "We have seen both approaches used. Many initially exchanged their hedged positions, which hadn't performed as anticipated, for buffer ETFs, and then decided to replace larger portions of their equity exposures or even fixed income exposures with buffers."

(continued)

(continued)

I asked, "Why not allocate nearly an entire portfolio in Buffer ETFs?" He replied:

> "Over time, progressive advisors are realizing that this will likely be the way to go in the future. Some have begun to transform their businesses already. The poor performance of 60/40 portfolios (60 percent stocks/40 percent bonds) over the last few years (2022–2024) has made investors and advisors realize that bonds aren't immune to downturns and that relying on historical correlations can be a big mistake."

During my interview with Karan Sood, CEO of Vest Financial LLC, he shared a compelling insight:

> "If advisors want to manage risk in a portfolio through buffer strategies in a meaningful way, it commonly takes a decent percentage allocation to the strategy to do that. For example, five percent of a portfolio in a buffer strategy has frequently not made as meaningful a difference to the overall risk characteristics of the portfolio. So, I have seen advisors migrate their usage of buffer strategies over time from a slice to more of a core holding."

Adjusting Your Approach Based on the Market Environment

Changes in the market environment may influence your approach to investing in buffer ETFs. For example, when stocks are in a bear market and valuations come back down to earth, you may not want your potential upside capped. You may also want to adjust your asset allocation to take advantage of opportunities in different asset classes, such as precious metals, bitcoin, or a specific stock market index; for example, international, emerging, and small caps.

REMEMBER

Regardless of the market environment, follow these three rules:

- Don't buy or sell during the intra-outcome period without a very good reason to do so.
- Don't assume that buffers eliminate the risk of loss — they don't. Their purpose is generally to provide a defined level of downside protection against initial losses.
- Don't overprotect at the expense of derailing your long-term growth goals.

Table 4-1 summarizes adjustments you may want to consider in response to various market environments.

TABLE 4-1 Responding to Changes in the Market Environment

Market Environment	Characterized By	Adjustments to Consider	Cautionary Advice
Strong bull market.	Low volatility. Elevated optimism.	Reduce allocations to buffer ETFs. Reduce downside protection by swapping out of moderate or deep buffers for buffers that provide less protection but higher caps. Use only for short-term capital needs and behavior risk management.	Think twice about making buffer ETFs a core holding. Consider buffer ETFs an insurance policy of sorts, not a vehicle for high growth.
Elevated volatility, market stress.	Sharp drawdowns. Sudden surges. Uncertainty.	Increase allocations to buffer ETFs.	Resist the urge to time the market (to try and wait for it to bottom out). Allocate unemotionally during market declines. Don't try to predict a market rebound; simply look to gradually increase your equity allocation, preferably, on market weakness.
Recovering market.	Volatility subsiding. Investor confidence rising.	Hold existing buffer ETFs if the potential outcome parameters still meet your investment objectives. Reassess whether you still need downside protection.	Avoid stepping up to a higher cap solely because the cap is nearly met in the current outcome period; consider the pros and cons. Avoid automatically rolling into a new outcome period without evaluating the potential outcomes. Be careful about trying to chase higher returns if doing so doesn't align with your risk profile.

(continued)

TABLE 4-1 *(continued)*

Market Environment	Characterized By	Adjustments to Consider	Cautionary Advice
Sideways, choppy markets.	Frequent reversals. Modest gains and losses. Absence of a clear trend.	Use buffer ETFs as a stabilizing tool.	Manage your expectations; don't expect high returns. Don't over-rotate into new buffer ETFs. Use buffers to help manage your emotions and behavior as an investor. Consider tax-loss harvesting in taxable accounts if positions show unrealized losses.
Deep bear market.	Rapid, severe drawdowns. Liquidity stress.	Recognize the limits of buffer protection. Reconsider your overall portfolio allocation; is it still appropriate for your risk profile and investment objectives? Consider reducing cash or bond holdings and increasing your exposure to equities — either in buffer ETFs with minimal protection or in unhedged equities with no upside cap.	Don't assume buffers replace defensive assets. Don't increase your allocation in buffer ETFs solely out of fear. If prices are already very depressed, it could be the wrong time to add protection and cap your upside. Buffers soften the landing, but most don't protect against crashes and deep bear markets, unless you own buffers with total protection. Consider tax-loss harvesting strategies and swapping into buffer ETFs with less protection and higher upside potential.

Choosing Funds Aligned with Your Preferences and Objectives

A key element of any approach to investing in buffer ETFs involves choosing funds that are tailored to your preferences and objectives. Here are some guidelines for choosing the right buffer ETFs for you:

- **Reference asset:** The *reference asset* is the underlying asset the fund tracks. If you're a U.S.-based investor, consider choosing a fund that tracks a broad, diversified index of large U.S. companies (for example, S&P 500). If you're willing to accept greater volatility for a potentially higher return, consider a fund that tracks the tech-heavy Invesco QQQ Trust (QQQ). For exposure to markets outside the U.S., look for a fund that tracks the MSCI EAFE index (EFA tracks large and mid-cap companies in Europe, Australasia, and the Far East) or the MSCI EM Index (EEM tracks large and mid-cap companies from 25 emerging market countries). You can also invest in buffer ETFs that track bitcoin, gold, and other asset classes.

TIP

Consider diversifying your portfolio by allocating portions of it to buffer ETFs that track different reference assets.

- **Type:** ETF types include buffer, barrier income, buffer income, accelerated, uncapped, laddered, step-up strategy, floor, dual-directional, deep buffer, and total protection. The ETF type or strategy reflects how the fund is structured, how it functions, and its overall level of downside protection. A buffer income ETF could be considered by risk-averse investors who favor income generation over growth. Accelerated buffer ETFs are generally a good choice when markets are rising slowly, with single-digit, average annual returns. Uncapped buffer ETFs could be attractive when prices are depressed, but poised for a quick and substantial recovery, for example, during the COVID-19 pandemic. Deep buffer ETFs appeal to investors who desire significant downside protection and are willing to give up a higher percentage of potential gains in exchange for it. See Part 4 for more about different types of buffer ETFs.
- **Buffer percentage:** The ETF type influences the level of downside protection, and you should know the exact percentage of protection you're getting before making a purchase. As discussed in Chapter 3, 15 percent protection is typically the sweet spot for most investors. This level of moderate protection provides reasonable protection in most market environments. However, you can opt for up to 100 percent downside protection. Just keep in mind that, generally, the deeper the buffer, the lower the cap.
- **Outcome period:** Outcome periods are typically 3, 6, or 12 months, and funds automatically roll into a new outcome period with the same buffer level and a newly calculated cap. To choose an outcome period, ask yourself how long you can leave the money invested in the fund (your investment time horizon) before you'll need it. If you're uncertain, opt for a shorter outcome period or don't invest. A longer outcome period could deliver a more predictable outcome and better terms (higher annualized upside gain potential), but upside cap levels are ever-changing, so this is not a given.
- **Cap:** The reference asset, ETF type, buffer percentage, outcome period, interest rates, and market volatility all influence cap levels. In recent years, caps have generally ranged from 10 to 14 percent annualized for a 12-month buffer ETF with moderate protection. Again, typically, the deeper the buffer, the lower the cap, so deep buffer ETFs have a relatively low cap. Before you

invest in a buffer ETF, check the estimated cap (they change daily) on the issuer's website and ask yourself how much upside you're willing to give up for the downside protection you want. If the reference asset gains 15 percent over the outcome period, and your return is capped at 10 percent, are you going to kick yourself because you missed out on the extra 5 percent gain?

Here are a few examples of how you may use these criteria to invest in buffer ETFs in a way that aligns with your preferences and objectives:

You're a conservative investor focused on preserving your investment capital:

- **Reference asset:** SPDR S&P 500 ETF Trust (SPY)
- **Type:** Deep or total protection, floor, or income
- **Buffer:** 20 to 100 percent
- **Outcome period:** 12 months or longer
- **Cap:** Low (as of this writing, 10 percent or less annualized — that's the price you pay for more downside protection)

You're a moderate risk investor, and you want the potential for growth, but can't afford to lose much of your investment capital:

- **Reference asset:** SPDR S&P 500 ETF Trust (SPY)
- **Type:** Moderate buffer
- **Buffer:** 15 to 20 percent
- **Outcome period:** 12 months
- **Cap:** Moderate (as of this writing, 10 to 13 percent)

Your objective is risk-managed growth:

- **Reference asset:** SPDR S&P 500 ETF Trust (SPY), Invesco QQQ Trust (QQQ)
- **Type:** Minimal buffer
- **Buffer:** 9 to 12 percent
- **Outcome period:** 12 months
- **Cap:** Relatively high (as of this writing, 13–18 percent)

IN THIS CHAPTER

» Finding the information you need

» Evaluating outcome parameters

» Comparing issuers

Chapter 5

Finding and Researching Buffer ETFs

The increasing demand for buffer ETFs has spawned a proliferation of funds and issuers, giving you more choices than ever. In this chapter, I provide guidance on how to research buffer ETFs, narrow the field, and check out what different issuers have to offer.

Tracking Down Buffer ETFs to Consider

Every issuer of buffer ETFs has a website where you can find information about the funds they offer. Table 5-1 leads you to the websites of the top issuers of buffer ETFs (as of this writing).

After accessing the website, poke around to find a product table or other tool that lists available buffer ETFs or enables you to search for buffer ETFs. Some websites are easier to navigate than others. For example, on Innovator's website, you simply select ETFs in the menu bar at the top and select Product Table to view all available ETFs. At the top of the table, you can select Buffer to display buffer ETFs exclusively (see Figure 5-1). Note, some issuers may require you to sign up (it's free) on their websites to access more advanced research tools.

TABLE 5-1 ETF Issuer Websites

Issuer	Website
Innovator	www.innovatoretfs.com
First Trust	www.ftportfolios.com
AllianzIM	www.allianzim.com/etfs
PGIM	www.pgim.com/us/en/intermediary/investment-capabilities/products/etf
BlackRock	www.ishares/outcomes
Calamos	www.calamos.com/funds/etf
Pacer	www.paceretfs.com
AllianceBernstein	www.alliancebernstein.com
TrueShares	www.true-shares.com/structured-outcome-etfs
Aptus	aptusetfs.com

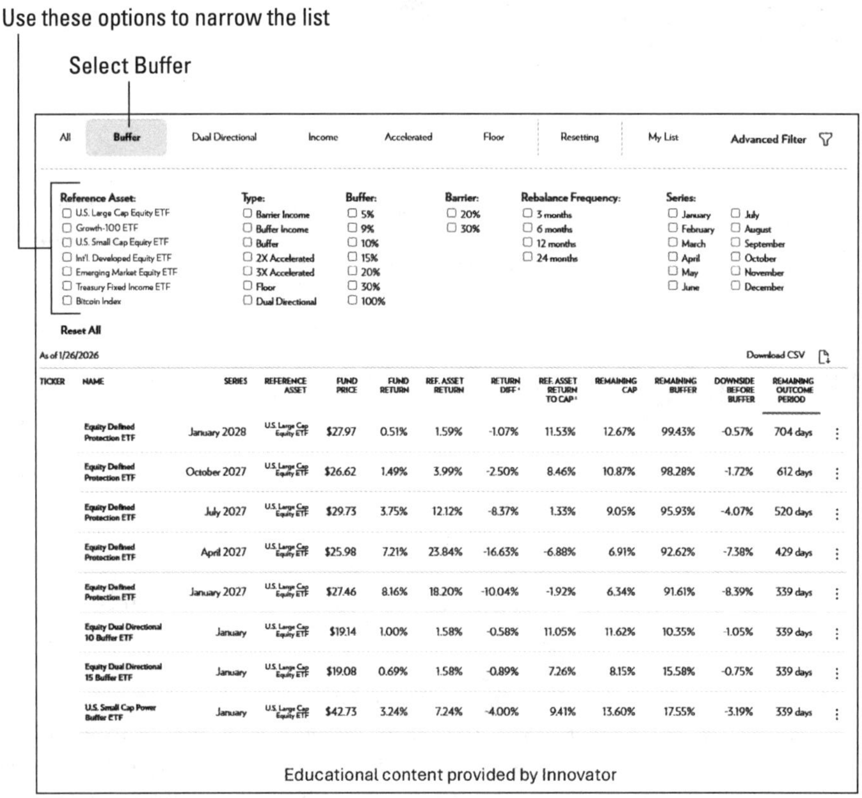

TICKER	NAME	SERIES	REFERENCE ASSET	FUND PRICE	FUND RETURN	REF. ASSET RETURN	RETURN DIFF¹	REF. ASSET RETURN TO CAP¹	REMAINING CAP	REMAINING BUFFER	DOWNSIDE BEFORE BUFFER	REMAINING OUTCOME PERIOD
	Equity Defined Protection ETF	January 2028	U.S. Large Cap Equity ETF	$27.97	0.51%	1.59%	-1.07%	11.53%	12.67%	99.43%	-0.57%	704 days
	Equity Defined Protection ETF	October 2027	U.S. Large Cap Equity ETF	$26.62	1.49%	3.99%	-2.50%	8.46%	10.87%	98.28%	-1.72%	612 days
	Equity Defined Protection ETF	July 2027	U.S. Large Cap Equity ETF	$29.73	3.75%	12.12%	-8.37%	1.33%	9.05%	95.93%	-4.07%	520 days
	Equity Defined Protection ETF	April 2027	U.S. Large Cap Equity ETF	$25.98	7.21%	23.84%	-16.63%	-6.88%	6.91%	92.62%	-7.38%	429 days
	Equity Defined Protection ETF	January 2027	U.S. Large Cap Equity ETF	$27.46	8.16%	18.20%	-10.04%	-1.92%	6.34%	91.61%	-8.39%	339 days
	Equity Dual Directional 10 Buffer ETF	January	U.S. Large Cap Equity ETF	$19.14	1.00%	1.58%	-0.58%	11.05%	11.62%	10.35%	-1.05%	339 days
	Equity Dual Directional 15 Buffer ETF	January	U.S. Large Cap Equity ETF	$19.08	0.69%	1.58%	-0.89%	7.26%	8.15%	15.58%	-0.75%	339 days
	U.S. Small Cap Power Buffer ETF	January	U.S. Large Cap Equity ETF	$42.73	3.24%	7.24%	-4.00%	9.41%	13.60%	17.55%	-3.19%	339 days

Educational content provided by Innovator

FIGURE 5-1: A partial list of Innovator buffer ETFs.

Courtesy of Innovator

Checkbox options above the product list enable you to narrow the list further based on various outcome parameters, as discussed in the next section.

To access details about a buffer ETF, select it from the list. A summary appears providing the outcome parameters and other information you need to make an informed choice, including the series, outcome period, rebalance frequency, starting cap, starting buffer, and exposure (see Figure 5-2). Scroll down, and you'll see links (on the right) for additional information.

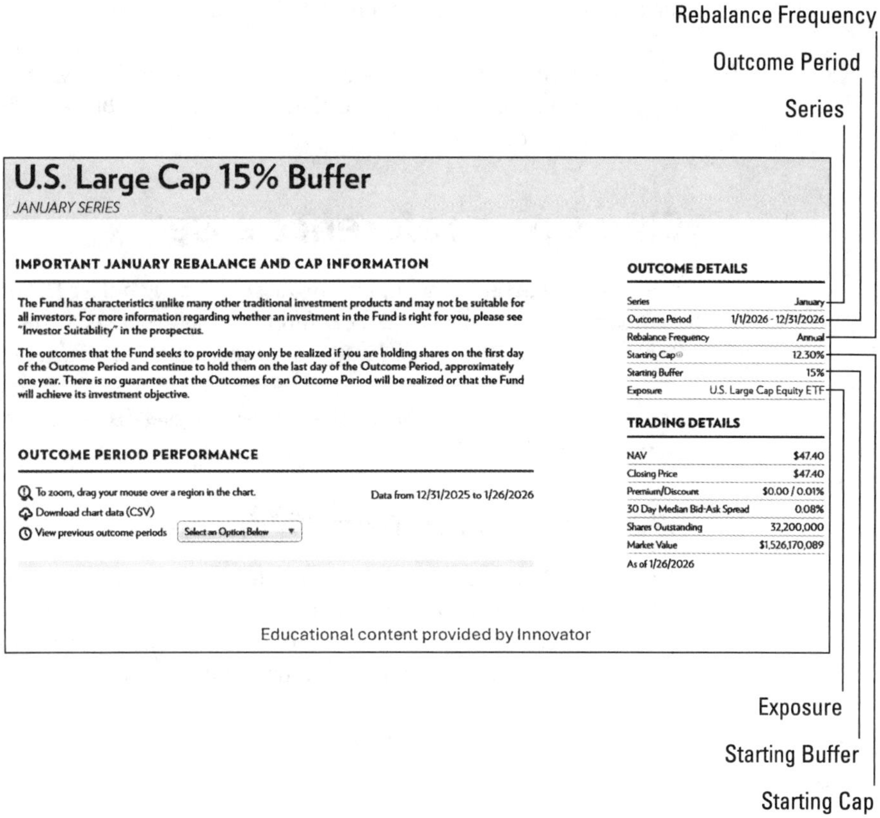

FIGURE 5-2: Key details of a 15 percent buffer ETF.

Courtesy of Innovator

In the following section, I provide guidance on how to interpret this information, so you can choose a buffer ETF that's a good match for you and your investment objectives.

Narrowing the Field: Choosing Outcome Parameters

Buffer ETF *outcome parameters* are the defined variables that determine how the ETF is expected to perform relative to its reference asset, over its set outcome period — how much it can potentially lose or gain, assuming you hold it for the specified number of days. These parameters include the reference asset, strategy/type, outcome period, buffer (downside protection), cap (upside participation), series (purchase month), and reset/rebalance frequency.

In this section, I explain each outcome parameter and provide guidance for evaluating it, so you can narrow the field to only those buffer ETFs that meet your investment objectives.

Choosing a reference asset

The reference asset is the underlying asset that the buffer ETF tracks. Buffer ETFs commonly track a large, diverse reference asset, such as SPDR S&P 500 ETF Trust (SPY) or Invesco QQQ Trust (QQQ), but they can track a variety of assets.

The following sections discuss the reference assets that buffer ETFs often track, along with their potential benefits and drawbacks.

SPDR S&P 500 ETF Trust (SPY)

The SPDR S&P 500 ETF Trust (SPY) tracks the Standard & Poor's 500 stock market index of the largest publicly traded U.S. companies across multiple industries, including technology, healthcare, finance, consumer goods, and more, which is why it's often used as a benchmark for overall U.S. stock market performance.

Buffer ETFs often use SPY as their reference asset because it offers the following advantages:

- Broad diversification
- Deep liquidity
- Long-term track record over many defined outcome periods, which allows investors to calculate the probability of various potential outcomes

SPY does have a few shortcomings when used as a reference asset:

- Given the historical volatility of the reference asset, some buffer ETFs may not provide enough protection during deep drawdowns.
- Historical returns can be "extreme," meaning they fall outside the parameters of a conventional buffer ETF. SPY rarely returns its average annual historical return of approximately 10 percent; rather, it often outperforms its average, and could also lose more than the protection offered by a minimal or moderate buffer during bear markets.
- The upside cap limits the potential gain when SPY outperforms its historical average, which is often the case in strong bull markets.
- The index is cap-weighted, meaning companies with larger market capitalization (market cap) have more influence over the performance. As of this writing, the index is heavily weighted in large technology companies, including NVIDIA, Apple, Microsoft, Amazon, and Alphabet (Google), creating a *concentration risk* (the potential for a significant loss if a large portion of an investment portfolio is focused on a single asset class or sector) if the tech sector suffers a deep decline.
- SPY is so widely used that it provides little differentiation across buffer ETFs that use it as their reference asset.

REMEMBER

SPY is the most popular reference asset for investors who want to reduce volatility or hedge in a buffer ETF that offers some protection against potential losses.

Invesco S&P 500 Equal Weight ETF (RSP)

The Invesco S&P 500 Equal Weight ETF (RSP) tracks the same companies as the SPDR S&P 500 ETF Trust (SPY) but gives all companies equal weighting, meaning it doesn't have the same concentration risk as SPY.

As a reference asset, RSP has the following advantages:

- Reduced concentration risk — broader representation across sectors
- Deep liquidity
- Potentially lower volatility than SPY given broader diversification of the dollars invested

Potential drawbacks of RSP include these:

- RSP is not a popular benchmark for performance.
- RSP tends to underperform SPY in markets driven by mega-cap stocks.
- Reduced exposure to the tech sector could adversely affect performance, as it has for many years. Tech has been an important driver of returns of the S&P 500, so diversifying away from tech in an equal-weighted index could continue to hurt performance.
- Buffer ETFs that track RSP are limited. Currently, only FT Vest offers a series of four ETFs that use RSP as the reference asset.

REMEMBER

RSP is best for diversifying exposure broadly across large-cap stocks. If you think the prices of the top 10 stocks in SPY, or the technology sector as a whole, are inflated, you may want to consider buffer ETFs that use RSP as their reference asset.

Invesco QQQ Trust (QQQ)

The Invesco QQQ Trust (QQQ) is an ETF that tracks the performance of the Nasdaq-100, which includes 100 of the largest non-financial companies listed on the Nasdaq stock exchange. This index is heavily weighted in technology stocks, including NVIDIA, Apple, Microsoft, Amazon, Meta Platforms, and Alphabet (Google) — that is, it's more heavily weighted than SPY in favor of the technology sector.

As a reference asset, the main benefit of QQQ is its strong long-term growth profile. According to *Morningstar*, over the past 15 years (ending March 31, 2026) it has delivered an average annual return of 17.66 percent and has outperformed SPY in seven of the past 10 years.

However, QQQ does have some drawbacks, including the following:

- Higher volatility than SPY: Historical performance shows it is typically 20 to 30 percent more volatile than SPY.
- Higher concentration risk: QQQ has greater exposure to tech stocks.
- Prone to deep drawdowns: QQQ has declined 30 percent or more during crashes and/or bear markets. A *drawdown* is a decline in the value of an asset from its highest point (peak) to its lowest point (trough).

REMEMBER

Consider choosing a buffer ETF that uses QQQ as its reference asset if you want to participate in the returns of high-growth tech companies, but with the benefit of some downside protection. Keep in mind, however, that you're exposing your investment capital to greater risk and volatility.

iShares Russell 2000 ETF (IWM)

The iShares Russell 2000 ETF (IWM) tracks the performance of the Russell 2000 index, which comprises the smallest 2,000 companies in the U.S. stock market. IWM is commonly used as a benchmark for the performance of investments in small-cap companies across numerous industries, including healthcare, financial services, technology, industrials, consumer products and services, and energy.

As a reference asset, the primary benefits of IWM are the exposure it provides to small-cap stocks and diversification away from large-cap stocks.

Disadvantages of IWM include the following:

- Higher historical volatility of returns: IWM has been approximately 20 percent more volatile than SPY.
- Given increased volatility, small-cap drawdowns could carry a higher risk of exceeding the buffer.
- Reduced earnings predictability when compared to investments in larger, more established companies.
- Poor recent performance relative to large-cap stocks. According to *Morningstar*, in the past 10 years (ending March 20, 2026), IWM has returned approximately 4.45 percent less, on average annually, than SPY (9.69 percent versus 14.09 percent).

REMEMBER

The more volatile the reference asset, the more valuable the buffer. Thankfully, the increased volatility of returns often results in a higher cap. As of this writing, according to Innovator, the upside cap for a 15 percent buffer ETF that tracks IWM is substantially higher than the equivalent buffer ETF that tracks SPY. The Innovator U.S. Small Cap Power Buffer ETF — January (KJAN) had a gross starting cap of 17.33 percent on December 31, 2025, while the Innovator U.S. Large Cap Power Buffer ETF — January (PJAN) had a gross cap of 12.30 percent. This extra 5 percent upside potential over the 12-month outcome period is *not* insignificant.

iShares MSCI EAFE ETF (EFA)

The iShares MSCI EAFE ETF (EFA) tracks the performance of large- and mid-cap companies in 21 developed countries outside the U.S. and Canada, including Europe, Australia, and the Far East. It serves as a benchmark for the performance of international equities.

For use as a reference asset, the primary benefit of EFA is that it allows you to diversify your portfolio by investing in companies in developed countries outside the U.S. and Canada.

Potential drawbacks include the following:

- » Exposure to currencies other than the U.S. dollar adds complexity and risk for U.S.-based investors.
- » Historically, EFA has underperformed U.S. equities. According to *Morningstar*, in the past 15 years (ending March 20, 2026), the iShares MSCI EAFE ETF (EFA) obtained a 6.42 percent average annual return compared to 13.44 percent for SPY.

iShares MSCI Emerging Markets ETF (EEM)

The iShares MSCI Emerging Markets ETF (EEM) tracks an index of large- and mid-cap companies in emerging markets. An *emerging market* is an economy that's transitioning from developing to developed status; it's characterized by rapid growth, increasing industrialization, and rising income levels.

The main benefits of investing in emerging markets are added diversification away from U.S. stocks and the potential for high growth, if the stars align.

Drawbacks of investing in emerging markets include the following:

- » Heightened risk and volatility.
- » Potential for high returns may not materialize. According to *Morningstar*, in the past 10 years (ending March 20, 2026), EEM has shown an average annual return of approximately 7.40 percent while SPY has returned 14.09 percent, on average annually.
- » Increased political and currency risks.

REMEMBER

For U.S.-based investors, buffer ETFs tied to the EEM index are generally better suited for a smaller allocation — around 10 percent to 20 percent of a portfolio — rather than serving as a core position. A similar approach applies to investments linked to the EAFE index.

iShares 20+ Year Treasury Bond ETF (TLT)

The iShares 20+ Year Treasury Bond ETF (TLT) tracks the performance of *20+ year Treasuries* — U.S. government bonds, which are considered very safe investments. However, long-term bonds are volatile and are very sensitive to changes in interest rates: if interest rates fall, their price rises, and if interest rates rise, their price falls.

The benefits of investing in TLT include the following:

- Sometimes TLT has been a good hedge against stock market drawdowns.
- Increased diversification away from stocks with the potential to reduce the overall volatility of a total portfolio.
- Potential for high returns in certain market environments, most notably rapidly declining interest rates.

TLT does have some drawbacks, including the following:

- Potential reduced upside compared to equities.
- Rising interest rates can cause prices to plummet on long-term bonds.
- Limited number of buffer ETF options available for investors to consider. Currently, there are only two buffer ETFs that track TLT, both issued by Innovator.

REMEMBER

20+ year Treasuries (TLT) can be volatile, and their value tends to rise and fall inversely (uncorrelated) to stock prices, so when used in tandem with stocks, they may reduce overall volatility across the portfolio. However, stocks and bonds don't always rise and fall inversely — in 2022, they both suffered double-digit percentage losses.

CME CF Bitcoin Reference Rate — NY Variant (BRRNY)

CME CF Bitcoin Reference Rate — New York Variant (BRRNY) is a real-time index calculated by the CME Group and CF Benchmarks, aggregating the trade flow of major spot bitcoin exchanges. (The word "spot" in this context refers to the immediate purchase, sale, or exchange of bitcoin.) BlackRock's iShares Bitcoin Trust (IBIT), the largest spot bitcoin ETF by assets under management, uses this rate as its benchmark. Also, Calamos, the issuer of many Bitcoin Structured Alt Protection ETFs, uses BRRNY as the reference asset in its funds. The main benefits of investing in a buffer ETF that tracks the bitcoin reference rate are the following:

- You gain exposure to the price movements of bitcoin without having to buy cryptocurrencies.
- You have a level of downside protection against potential losses in a very volatile asset class prone to large drawdowns.
- Bitcoin 100 percent buffer ETFs are available with fairly compelling upside caps. Given the volatility of the reference asset, upside caps can potentially exceed those offered by equity benchmarks.
- Diversification away from stocks and bonds. Bitcoin has consistently maintained a low correlation with traditional asset classes.

Investing in a buffer ETF that tracks the bitcoin reference rate has several potential drawbacks, including the following:

- Extreme volatility, which may overwhelm buffers
- Outcomes that are very sensitive to market timing
- Structural and regulatory risks
- Limited investment options compared to conventional buffer ETFs that track stock asset classes
- Non-conventional buffer levels: Most bitcoin buffer ETFs function as floor products, subjecting shareholders to initial losses (for example, investors absorb the first 10 or 20 percent loss), but then provide full protection below the floor level

WARNING

Given the volatility of this asset class, investing in bitcoin should be considered highly speculative. Consider investing only a small percentage of your portfolio for added diversification.

SPDR Gold Shares ETF (GLD)

The SPDR Gold Shares ETF (GLD) tracks the price of gold bullion.

The main benefits of investing in a buffer ETF that tracks the price of gold bullion are the following:

- You gain exposure to gold without having to buy and store the metal.
- Gold can serve as a hedge against equities — it's typically uncorrelated.
- Gold can be an important diversifier in a total portfolio.
- Gold has proven to be a valuable store of wealth for centuries.
- Gold can act as a hedge against inflation.
- The buffer gives you some downside protection in case the price of gold declines.

Potential drawbacks of investing in a buffer ETF that tracks gold include the following:

- The cap can limit upside potential during a strong gold rally.
- Returns can be flat over long periods and underperform equities.
- Investment options are limited. As of this writing, only one buffer ETF tracks the price of gold — FT Vest Gold Strategy Quarterly Buffer ETF (BGLD).

REMEMBER

A buffer ETF that tracks the price of gold is useful primarily for diversifying a total portfolio to help offset the risks of investing in stocks. Gold has much greater upside potential than bonds or cash-equivalent investments. And at times, gold can act as a hedge against inflation. However, precious metals, including gold, can be very volatile, so having a buffer in place may appeal to many investors.

Deciding on a strategy/type

A buffer ETF's *type* or *strategy* reflects how it is structured to provide the defined outcome — how much downside it absorbs, how much upside it allows, the overall timeframe, and how often it resets (to provide a fresh buffer and new cap). Like the reference asset, it has a great deal of influence over the fund's performance. In fact, two buffer ETFs that track the same reference asset can deliver vastly different outcomes depending on how they are structured.

Buffer ETF strategies/types include the following:

- **Accelerated:** Seeks to double or triple the performance of the reference asset to a cap, which can be useful in a single-digit return environment. Some have a level of protection, and some do not.
- **Barrier income:** Provides quarterly income over the outcome period with downside protection. However, the protection applies only if losses remain above a preset barrier level. For example, if the barrier is 20 percent and the reference asset drops 19 percent, your investment is protected, but if the reference asset falls 21 percent, it's not. You may receive a competitive yield with barrier income ETFs, but if the barrier is breached at the end of the outcome period, you absorb the entire loss.
- **Buffer:** Allows participation in the reference asset to a cap while providing a defined level of downside protection against initial losses to a specified percentage.

  REMEMBER

  A buffer may provide a specific level of protection, such as protecting against the first 10 percent loss, or it may provide a range of downside protection, such as –5 to –30 percent, which means you absorb the first 5 percent loss, you are protected against the next 25 percent loss, and then you absorb any loss beyond 30 percent.
- **Buffer income:** Generates income over the outcome period, typically with monthly distributions, while providing a level of downside protection against initial losses.
- **Buffer step-up strategy:** Automatically resets to a higher cap if the reference asset reaches a certain upside threshold. It will also automatically reset the buffer if the reference asset declines by a certain percentage. This is an actively managed strategy that does the work for you.
- **Dual-directional:** Offers the potential for positive returns in both rising and declining markets while also providing a level of downside protection.
- **Floor:** Protects against losses beyond a predetermined level; for example, you may absorb the first 10 percent loss, but are protected against any loss exceeding that level.
- **Laddered:** Holds typically 12 underlying buffer ETFs with different reset months (or sometimes four buffer ETFs with quarterly resets), so you always have some holdings early, in the middle of, and near the end of an outcome period. This diversified managed strategy is particularly popular with investors and investment advisors wanting a sleeve of a total portfolio invested in buffer ETFs.

- **Uncapped:** Allows for unlimited upside growth potential beyond what is known as the "spread" while also providing a level of downside protection, typically 15 percent. As of this writing, the net spread equals approximately 4 percent (before fees) for an uncapped buffer ETF with 15 percent protection that tracks the SPDR S&P 500 ETF Trust (SPY). A spread of 4 percent means an investor gives up the first 4 percent positive return over the outcome period but captures all the upside (no cap) beyond 4 percent.

See Chapters 11–18 for more in-depth coverage of buffer ETF strategies.

Settling on an outcome period

A buffer ETF's *outcome period* is the time over which the upside cap and downside buffer are in effect, typically 3, 6, or 12 months. The outcome period influences timing risk, flexibility, and predictability. All buffer ETFs are highly liquid (you can sell at any time during the outcome period), regardless of the length of the outcome period. However, it's typically advisable to buy and hold from the start to the end of your chosen outcome period, so you should choose wisely. Use the following guidelines when choosing an outcome period:

- Shorter outcome periods allow for a shorter time commitment with regard to the performance of the reference asset. If you need to cash out in three months rather than waiting 12 months, consider a quarterly buffer ETF.
- Buffer ETFs with longer outcome periods typically have higher caps, though not necessarily on an annualized basis. Those with shorter outcome periods reset more frequently, giving you a fresh buffer and new cap. Generally speaking, assuming the same buffer level — for example, 10 percent — a shorter outcome period would be considered more conservative. For example, a quarterly buffer with 10 percent protection resets and provides new protection four times per year, while a 12-month buffer resets only once per year. Neither would provide significant protection in a fast-plunging market, but in a slowly declining market, the quarterly buffer with more frequent resets would likely perform much better over the course of 12 months, given the more frequent buffer resets.
- Typically, the longer the outcome period, the more predictable the outcome. Shorter periods can be more sensitive to short-term price changes in the reference asset.

TIP

Buffer ETFs generally offer the most predictable outcome when held for the entire outcome period. If you don't have the patience to hold a fund for at least 12 months, consider investing in a buffer ETF with a shorter outcome period (3 or 6 months). After seeing how a short-term buffer ETF performs (very likely it will be in line with the published outcome parameters), you may be more comfortable investing over a 12-month outcome period.

Gauging how much downside protection you want

Deciding on a level of downside protection comes down to figuring out how much loss you're trying to avoid and how much upside you're willing to give up to avoid it. Here are a few rules of thumb:

- The greater the downside protection, the higher the cost (the lower the cap).
- Protection against the first 5 percent loss is the most expensive.
- Buffer ETFs that protect against the first 15 or 20 percent loss should provide a sufficient level of protection to help mitigate losses in most market environments (see Chapter 3 for details). You may want a deeper buffer if you are very risk-averse, valuations are stretched, the reference asset is more volatile than the S&P 500, or your market outlook warrants greater protection. Consider a smaller buffer with a higher cap if the reference asset is already deep in bear-market territory and valuations are attractive.

TIP

Consider the specific role the ETF plays in your portfolio:

- **Tactical or satellite position:** Minimal buffer — you can tolerate more risk in pursuit of an opportunity for a higher return.
- **Core holding:** Minimal to moderate buffer — you want to stay invested (not try to time the market) but are concerned about losing money. 10 to 20 percent protection for a portfolio with core buffer ETF positions is generally sufficient and reduces the risk of large drawdowns.
- **Volatility damper or defensive sleeve:** Deep buffer — you want to protect a portion of your portfolio against deep losses, but still want some upside gain potential beyond what bonds or risk-free investments offer.

Choosing a series/purchase month

When you buy a buffer ETF can affect the outcome as much as or more than *what* you buy. Buying at the start of an outcome period ensures that you're getting the published downside protection (buffer) and upside participation (cap) the fund offers.

When you're shopping for a buffer ETF, look for a series that's nearing the start of a new outcome period; for example, in December, look for funds with a new outcome period that starts on January 1 (actually January 2 in practice, because markets are closed on New Year's Day), and wait to buy it in the closing hours of trading on the reset date (the last trading day before the start of the new outcome period).

REMEMBER

You can buy ETFs during the intra-outcome period, but before you do, be sure you understand how much downside protection and upside participation remain in the period. Be certain to check the downside-before-buffer risk if you're considering an intra-outcome purchase. You can find this information on the issuer's website. See Part 3 for additional guidance on buying buffer ETFs during the intra-outcome period.

Comparing expense ratios and total cost of ownership (TCO)

Fund issuers are required to publish their *expense ratios* — the fees they charge for managing the fund — and this number can be helpful when you're comparing the cost of different funds. Typically, buffer ETF fees range from 0.50 percent to 0.90 percent annualized. As with other ETFs, these fees come directly out of the net asset value (NAV) of the ETFs over the course of the outcome period. (*NAV* represents the dollar value of one share.)

Investors may initially balk at buffer ETF fees because they're higher than passively managed stock ETFs. However, recognize that you really can't do this yourself; you can't purchase four option contracts in a tax- and cost-efficient manner and achieve the same outcome parameters as the large issuers of buffer ETFs. They have scale and can likely get an upside cap far greater than you would be able to obtain on your own, trading much smaller dollar amounts. Personally, I wouldn't attempt to trade the options myself, despite my many decades of advisory experience, but you may think differently.

TIP

What's most important when comparing fees of different buffer ETF issuers is how the fee impacts the net upside cap. I would suggest you simply compare the caps of ETFs that have the same level of downside protection, the same starting date of the outcome period, and the same duration of the outcome period ("apples-to-apples"). Then, go with the series that offers the highest net upside cap.

If you feel compelled to scrutinize the TCO more closely, take into account the following potential costs:

- **Expense ratio:** The management fee, which is a percentage of your total investment in the fund. If the expense ratio is 0.79 percent per year, you multiply 0.0079 by the total you invested in the fund; for example, 0.0079 × $40,000 = $316.

  REMEMBER

  Issuers that offer buffer ETFs with shorter-term outcome periods also publish their expense ratios on an annualized basis. So, if you're buying a quarterly buffer with an annualized fee of 0.85 percent, simply divide it by four to know the approximate fee you're paying per 3-month outcome period.

- **Bid-ask spread:** The cost of buying and selling your shares. You buy at the ask price and sell at the bid price; the difference is the bid-ask spread, which is the price you pay. To convert it to a percentage, use the following formula: (Ask price – Bid price)/Mid Price. So, if the ask price is $49.93, the bid price is $49.82, and the midpoint is $49.88: ($49.93 – $49.82)/$49.88 = $0.11/$49.88 = 0.0022 or 0.22 percent.

  REMEMBER

  You pay the bid-ask spread both when you buy and sell, so the total cost could be double (or more) than the cost you paid when buying shares.

  Calculating and comparing bid-ask spreads is really tough. When I enter orders, I'm typically happy to get in the middle of the spread or better. In a fast-moving market, the bid-ask may be the least of your concerns — the market movement itself can help or hurt you more than the spread. Still, no doubt you want the spread as tight as possible: a few pennies or so, hopefully even tighter.

- **Opportunity cost:** The greatest potential opportunity cost in a buffer ETF is the return you could miss out on if the return of the reference asset exceeds the cap at the end of the outcome period. You can't calculate opportunity cost into the TCO until the end of the outcome period or when you sell your shares, but you should obviously consider differences in caps when comparing buffer ETFs.

- **Dividend forfeiture:** With most buffer ETFs, dividends don't pass through to shareholders. You won't know exactly how much money this represents in advance of the dividends being paid, so you can't calculate it into the TCO, but you should be aware of it when comparing investment options — for example, if you're choosing between a buffer ETF and a traditional ETF that focuses on companies that pay dividends. Note, some buffer ETF structures, like those employed by BlackRock, pay annual dividends, but most buffer ETFs do not (other than those specifically designed to produce income).

KEEPING DIVIDENDS IN PERSPECTIVE

Some investors prefer not to receive dividends. Why? Well, on the day an individual stock or ETF trades *ex-dividend*, its price declines by the amount of the dividend. Say it declares a dividend of $1 per share. On the ex-dividend date, when the stock trades without the dividend for shareholders buying it, the stock trades down by $1 plus or minus the market action for that day. When the shareholder receives the dividend, typically up to a week later, in a taxable account, it's a taxable event. So, the shareholder will likely owe some taxes for receiving the dividend, even if it wasn't wanted.

I could argue that I'd rather receive no dividends (think Berkshire Hathaway stock) and simply sell at a long-term capital gain tax rate if I need to raise cash for whatever reason. So, I don't view the fact that most buffer ETFs don't pay dividends as a disadvantage.

TIP

When you're choosing between two buffer ETFs that track the same reference asset and have nearly the same buffer and cap, compare their costs in terms of expense ratio + bid-ask spread. For example, suppose Fund A has an expense ratio of 0.70 percent, and a bid-ask spread of 0.40 percent — its TCO is 1.10 percent. Fund B has an expense ratio of 0.85 percent and a bid-ask spread of 0.10 percent, so its TCO is 0.95 percent. Although Fund B has a higher expense ratio, its total cost is less than Fund A's.

REMEMBER

CONSIDER THE TCO

I asked Burke Ashenden, Director of Capital Markets at Innovator Capital Management, his opinion about buffer ETF expense ratios and TCO. Here's how I phrased it:

> "A typical advisor or investor could look at the expense ratio of a buffer ETF and decide they are quite a bit more expensive than other ETFs, but you've mentioned to me in the past that the publicized expense ratio doesn't tell the whole story. You've said the total cost of ownership is what's critical to understand. Please explain further."

Burke responded as follows:

> "Most investors only think about the management fee when evaluating the cost of a financial product. As a former trader, my perspective is a little different. I like to consider all the variables that affect my return when I make a purchase. So, one thing I would call investors' attention to is the bid-ask spread and execution costs when evaluating an ETF."

(continued)

(continued)

"How wide is the ETF's bid-ask spread? 'Let's say an ETF has an expense ratio of 0.25 percent with a 0.75 percent bid-ask spread. 'We'll call that ETF A. ETF B has the same exact exposure but offers a 0.30 percent expense ratio with a bid-ask spread of 0.10 percent."

"Most investors will choose ETF A because of the lower expense ratio, but ETF B is actually cheaper from a TCO perspective. Think about that for a second. Assuming equivalent performance, it'll take the investor of ETF A several years to recoup the spread costs for it to truly be less expensive than ETF B."

As with all ETFs, buffer ETF trading costs are higher if you buy and sell frequently, because each time you buy or sell, you're having to pay some difference in the bid-ask spread. Keep this in mind if you are planning to actively trade buffer ETFs.

Getting to Know the Issuers

The two big players in the buffer ETF space are Innovator and First Trust Vest (FT Vest). AllianzIM, AllianceBernstein, BlackRock (iShares), also offer buffer ETFs, as do PGIM (formerly known as Prudential Global Investment Management), Calamos, and others. Issuers can differ in the following ways:

- **Size:** Larger issuers may allow for tighter bid-ask spreads, greater liquidity, and lower trading friction. Smaller issuers may offer niche products or tweaked versions (different buffer levels, reference assets, or outcome periods) of some of the larger issuer offerings that may appeal to you.
- **Selection:** Larger issuers offer dozens of different ETFs that track different reference assets, employ varied outcome strategies, and have different outcome periods, buffers, caps, and costs. Other issuers may have only a few limited offerings.
- **Skills, experience, and partnerships:** Some issuers have been in the business longer than others. Some outsource their portfolio management or options trading to sub-advisors. Expertise and the right partnerships can translate into lower costs, greater liquidity, higher caps, and more predictable outcomes.

» **Transparency:** Look for an issuer that demonstrates a commitment to transparency — one that makes it easy to comparison shop and access the information you need to make well-informed investment decisions. Especially important is having easy access to buffer and cap updates daily and throughout the trading day. Some issuers update the potential outcome parameters frequently during the trading day, and others do not.

Innovator

Innovator introduced the first buffer ETFs, launching the category in 2018 and helping to define it. The company excels in the following areas:

» **Selection:** Innovator offers a broad selection of buffer ETFs characterized by:

- Multiple buffer levels: 9, 15, 20, 30, and even 100 percent
- Numerous outcome periods, ranging from 3, 6, 12, and 24 months, make it easier to buy at or near the start of a new outcome period, choose a fund that meets your investing timeline, and consider implementing a laddered investment strategy (see Chapter 12 for more about this strategy)
- A variety of reference assets, including SPY, QQQ, IWM, EFA, EEM, and TLT

» **Innovation:** Innovator offers several novel products, including accelerated, dual-directional, step-up strategy, buffer income, and floor ETFs.

» **Track record:** Innovator has completed more outcome periods than most other issuers and has a solid track record of meeting its outcome targets.

» **Investor education and transparency:** You can find all the information you need to research Innovator's buffer ETFs on its website at `www.innovatoretfs.com`.

» **Industry recognition and backing:** Innovator has a strong market presence and reputation in the industry. Noticing Innovator's powerful market position, Goldman Sachs acquired Innovator on April 2, 2026.

REMEMBER

To research Innovator's buffer ETFs, start with its Product Table at `www.innovatoretfs.com/define/etfs/#buffer` or its ETF Finder at `www.innovatoretfs.com/etf/finder`. Check out the Tools menu, where you'll find links to Innovator's Potential Outcome Analyzer, Previous Outcome Period, Personal Outcome Analyzer, and more. These tools can help you get a better sense of how a buffer ETF is likely to perform before you invest in it. (You may need to create a user ID and password and log in to gain access to certain tools on the site.)

First Trust (FT) Vest

According to *Morningstar*, FT Vest is the largest issuer of buffer ETFs, as measured by assets under management (AUM). First Trust (FT) and Vest are independent investment firms that formed a partnership to launch a series of FT Vest products. (Vest Financial launched the first mutual fund with an explicit buffer strategy in 2016.) FT Vest is focused on managing downside risk while delivering consistent outcomes for investors. It excels in the following areas:

- **Size:** FT Vest is the largest issuer in the buffer ETF category, which gives it several advantages over its competitors, including potentially tighter bid-ask spreads, easier execution of large trades, and increased liquidity.
- **Skills and experience:** Through its strategic partnership (First Trust and Cboe Vest), FT Vest has deep options-based risk-management expertise behind its products.
- **Selection:** FT Vest has a large selection of target outcome investments, including buffer funds, buffer and premium income funds, enhance and moderate funds, floor funds, laddered funds, and max buffer funds. Many funds have varied/multiple reset dates to meet your timing needs, stagger your exposure, and enable you to implement a laddered strategy.

  TIP

  FT Vest has two funds that enable you to implement a laddered strategy by investing in a single fund with a single ticker symbol: FT Vest Laddered Buffer ETF (BUFR) and FT Vest Laddered Deep Buffer ETF (BUFD). With over $8.5 billion in assets, BUFR is by far the largest buffer ETF by AUM in the industry. It's a very popular selection of the investment advisory community because it allows for immediate diversification of a slice of the overall asset allocation pie within the buffer ETF space. A laddered buffer ETF is essentially an "ETF of ETFs" or a "fund of funds."
- **Track record:** Like Innovator, FT Vest has been in the buffer ETF space for many years and has completed more outcome periods than most of its competitors. The company has a solid track record of meeting its outcome targets.
- **Investor education and transparency:** You can access all the information you need to research FT Vest's buffer ETFs on its website at `www.ftportfolios.com`.
- **Industry recognition and backing:** Like Innovator, FT Vest has a strong market presence and reputation in the industry.

Other issuers

Other players in the buffer ETF space are definitely worth checking out. In this section, I provide a brief overview of AllianzIM, PGIM, BlackRock, Calamos, Pacer, AllianceBernstein, TrueShares, and Aptus.

Allianz Investment Management

Allianz Investment Management (AllianzIM) is unique in that it's best known for its insurance products, including annuities. Because its core business is squarely focused on risk management, buffer ETFs are a natural extension. AllianzIM has made significant inroads in the buffer space and now has over $4.5 billion AUM in its buffer ETFs. Here's how AllianzIM stacks up in respect to key criteria:

- **Size:** Allianz is one of the biggest options traders in the U.S., accounting for billions of dollars in options trades daily and trillions of dollars per year.
- **Skills and experience:** Because options trading is at the heart of executing various buffer ETF investment strategies, AllianzIM has the skills and experience to design and build funds that deliver targeted outcomes.

  REMEMBER

  AllianzIM's size, skills, and experience translate into lower costs. The company prides itself on being the lowest-cost S&P 500 buffer ETF provider among the top three players by AUM.
- **Selection:** AllianzIM has consistently expanded its buffer ETF offerings since entering the space. It has funds that offer protection ranging from 10 to 100 percent and floor ETFs; capped and uncapped funds; laddered funds; funds with outcome periods of 3, 6, or 12 months; and many series with starting dates for every month of the year. Note, AllianzIM has a deep lineup of uncapped buffer ETFs (available for every month of the year) and has more 6-month outcome period ETFs than its competitors.
- **Track record:** AllianzIM has decades of experience in options trading and risk management and a solid reputation for delivering quality products and service.
- **Investor education and transparency:** You can find all the information you need to research AllianzIM's buffer ETFs on its website at `www.allianzim.com/etfs`.
- **Industry recognition and backing:** Allianz has a strong global reputation in the insurance industry.

REMEMBER

What sets AllianzIM apart from other players in the buffer ETF space is that they do it all themselves, in-house. They don't outsource portfolio management or options trading. They don't use sub-advisors. When you invest in AllianzIM buffer ETFs, you're doing business with the firm that manages your money.

PGIM

PGIM's headline differentiator is cost. All its buffer ETFs have a net expense ratio of about 0.50 percent compared to similar offerings from some larger issuers that routinely have expense ratios closer to 0.74 to 0.85 percent. Keep in mind, however, the expense ratio is only one item that factors into the TCO (see the earlier section "Comparing expense ratios and total cost of ownership (TCO)" for details).

PGIM offers buffer ETFs that track SPY or QQQ with buffers of 12, 20, or 100 percent and a series with starting dates for every month of the year. Like FT Vest and others, PGIM offers laddered buffer ETFs — each is an "ETF of ETFs" with staggered outcome periods, reducing the cost and hassle of implementing a laddered strategy on your own.

Another differentiator is PGIM's decision to go with a series of 12 percent buffers. Other issuers typically offer protection of 9, 10, or 15 percent, but PGIM chose protection for a series of its buffers in the range I refer to as "minimal protection" (9–12 percent), at a level that could be considered a "sweet spot" of sorts, and it definitely sets PGIM apart. If you think 15 percent protection is a bit too much for the outcome period you're looking at, and 9 or 10 percent is too little, then you should consider the 12 percent buffers offered by PGIM.

For more about PGIM's buffer ETFs, visit `www.pgim.com/us/en/intermediary/investment-capabilities/products/etf`.

BlackRock

BlackRock is the largest asset manager in the world as measured by AUM, with trillions of dollars under management and its own ETF brand — iShares. Thanks to its tremendous size and scale, it has deep ETF infrastructure and distribution channels, strong institutional relationships, and broad platform support. These strengths translate into reliability, competitive pricing, and easier access across brokerages and advisor platforms.

Similar to PGIM, BlackRock has undercut many of its competitors in the buffer ETF space with expense ratios coming in around 0.50 percent annually. In addition — and this is critical — BlackRock's buffer ETFs are structured with only three option contracts rather than the conventional four-option strategy employed by other issuers. Instead of buying a deep-in-the-money call option to track the return of the reference asset, BlackRock purchases iShares Core S&P 500 ETF (IVV) and has three option contracts around this core holding. Lately, this "new and improved" structure has delivered higher caps compared to the competition. Note, BlackRock passes on much of the annual dividend paid by IVV to its shareholders. So, unlike most other buffer ETF offerings, you will receive some dividend income, typically paid in December.

BlackRock's buffer ETFs are generally grouped by buffer: 10 percent buffer, max buffer, moderate quarterly laddered buffer, and deep quarterly laddered buffer.

For more about BlackRock's buffer ETFs, visit `www.ishares.com/outcomes`.

Calamos

Calamos offers competitive pricing and exposure to more asset classes than some of its larger competitors. Specifically, Calamos offers buffer ETFs (which it refers to as "structured protection ETFs") that provide exposure to the following reference assets: bitcoin, S&P 500, Nasdaq-100, and Russell 2000. Calamos specializes in funds that offer 100 percent downside protection.

If you're interested in exposure to bitcoin but are afraid of the volatility and risk of deep losses, the Structured Alt Protection ETFs offered by Calamos could provide a solution. The structures are varied: some of these funds provide total protection against any loss; others employ a floor strategy (for example, no protection for an initial loss of 10 or 20 percent but protection against any losses deeper than the specified floor). The floor products typically offer very attractive upside caps, so if you're bullish on the price of bitcoin, but want some level of protection and are willing to risk an initial 10 to 20 percent loss, these could appeal to you. In addition, Calamos has several laddered buffer bitcoin ETFs worth checking out.

After reaching its website, scroll down to the Calamos Structured Protection EFT Focus Tool box and select Open Tool to access the product table.

Pacer

Pacer may have a niche product that aligns with your risk profile and investment objectives. Most Pacer Swan Structured Outcome Series (SOS) ETFs track the SPDR S&P 500 ETF Trust (SPY), and the following buffer levels generally differentiate them:

- **Moderate:** 15 percent
- **Conservative:** –5 to –30 percent
- **Flex:** The fund buffers against the first 20 percent loss; from –20 to –40 percent, you lose 2 percent for every 1 percent the reference asset loses; and from –40 percent down, you lose 1 percent for every 1 percent the reference asset loses.

  Note, the "Flex" offerings are a hybrid of sorts — providing a level of protection against initial losses but then accelerated losses if the buffer is breached at the end of the outcome period. These offerings may appeal to more sophisticated investors with a very defined outlook on the performance of the reference asset over the outcome period.

Pacer also offers a managed "ETF of ETFs" with a single ticker symbol (PSFF), which simplifies the process of implementing a laddered strategy.

For more about Pacer's buffer ETFs, visit www.paceretfs.com. After reaching the site, open the Pacer ETFs menu and select Structured Outcome to access a product table of its buffer ETFs.

AllianceBernstein

AllianceBernstein offers a couple of buffer ETFs that provide protection while tracking the S&P 500. It also offers a buffer ETF that tracks the iShares MSCI EAFE ETF (EFA). Its largest buffer ETF, with approximately $1 billion in AUM, is AB Conservative Buffer ETF (BUFC). It seeks 15 percent protection with some upside participation in the S&P 500.

For more about AllianceBernstein's buffer ETFs, visit www.alliancebernstein.com/us/en-us/investments/products/etf.html. After reaching the site, scroll down to view the ETFs with "buffer" in their name.

TrueShares

TrueShares (TrueMark Investments LLC) also offers buffer ETFs — referred to as Structured Outcome ETFs. Most target 10 percent downside protection while tracking the S&P 500. It currently has a buffer series for every month of the year. TrueShares pioneered the uncapped format within the buffer ETF space in 2020.

For more about TrueShares' buffer ETFs, visit www.true-shares.com/structured-outcome-etfs.

Aptus

Aptus is a newcomer in the buffer ETF space. It offers a low-cost alternative in four ETFs designed to provide protection against the first 15 percent of losses while tracking the SPDR S&P 500 ETF Trust (SPY). It also offers a laddered buffer ETF comprised of its four buffer ETFs.

For more about Aptus buffer ETFs, visit aptusetfs.com.

IN THIS CHAPTER

» Brushing up on basic guidelines

» Evaluating different levels of protection

» Making well-informed trade-offs

Chapter 6

Choosing a Level of Downside Protection

One of the most significant distinctions between buffer ETFs is the level of downside protection they offer. Whether you're comparing offerings from the same or different issuers, you'll find buffer ETFs with downside protection ranging from about 9 to 100 percent. You'll notice other buffer-related differences as well, such as funds that provide a range of protection (for example, −5 to −30 percent), and floor ETFs that protect against any loss greater than a specified percentage.

Of course, all this protection comes at a price, mostly in the form of an opportunity cost. Generally, the deeper the downside protection, the lower the cap. So, choosing the right level of downside protection for you is all about making trade-offs and deciding whether the cost of protection is worth the amount of upside above the cap (potential gains in the reference asset during the outcome period) that you're giving up. Of course, we can't know in advance if the return of the reference asset will exceed the cap in any given outcome period. Still, in this chapter, I explain your options and provide guidance on how to make well-informed decisions.

REMEMBER

Keep in mind that buffer ETFs may not be the best choice for all investors. If your investment objective is long-term growth, and you have an investment time horizon of decades, for example, you're likely better off investing in traditional index-based stock ETFs — investments that aren't capped. Of course, if you have no protection in your stock portfolio, you'll want to be certain your temperament will allow you to ride out the inevitable downturn in your portfolio when it may temporarily lose 30 percent or more during a crash and/or bear market. If you're nearing retirement or already retired, it's not easy to watch your wealth evaporate, and it's very tough to stay the course. But if you have a long time horizon, a strong stomach, and no concerns about volatility or temporary losses, you will likely perform better over the long haul with no protection and no cap.

Starting with a Few Guidelines

Nobody can tell you the level of downside protection that's perfect for you and your personal financial situation. The best anyone can do is provide you with some guidelines that can help you decide for yourself. In this section, I highlight key considerations for making a well-informed choice about the level of downside protection to look for in a buffer ETF.

Consider the buffer's purpose

Why you want a buffer is an important consideration when choosing *how much* protection you want. For example, if you're using the buffer to prevent yourself from making impulsive investment decisions in response to market volatility, a minimal buffer may be sufficient, but if you're retired and need to preserve capital, you'll likely want a deeper buffer. Consult the following table for general guidance:

Buffer's purpose	Buffer range
Dampen volatility/emotions	9–10%
Replace core equity position	9–15%
Mitigate risk in pre-retirement or retirement	9–30%
Preserve capital for near-term spending	20–100%

BUFFERING FOR RETIREMENT

I asked Bruce Bond, co-founder and CEO of Innovator Capital Management LLC, the following question: "For moderate risk investors already in retirement or nearing retirement, which of your offerings might be the most appropriate for them?" His response:

> "One of our most successful offerings is the 15 percent buffer strategy. This seems to be the level of protection that has had the greatest appeal to investors in or nearing retirement. Our 20 percent quarterly buffer strategy is another one that has seen steady inflows as investors have used it for a defensive allocation that doesn't carry any interest-rate risk or credit risk."

Gauge your tolerance for loss and missed opportunities

Fear and greed can cause even experienced investors to make poor investment decisions. Buffer ETFs can help regulate emotions. To determine how much downside protection you need to satisfy your loss tolerance, ask yourself, "At what percentage drawdown (decline in the market) would I panic, sell, or regret the investment?" How would you feel about a decline of 10, 15, or 20 percent? Consider selecting a buffer that's slightly deeper than that number; for example, if you'd start to feel the pain at 15 percent, consider a fund with a 20 percent buffer.

REMEMBER

Also consider how you'd feel if you missed out on a surge in the market. What if the market soared 30 percent during the outcome period, but your buffer ETF was capped at 15 percent? If you'd kick yourself for missing out on extra gains, then think twice about how much upside potential you're willing to sacrifice for downside protection.

Assess your time horizon

Buffer ETFs are helpful for preserving capital, especially when you can't afford to ride out market drawdowns. Generally, the shorter your investment time horizon, the deeper the buffer should be:

- **Longer time horizon (5+ years):** 9–10 percent
- **Mid-range time horizon (3–5 years):** 9–15 percent
- **Near- to mid-range time horizon (1–3 years):** 15–20 percent
- **Near-term time horizon (0–1 year):** 20–100 percent

Account for sequence risk

Sequence risk (also called *sequence-of-returns* risk) is the potential negative impact on an investment portfolio's value due to the timing of withdrawals, and it can be a significant risk in the early years of retirement. For example, if you sell stocks and withdraw money after a meaningful market decline, it can significantly reduce your portfolio's potential future value. If you withdraw money to cover expenses when the market is at a peak, the impact on the portfolio's value could be significantly reduced.

REMEMBER

Sequence risk reinforces the need to consider your time horizon carefully. You don't want your portfolio's value to be depressed when you need to liquidate a high percentage of your investments. Once you liquidate and withdraw funds from your portfolio, the withdrawn assets will obviously never be able to recoup any losses they suffered prior to being withdrawn.

Think in terms of scenarios

Estimating a desired level of downside protection can be difficult when you're just comparing percentages, so consider various what-if scenarios, instead, such as the following:

- **What if the reference asset drops 20 percent during the outcome period?** With 10 percent downside protection, your investment is still down 10 percent (before fees). With 20 percent downside protection, your return would be close to break-even.
- **What if the reference asset rises 20 to 30 percent, and your return is capped at 15 percent?** Will you regret forfeiting a 5 percent gain? How will you feel about giving up a 15 percent gain if the reference asset surges 30 percent during the outcome period?

Factor in the market environment

Every buffer ETF tracks the performance of an underlying reference asset, such as SPDR S&P 500 ETF Trust (SPY), Invesco QQQ Trust (QQQ), iShares Russell 2000 ETF (IWM), bitcoin, gold, or some other asset. Some of these reference assets are more volatile than others, so factor in their relative risk when deciding on a level of downside protection. The following table provides some useful comparisons:

Reference asset	Typical drawdowns	Historical severe drawdowns	Typical buffer range
SPY	-10% to -15%	-30% to -50%	9–20%
QQQ	-10% to -20%	-50% to -80%	10–20%
IWM	-15% to -25%	-50%+	15%
EFA and EEM	-15% to -25%	-50%+	15%
Bitcoin	-30%+	-70%+	10–100%

REMEMBER

A 15 percent buffer that's likely to protect against most losses on SPY may not provide sufficient downside protection for more volatile assets.

Also, keep in mind that historically, the S&P 500 has recovered faster than other markets. Small caps and international equities can stay depressed longer. Still, the S&P 500 has had several periods when it took many years to recoup losses — Great Depression (1929–1939), Great Inflation (1970s), Dot-Com Bubble/Great Recession (2000–2008) — so we just don't know how long it will take for any particular reference asset in a buffer ETF to recover after its next severe downturn.

WARNING

Unless you absolutely can't afford any losses and you are extremely risk-averse, don't make the mistake of buying too much protection. Paying extra (accepting a much lower cap) for 100 percent protection for an ETF that tracks the S&P 500 likely doesn't make sense for most investors, because such a loss is highly unlikely. Instead, think in terms of buying *meaningful* downside protection.

STRATEGIES FOR DIFFERENT MARKETS

I asked Bruce Bond, co-founder and CEO of Innovator Capital Management LLC, the following questions: "What strategies are typically recommended by advisors if we are deep in a bear market? And, what would be a recommended strategy if we are at very lofty stock-market valuations or even potentially in a euphoric bubble?" Here's his response:

> "Whether we are in a bull market or a bear market, the preferred buffer level typically boils down to the risk tolerance of the investor and where we are in the market cycle. For example, after an extended bull market, valuations are often stretched. In that kind of scenario, investors begin to believe the market could reverse course, causing them to get out of stocks, or at the very least to stop adding exposure. This approach is beneficial if the market falls, but detrimental if the market continues to climb. We see greater demand for buffer strategies in circumstances like this; if the market does go down, the buffers provide built-in protection, but if it doesn't, the strategy will participate in the continued positive performance."

Compare buffer ranges: Buffers, floors, and barriers

Not all downside protection is the same. It can be structured in different ways, as explained in the following sections.

Buffer

A *buffer* protects the initial X percent of losses or a range of losses over a defined outcome period. For example, a 15 percent buffer protects up to 15 percent of any initial loss (from 0 to 15 percent). With some buffers, you absorb an initial loss before the protection kicks in; for example, with a buffer of −5 to −30 percent, you absorb the first 5 percent loss, are protected against the next 25 percent loss, and then absorb any loss beyond 30 percent.

A buffer is best for smoothing out volatility, calming emotions, and providing a reasonable level of downside protection — hopefully without forfeiting too much upside potential.

Floor

A *floor* defines the maximum amount you can lose. For example, a floor of −10 means you absorb the first 10 percent loss and are protected against any further loss.

Floor ETFs are best for protecting capital against very deep declines, but you have to be willing to accept an initial percentage loss before the buffer will provide protection.

Barrier

A *barrier* provides conditional downside protection; you're protected only if losses don't breach the defined barrier at the end of the outcome period. If losses exceed the barrier, you lose all protection.

Barrier income products often allow for relatively high yields and are attractive in stable markets; however, they could perform poorly in volatile or bear markets and provide no protection — if a barrier is breached. They're designed for more sophisticated investors who understand *tail risk* — low-probability events that can result in significant losses. They're less suitable for novice investors.

Consider splitting your allocation

Downside protection isn't necessarily a one-and-done decision. You can allocate your portfolio among two or more ETFs with different levels of downside protection. Here are a few ways to achieve a blend of downside protection:

Two-tier protection: Two-tier protection could be considered for core equity replacement when you're unsure exactly how much protection you need:

- 50 percent in a 10 percent buffer ETF
- 50 percent in a 20 percent buffer ETF

Three-tier protection: Three-tier protection can help balance moderate growth and capital preservation:

- 30 percent in a 10 percent buffer ETF
- 40 percent in a 15 percent buffer ETF
- 30 percent in a 20 percent buffer ETF

Balanced growth/protection: Balanced growth/protection could be considered for long-term investments when some downside protection is desired:

- 70 percent in a 10 percent buffer ETF
- 30 percent in a 20 percent buffer ETF

REMEMBER

You can also split your allocation among ETFs that track different reference assets. For example, for a more aggressive portfolio, you may want to invest 70 percent in an ETF with a 10 or 15 percent buffer that tracks QQQ and 30 percent in an ETF with a 10 percent buffer that tracks SPY. The possibilities are endless. See Chapter 7 for more about building a portfolio.

Exploring Levels of Downside Protection

For simplicity, you can think of downside protection as consisting of four levels: minimal, moderate, deep, and total, as shown in the following table.

Downside protection level	Range
Minimal	9–12%
Moderate	15–20%

Downside protection level	Range
Deep	25–30%
Total	100%

In this section, I describe each level of protection and provide guidance to help you choose a level that's right for you and your investment objectives.

Minimal

The two big players in the ETF space — Innovator and FT Vest — offer an ETF series each month that provides minimal downside protection, typically with a very attractive upside cap. Innovator offers ETFs that provide 9 percent protection, and FT Vest offers ETFs with 10 percent protection. AllianzIM also offers a full series with 10 percent protection. BlackRock offers a series of four buffer ETFs with 10 percent protection. If you want a little bit more protection, PGIM offers a series of buffer ETFs with minimal downside protection of 12 percent. (See Chapter 5 for details about buffer ETF issuers.)

You may find minimal downside protection most appealing in the following situations:

- **The reference asset recently experienced a meaningful decline.** Suppose you're in the middle of a bear market and the underlying index you want to track (for example, the S&P 500) is already trading down 20 percent from its recent peak. You could purchase a buffer ETF that offers minimal downside protection in case the market continues to drop, but also allows you to participate nicely in the upside if the market rebounds. Buffer ETFs with minimal protection typically offer the highest caps, so your profit potential should be quite attractive.
- **You're looking to transition from a buffer ETF with a moderate or deep buffer to one with less protection and a higher cap.** If you own a buffer ETF with moderate or deep downside protection, and the reference asset has already experienced a significant decline, consider swapping to a buffer ETF with less downside protection and a higher cap. For example, if the ETF is tracking the S&P 500 and the reference asset is already down 20 percent from its peak, you could be paying for more protection than you need; another drop of 15 or 20 percent is highly unlikely, so perhaps at that point, 10 percent downside protection is enough for you.

Depending on the current parameters of your moderate or deep buffer ETF (remaining buffer, remaining cap, and downside before buffer), you may prefer more upside potential in a buffer ETF with minimal protection coming out of a downturn. Simply compare the caps and remaining protection to help with your decision.

» **You want to add some downside protection to your unhedged stock portfolio.** If you have an unhedged (no holdings with any protection against losses) stock portfolio, you can use a buffer ETF to add protection while remaining fully invested in stocks. This approach could be an attractive alternative to reducing your allocation in stocks. Rather than selling stocks to sit in low-yielding cash or bonds, simply swap some of your unhedged stock portfolio for buffer ETFs offering minimal protection to keep you invested in equities. This strategy may also provide you with some peace of mind that you didn't have with your unhedged stock portfolio.

Moderate

Most issuers of buffer ETFs offer a series with moderate downside protection. Innovator and FT Vest have funds that protect against the first 15 percent loss during the outcome period. AllianzIM and PGIM have funds that protect against the first 20 percent loss.

BUFFERS IN DECLINING MARKETS

During my interview with Johan Grahn, former Head ETF Strategist at Allianz Investment Management LLC, I mentioned the fact that buffer ETFs always outperform their reference asset in a declining market. His response:

> That's right. Over the outcome period, no matter how far down it goes, you will still outperform. And if it goes up, you will participate all the way up to the cap, and it's only if the market blows beyond the cap that you're underperforming. But keep in mind here, importantly, you're underperforming the S&P 500 in that scenario. But, if you're replacing an alternative allocation or a bond allocation, for example, and let's say you get capped out and make 12 percent in your buffered ETFs, for example, you'll likely still outperform the bond allocation and potentially the alternative allocation as well. So, you might still be a winner depending on how you're thinking about this.

REMEMBER

Moderate downside protection should be sufficient in most market environments for a buffer ETF that tracks the S&P 500. A deeper buffer may be appropriate for a reference asset that tends to be more volatile or if you're concerned about the possibility of a deep bear market. Less downside protection (and a higher cap) may be attractive if the reference asset has already experienced a recent meaningful decline.

You may opt for moderate downside protection for all the same reasons you'd choose a buffer ETF with minimal protection. The only difference is that you're getting more protection and less upside potential.

Deep

Some issuers of buffer ETFs offer a series with deep downside protection. Innovator's offerings provide protection against a 30 percent loss (–5 to –35 percent) during the outcome period, and FT Vest has funds that protect against a 25 percent loss (–5 to –30 percent).

WARNING

Deep buffer ETFs typically don't protect against the first 5 percent loss. They forgo protection on the first 5 percent loss so they can offer a more competitive cap. (The first 5 percent level of protection is the costliest.)

Here are a few good reasons to consider a deep buffer ETF:

- You're willing to give up protection on the first 5 percent loss in exchange for a higher cap.
- You're not very concerned about losing 5 percent. What keeps you up at night is the thought of losing significantly more than that in the event of a steep market decline.
- You're a conservative investor who would like more upside potential than bonds are offering.
- You have an unhedged stock portfolio and would like to protect against potentially deep market losses.
- You're risk-averse and concerned about potential losses, but you recognize the need for some growth potential in your portfolio.

REMEMBER

If you're investing in an ETF that tracks the S&P 500, 25 or 30 percent downside protection should shield your portfolio from deep losses in the average historical bear market decline of approximately 34 percent. Keep in mind, however, that most deep buffer ETFs don't protect against the first 5 percent loss.

Total

Most buffer ETF issuers offer ETFs with total (100 percent) downside protection. Calamos specializes in this area. It offers full downside protection (a series for every month) while providing S&P 500 equity exposure to a defined cap, while protecting against 100 percent of losses over a one-year period (before fees and expenses). It also offers a series of four ETFs that track the Nasdaq-100 and another series of four ETFs that track the Russell 2000, with total downside protection.

In addition, Calamos offers Protected Bitcoin ETFs that provide 100 percent protection. Note, some of its deep buffer ETFs that track bitcoin don't protect against initial losses; for example, its Bitcoin 80 Series Structured Alt Protection ETF limits the maximum loss to 20 percent, protecting from −20 to −100 percent over a one-year outcome period.

Issuers structure total downside protection ETFs in various ways. For example, Innovator's Equity Defined Protection ETF (TJUL) tracks the return of the SPDR S&P 500 ETF Trust (SPY), up to a cap of 13.60 percent (before fees, as of this writing) while buffering investors against 100 percent of losses over a two-year outcome period. Investors forgo dividend income and pay an annual expense ratio of 0.79 percent. Note, the outcome period for investors seeking full downside protection in TJUL is double the standard outcome period of 12 months. So, investors need to be prepared to stay invested for the entire two-year period to realize the defined outcome.

BlackRock's iShares Large Cap Max Buffer — June (MAXJ) is another example of a 100 percent buffer ETF that offers total downside protection. Its 12-month outcome period is the most common duration offered by issuers. At its most recent reset date (June 30, 2025), MAXJ offered a gross starting cap of 7.06 percent. Its annual expense ratio is 0.50 percent.

You may want to consider investing in an ETF that offers 100 percent downside protection if any of the following statements describe you:

- You're extremely conservative and want total protection of your principal, though with some upside gain potential beyond what bonds and cash equivalent investments are paying.

- You're wary of high stock market valuations, and you believe the downside risk in the market is far greater than losses experienced in a typical bear market decline.
- You fear we may be heading for a market crash, but you'd like to hedge against being wrong and remain invested with some upside potential if your fears prove unwarranted.

REMEMBER

Many investors purchase annuities, structured notes, or market-linked CDs that protect against losses but come with higher fees, high investment minimums, long lock-up periods, and unfavorable tax treatment. Total protection buffer ETFs offer downside protection but without many of the disadvantages of investing in structured notes and annuities.

Weighing the Cost of Downside Protection

Whether you're deciding if a buffer ETF is right for you or trying to figure out which level of downside protection is best, your decision ultimately boils down to cost versus benefit. How much potential gain are you willing to give up for the level of downside protection you want?

Everything else being equal, the benefit is a certain level of downside protection, and the cost is the amount of upside participation you forfeit (although you should certainly consider other costs, as well, as explained in Chapter 5). The following table illustrates the relationship between buffer (downside protection) and cap (upside participation) for different Innovator buffer ETFs that track the SPDR S&P 500 ETF Trust (SPY) with a 12-month outcome period. (Starting caps shown are net of fees on the most recent reset dates (February 28, 2026) and are calculated at the beginning of each outcome period, so they're subject to change.)

Starting buffer	Starting cap
9%	16.18%
15%	12.00%
30% (-5% to -35%)	11.28%
100%	5.94%

REMEMBER

SMALLER BUFFER, HIGHER CAP

I asked Wes Mathews, former Principal, Director of Portfolio Solutions at Milliman Financial Risk Management LLC, "Of the various buffer levels offered by Innovator, which level of protection is the most popular?" His response:

> "It's definitely the 15 percent buffer. Investors gravitate towards the 15 percent level of protection, which they seem to think is the most desirable trade-off. I think most advisors I've spoken with are looking at what has the S&P 500 done, on average, in bad years. They ask themselves, "How much of the downside am I interested in cutting off in exchange for what portion of the upside in the S&P?" With a smaller buffer, you would see a higher cap, and vice versa with a larger buffer."

Buffer versus cap isn't the only trade-off to think about. Here are a few other considerations:

- **Outcome period:** Depending on the current market environment, ETFs with longer outcome periods may offer more generous caps, but it's not a given.

  REMEMBER

  When comparing buffers and caps of ETFs with different outcome periods, consider the number of months each buffer or cap covers. A 24-month outcome period with a 16 percent cap is really providing a potential return of approximately 8 percent annualized. A 3-month outcome period with a 4 percent cap is effectively giving you approximately 12 percent annualized upside potential.
- **Reference asset:** Upside caps can vary a great deal depending on the underlying reference asset. Typically, the more volatile the reference asset, the higher the potential upside.
- **Expense ratios and other costs:** Although expense ratios and other costs may not be directly related to the buffer and cap, you should certainly consider these costs when evaluating buffer ETFs. Issuers publish the net caps on their websites, so always comparison shop.

IN THIS CHAPTER

- » Brushing up on different layering strategies
- » Checking out sample portfolio allocations
- » Rebalancing your portfolio

Chapter 7
Building a Buffer ETF Portfolio

Building a buffer ETF portfolio begins with a deceptively simple choice: whether to invest in a single buffer ETF or to allocate your investment capital across multiple funds. A single fund provides a clean, defined outcome, but it concentrates your exposure to one reference asset, one buffer level, one cap, and one outcome period. Allocating across multiple buffer ETFs enables you to blend different buffers, caps, reference assets, and reset dates to shape risk, return, and liquidity more precisely.

This chapter reveals various strategies for layering your portfolio across multiple buffer ETFs and presents sample portfolios to consider for different investment goals — moderate to aggressive growth or something more conservative.

Exploring Different Ways to Layer Your Allocation

Buffer ETF outcome parameters — buffer, cap, reference asset, and outcome period — give you several ways to layer your allocation. (*Outcome parameters* are variables that affect a buffer ETF's performance; see Chapter 1 for details.) Consider the following approaches:

- **Build layers across buffer depths and caps.** This approach provides a better balance between downside protection and upside participation. For example, you might consider allocating roughly one-third (or another portion) of your portfolio to each of the following buffer ETF types:
  - Minimal buffer (9, 10, or 12 percent) to increase your upside potential (higher cap) for a portion of your portfolio
  - Moderate buffer (15 or 20 percent) to protect a portion of your portfolio against deeper losses while still allowing for substantial upside participation
  - Deep buffer (25 or 30 percent) to protect a portion of your investment capital in the event of a market crash

  A slightly more aggressive approach might be to invest 25 percent in a traditional ETF (without a buffer or cap) and 25 percent in each of the three buffer ETF types listed above.
- **Build layers across different reference assets.** This approach spreads your exposure across asset classes, such as U.S. large cap (S&P 500 or Nasdaq-100), U.S. small cap (Russell 2000), international equities (the Morgan Stanley Capital International [MSCI] index), bitcoin, gold, 20+ year Treasuries, and so on. For example, you could layer your investment capital as follows:
  - 50 percent buffered U.S. large-cap blend (S&P 500)
  - 20 percent buffered U.S. large-cap growth (Nasdaq-100)
  - 20 percent buffered international developed markets (EFA)
  - 10 percent unbuffered equities
- **Stagger allocations across outcome periods.** This "laddered" approach spreads your exposure across time, reducing *timing risk* (investing all your capital at once when the market is near a peak, for example), providing a more consistent risk/return profile, and ensuring ongoing access to downside protection (with a staggered allocation, part of your portfolio will have more frequent resets with fresh buffers and new caps). To implement a laddered strategy, take the following steps:

1. **Divide your allocation into equal parts.**
2. **Invest each part in a buffer ETF with a different outcome period, such as January, April, July, and October.**

See Chapter 12 for more about laddering.

TIP

An easier way to implement a laddering strategy is to invest in a buffer ETF that does it for you, such as one of FT Vest's Laddered Buffered ETFs. By investing in a laddered buffer ETF, you don't need to spread your investment across multiple ETFs.

Keep in mind that you can combine these three layering strategies to spread allocations across buffers/caps, reference assets, and outcome periods. For example:

- **Allocate 60 percent of your investment capital to U.S. large-cap buffer ETFs that are**
  - Spread across funds with minimal to moderate buffers
  - Laddered monthly
- **Allocate 25 percent to higher growth or tech-focused buffer ETFs that are**
  - Spread across funds with moderate to deep buffers
  - Laddered quarterly
- **Allocate 15 percent to international buffer ETFs that are**
  - Spread across funds with minimal to deep buffers (according to your preference)
  - Laddered quarterly

Checking Out Sample Buffer ETF Portfolios

How you layer your overall allocation across multiple buffer ETFs is limited only by your imagination. In this section, I present five sample portfolios to be considered for different risk profiles — moderate growth, growth, aggressive growth, conservative, and ultra-conservative. You can choose one of these allocation frameworks and use it "as is" or tailor it to your investment style and objectives.

REMEMBER

In each sample portfolio, I list several buffer ETFs to consider, some of which track the same reference asset and provide the same level of downside protection. You may decide to buy only one of these buffer ETFs, and that's fine. For example, in the sample growth portfolio, I suggest a 60 percent allocation in funds with a 9 to 10 percent buffer. You may decide to invest in only one of the funds or spread your allocation across two or more of them. Either approach is fine. Each buffer ETF offers plenty of diversification because the underlying reference asset typically provides exposure to a benchmark index (for example, S&P 500) comprised of hundreds of stocks.

REMEMBER

To ensure the buffer ETFs you invest in perform in line with the issuer's published outcome parameters, purchase your shares on the fund's reset date (in the market's closing hours on the last trading day of the outcome period). For example, if you're building your portfolio at the start of the year, look for buffer ETFs with an outcome period that starts January 1, and buy your shares in the closing hours of trading on December 31. Likewise, if you're building a portfolio starting midyear, look for buffer ETFs with an outcome period that starts on July 1, and buy your shares in the closing hours of trading on June 30.

Nearly all buffer ETF issuers, with the exception of FT Vest, offer ETFs that reset on the last business day of the month. FT Vest offers buffer ETFs that reset on the third Friday of the month (options expiration). FT Vest takes this approach at least partially to reduce exposure to roll risk, and to ensure liquidity is at a "high point." (See the nearby sidebar, "Reducing Exposure to Roll Risk".)

TECHNICAL STUFF

REDUCING EXPOSURE TO ROLL RISK

I asked Karan Sood, CEO of Vest Financial LLC, "Most of your competitors chose the last business day of the month as the roll/reset date for their buffer ETFs. FT Vest chose the third Friday of the month. Why is that?" His response:

> "We generally like the third Friday because that, in our view, is the high point of liquidity for options. There is not an immediate danger, but at some point, there could be [an] elevated concentrated roll risk on the last business day of the month. Because these are transparent ETFs, you are announcing the roll date to the world. And so, it gives us also the ability to say we are not with the rest of the wider market, so we are protected from [the] concentration of that end-of-month roll risk."
>
> "There are also mutual fund versions of these structures, which are actually currently bigger than many of the biggest ETF versions. And they are rolling on the last business day of the month, too. There has been news about the month-end roll now becoming something that market participants are taking advantage of."

Moderate growth portfolio

Moderate growth is a popular investment objective for many investors. They seek to balance growth and capital preservation with the objective of outpacing inflation and taxes over the long term. A traditional portfolio allocation for a moderate growth portfolio is 60 percent stocks and 40 percent bonds. However, for a portfolio fully invested in buffer ETFs, you replace the bond allocation with buffer ETFs.

REMEMBER

Buffer ETFs are often used as a complement or alternative to the fixed-income portion of a total portfolio, allowing for increased stock exposure and higher upside potential.

Here's a sample moderate growth portfolio that would be ideal for starting at the beginning of the year (because most of the ETFs included in this sample reset on December 31). However, you can build this portfolio at the end of any month or quarter by choosing funds that reset closer to the date you're building your portfolio.

- **30 percent in buffer ETFs with 9 to 10 percent protection:** Consider one or more of the following funds:
  - iShares Large-Cap 10% Target Buffer ETF — December (TEND)
  - Innovator Equity Buffer — January (BJAN)
  - FT Vest U.S. Equity Buffer — December (FDEC)
  - AllianzIM U.S. Equity Buffer10 — January (JANT)
- **30 percent in buffer ETFs with 15 percent protection:** Consider one or more of the following funds:
  - Innovator U.S. Equity Power Buffer — January (PJAN)
  - FT Vest U.S. Equity Moderate Buffer — December (GDEC)
  - Innovator International Developed Power Buffer — January (IJAN)
- **20 percent in buffer ETFs with 20 percent protection:** Consider one or more of the following funds:
  - PGIM S&P 500 20 Buffer — January (PBJA)
  - AllianzIM U.S. Equity Buffer 20 — January (JANW)
- **20 percent in buffer ETFs with 25 to 30 percent protection:** Consider one or more of the following funds:
  - Innovator U.S. Equity Ultra Buffer — January (UJAN)
  - FT Vest U.S. Equity Deep Buffer ETF — December (DDEC)

TIP

You could build a moderate growth portfolio at any time during the year by investing in buffer ETFs that reset closer to the time you're building your portfolio. However, you may need to wait until the end of the month or the end of the quarter to ensure that you're getting in at the start of the outcome period.

Growth portfolio

In my experience, most investors, regardless of age, have a primary investment objective of growth. They seek growth with the objective of outpacing inflation, taxes, and portfolio withdrawals over the long term. A traditional allocation for a growth-oriented portfolio could be 75 percent stocks and 25 percent bonds, but for a portfolio that's fully invested in buffer ETFs, you would replace the bond allocation with buffer ETFs.

Here's a sample growth portfolio that would be ideal for starting at the beginning of the second quarter (in April), because most of the ETFs included in this sample reset on March 31. However, you can build this portfolio at the end of any month or quarter by choosing funds that reset closer to the date you're building your portfolio.

- **60 percent in buffer ETFs with 9 to 10 percent protection:** Consider one or more of the following funds:
  - iShares Large-Cap 10% Target Buffer ETF — March (TENM)
  - Innovator Equity Buffer — April (BAPR)
  - AllianzIM U.S. Equity Buffer10 — April (APRT)
  - FT Vest U.S. Equity Buffer — March (FMAR)
- **25 percent in buffer ETFs with 12 to 15 percent protection:** Consider one or more of the following funds:
  - Innovator U.S. Equity Power Buffer — April (PAPR)
  - FT Vest U.S. Equity Moderate Buffer — March (GMAR)
  - Innovator International Developed Power Buffer — April (IAPR)
  - PGIM S&P 500 12 Buffer — April (APRP)
- **15 percent in buffer ETFs with 20 percent protection:** Consider one or more of the following funds:
  - PGIM S&P 500 20 Buffer — April (PBAP)
  - AllianzIM U.S. Equity Buffer 20 — April (APRW)

Aggressive growth portfolio

Investors seeking aggressive growth are willing to accept above-average losses and elevated volatility in the hopes of achieving their high growth investment objectives over the long term. A traditional portfolio allocation for an aggressive growth portfolio would be 100 percent stocks. For an aggressive growth portfolio fully invested in buffer ETFs, add holdings that track more volatile reference assets with higher growth potential, such as Invesco QQQ Trust (QQQ). In addition, you can allocate a percentage of your portfolio to ETFs that offer accelerated or uncapped returns.

Here's a sample aggressive growth portfolio that would be ideal for starting at the beginning of the third quarter (in July), because most of the ETFs included in this sample reset on June 30. However, you can build this portfolio at the end of any month or quarter by choosing funds that reset closer to the date you're building your portfolio.

- **60 percent in buffer ETFs with 9 to 10 percent protection:** Consider one or more of the following funds:
  - iShares Large-Cap 10% Target Buffer ETF — June (TENJ)
  - Innovator Equity Buffer — July (BJUL)
  - AllianzIM U.S. Equity Buffer10 — July (JULT)
  - FT Vest Nasdaq-100 Buffer ETF — June (QJUN)
- **10 percent in buffer ETFs with 15 percent protection:** Consider Innovator U.S. Small Cap Power Buffer ETF — July (KJUL)
- **10 percent in uncapped buffer ETFs with 15 percent protection:** Consider AllianzIM Buffer 15 Uncapped — July (JULU)
- **10 percent in accelerated buffer ETFs with 9 percent protection:** Consider U.S. Equity Accelerated 9 Buffer ETF — July (XBJL)
- **10 percent in Bitcoin Floor ETFs with a 10 or 20 percent floor:** Given the attractive upside potential of bitcoin, even with a floor product structured so that shareholders absorb a certain percentage of initial losses, a buffered bitcoin ETF could be included in an aggressive growth portfolio. Consider one or more of the following Bitcoin Floor ETFs:
  - Calamos Bitcoin 90 Series Structured Alt Protection ETF — July (CBXY)
  - Calamos Bitcoin 80 Series Structured Alt Protection ETF — July (CBTY)

Conservative portfolio

A conservative portfolio would typically be appropriate for risk-averse investors — those committed to limiting their annual losses to a single-digit percentage. If your primary investment objective is capital preservation, this conservative approach may be suitable for you.

A traditional portfolio allocation for a conservative portfolio is 25 percent stocks and 75 percent bonds. However, for a portfolio fully invested in buffer ETFs, replace the bond allocation with buffer ETFs.

Here's a sample conservative portfolio that would be ideal for starting at the beginning of the fourth quarter (in October), because most of the ETFs included in this sample reset on September 30. However, you can build this portfolio at the end of any month or quarter by choosing funds that reset closer to the date you're building your portfolio.

- **20 percent in buffer ETFs with 15 percent protection:** Consider one or more of the following funds:
  - Innovator U.S Equity Power Buffer — October (POCT)
  - FT Vest U.S. Equity Moderate Buffer — September (GSEP)
  - Innovator International Developed Power Buffer — October (IOCT)
- **15 percent in buffer ETFs with 20 percent protection:** Consider one or more of the following funds:
  - PGIM S&P 500 20 Buffer — October (PBOC)
  - AllianzIM U.S. Equity Buffer 20 — October (OCTW)
- **15 percent in buffer ETFs with 25 to 30 percent protection:** Consider one or more of the following funds:
  - Innovator U.S. Equity Ultra Buffer — October (UOCT)
  - FT Vest U.S. Equity Deep Buffer ETF — September (DSEP)
- **50 percent in buffer ETFs with 100 percent protection:** Consider one or more of the following funds:
  - iShares Large Cap Max Buffer ETF — September (SMAX)
  - PGIM S&P 500 Max Buffer ETF — October (PMOC)
  - Innovator Equity Defined Protection ETF — October (ZOCT)
  - Calamos S&P 500 Structured Alt Protection ETF — October (CPSO)

- Calamos Nasdaq-100 Structured Alt Protection ETF — September (CPNS)
- Calamos Russell 2000 Structured Alt Protection ETF — October (CPRO)
- Calamos Bitcoin Structured Alt Protection ETF — October (CBOO)

Ultra-conservative portfolio

An ultra-conservative portfolio would be appropriate for risk-averse investors with little tolerance for losses. The primary investment objective is capital preservation. A traditional portfolio allocation for an ultra-conservative portfolio is 100 percent bonds or Treasury bills. If you want to be fully invested in buffer ETFs, you can replace the bond/Treasury bill allocation with deep buffer and 100 percent protection ETFs.

Here's a sample ultra-conservative portfolio that would be ideal for starting at the beginning of the year (in January), because most of the ETFs included in this sample reset on December 31. However, you can build this portfolio at the end of any month or quarter by choosing funds that reset closer to the date you're building your portfolio.

- **25 percent in buffer ETFs with 25 to 30 percent protection:** Consider one or both of the following funds:
  - Innovator U.S. Equity Ultra Buffer — January (UJAN)
  - FT Vest U.S. Equity Deep Buffer ETF — December (DDEC)
- **75 percent in buffer ETFs with 100 percent protection:** Consider one or more of the following funds:
  - iShares Large Cap Max Buffer ETF — December (DMAX)
  - PGIM S&P 500 Max Buffer ETF — January (PMJA)
  - Innovator Equity Defined Protection ETF — January (ZJAN)
  - Calamos S&P 500 Structured Alt Protection ETF — January (CPSY)
  - Calamos Nasdaq-100 Structured Alt Protection ETF — December (CPNQ)
  - Calamos Russell 2000 Structured Alt Protection ETF — January (CPRY)
  - Calamos Bitcoin Structured Alt Protection ETF — January (CBOJ)

Adjusting Allocations as Conditions Change

Building an investment portfolio isn't a set-it-and-forget-it proposition. Your investment objectives are likely to change over time. Market conditions can change. You may need to cash out some funds to cover emergency expenses. To ensure that your portfolio remains aligned with your objectives, check it regularly and consider making adjustments.

Assuming you spread your investment capital across multiple buffer ETFs, and perhaps other investment assets, you should have plenty of opportunities to make adjustments on or between reset dates. (See Part 3 for more about buying and selling buffer ETFs during the intra-outcome period.)

Here are a few approaches to rebalancing you may want to consider:

- **End-of-outcome-period rebalancing:** The last trading day of the outcome period provides the perfect opportunity to reevaluate a buffer ETF. Depending on current market conditions and where you believe the market is heading, you may want to shift an allocation to a buffer ETF with a shallower buffer (higher cap) or deeper buffer (lower cap), or to a fund that tracks a different reference asset.

  REMEMBER

  Consider the tax implications of selling shares. Whenever you exit a position in a buffer ETF, you have a gain or loss that may be reportable on your tax return. Allowing your investment to roll into a new outcome period allows you to defer taxes on any gains. Of course, if you're holding your buffer ETFs in a tax-deferred account, such as a traditional or Roth IRA, you needn't be concerned about the tax implications of selling shares.
- **Buffer-decay rebalancing:** In a declining market, a buffer ETF can consume some or all of its buffer. If a buffer ETF has little or no downside protection remaining, you may want to sell it and swap into a fund with more downside protection.
- **Rebalancing to raise the cap:** In a rising market, caps can become restrictive, limiting your remaining upside potential. If you're halfway through the outcome period, and your buffer ETF is already close to its cap, you may want to swap into a buffer ETF with a higher cap.
- **Reference-asset rebalancing:** The risk/return profile of different reference assets changes over time, providing potential opportunities to improve your portfolio's performance. For example, if the Nasdaq-100 declines more than

the S&P 500 during a market crash, you may want to reallocate some of your investment capital to a buffer ETF that tracks the Nasdaq-100 with the hope that it will experience a dramatic rebound.

- **Cash-flow rebalancing:** This type of rebalancing is in response to new money you have to invest or the need to cash out of some of your holdings. If you have cash to put to work, you need to decide how you're going to invest it in a way that aligns with your investment objectives. Or, if you need cash, and all your positions show a profit, consider which buffer ETFs can be sold in the most tax-efficient manner — for example, you'll probably want to sell shares from funds that you've held for at least a year (so your gains are subject to lower long-term capital gains tax rates). You could also sell your funds that have the lowest percentage gain in your portfolio, are near their cap, and have already obtained long-term tax status — this would likely result in the least amount of taxes owed.

REMEMBER

Consider taking a gradual approach to rebalancing by making small adjustments over long periods instead of big adjustments over short periods. Imagine changing course while sailing from your point of departure to your desired destination. Shifting course a few degrees at a time may be sufficient to keep you on track.

3

Investing in Buffer ETFs during Intra-Outcome Periods

IN THIS PART . . .

Evaluate buffer ETF outcome parameters during the intra-outcome period, so you fully understand what you're getting.

Figure out what to do when your buffer or cap is nearly exhausted during the intra-outcome period.

Gain insight into how buffer ETFs behave in bear markets, bull markets, and bear-to-bull markets.

IN THIS CHAPTER

- » Shifting focus to intra-outcome parameters
- » Investing in buffer ETFs during the intra-outcome period
- » Avoiding common pitfalls of buying and selling during the intra-outcome period

Chapter 8

Tracking Key Intra-Outcome Parameters

When you're looking to buy a buffer ETF at the beginning of its outcome period, your focus is on initial outcome parameters such as outcome period, reference asset, starting buffer, and starting cap. These outcome parameters define each buffer ETF's risk-return profile and shape investor expectations for its end-of-period performance.

However, *during* the outcome period, those starting parameters become less significant. The outcome period becomes shorter, and the remaining buffer and cap fluctuate in response to price changes in the reference asset. If you're buying at the beginning of the outcome period and holding at least until the end of that period, you can pretty much ignore intra-outcome price volatility and the fund's value in relation to its cap and buffer. But if you're buying or selling a buffer ETF *during* the outcome period (intra-outcome), you need to focus on *intra-outcome parameters*, such as the *remaining buffer*, *remaining cap*, and *downside-before-buffer risk*. By paying careful attention to these and other key intra-outcome parameters, you'll be better equipped to assess whether a buffer ETF is a good choice at any specific point in time.

This chapter provides you with a framework for using intra-outcome parameters as practical tools for timing entries and exits, managing portfolio risk, and making well-informed investment decisions.

Defining Intra-Outcome Parameters

Intra-outcome parameters are the variables that change over the course of the outcome period. The following are intra-outcome parameters you need to pay attention to when buying or selling buffer ETFs during the intra-outcome period:

- **Fund return:** The percentage the buffer ETF has gained or lost since its most recent reset date.
- **Reference asset return:** The percentage the reference asset has gained or lost since the buffer ETF's most recent reset date.
- **Return difference:** The percentage difference in performance between the reference asset and the buffer ETF. If the value is positive, the buffer ETF is outperforming its reference asset. If the value is negative, the buffer ETF is underperforming its reference asset.
- **Reference asset return to cap:** How much the reference asset would need to appreciate for the buffer ETF to reach its upside cap.
- **Remaining cap:** The maximum percentage the buffer ETF can gain in the remaining outcome period. If the buffer ETF has appreciated since its last reset date, its remaining cap will be less than its starting cap. If the buffer ETF has lost value, its remaining cap will be greater than its starting cap.
- **Remaining buffer:** In a declining market, pay attention to how much buffer is left. If the buffer is depleted (or nearly so), you could sell and swap into an ETF with more downside protection. However, doing so could mean locking in a loss (if the reference asset loss exceeds the buffer), so it's not always an easy decision. Much will depend on the amount of remaining protection, your risk profile, and your outlook for the performance of the reference asset over the remainder of the outcome period.
- **Downside before buffer:** The percentage a shareholder could lose, from the current price level of the buffer ETF, before the buffer's protection kicks in. If the ETF has gained value since its last reset date, that gain is unprotected and represents the "downside-before-buffer" risk. For example, if you buy a buffer ETF that has gained 7 percent midperiod, you could lose 7 percent (downside before buffer) before you get any protection.
- **Remaining outcome period:** The number of days remaining before the next reset date.

Buffer ETF issuers typically provide updated intra-outcome parameters on their websites on a daily basis. Figure 8-1 shows a partial list of Innovator buffer ETFs that track the Invesco QQQ Trust (QQQ), complete with current values and key intra-outcome parameters as of April 17, 2026. The location of this information may differ slightly among issuers. For example, Innovator and FT Vest display pertinent information in their product tables, but for AllianzIM and BlackRock ETFs, you need to access the buffer ETF's page and then scroll down to view the current outcome parameters, as shown in Figure 8-2.

NAME	SERIES	REF. ASSET	FUND RETURN	ASSET RETURN	RETURN DIFF	ASSET RETURN TO CAP	REM. CAP	REM. BUFFER	DOWN BEFORE BUFFER	REM. OUT-PERIOD
Growth-100 15% Buffer ETF	April	Growth-100 ETF	5.04%	11.89%	-6.85%	4.77%	10.82%	18.44%	-5.59%	348
Growth-100 15% Buffer ETF	March	Growth-100 ETF	3.14%	6.34%	-3.21%	8.97%	11.56%	16.24%	-3.83%	317
Growth-100 15% Buffer ETF	February	Growth-100 ETF	2.34%	3.85%	-1.51%	10.83%	11.67%	15.07%	-3.08%	289
Growth-100 15% Buffer ETF	January	Growth-100 ETF	3.03%	5.13%	-2.10%	9.06%	10.48%	15.41%	-3.73%	258
Growth-100 15% Buffer ETF	December	Growth-100 ETF	3.50%	4.29%	-0.79%	10.64%	10.69%	14.32%	-4.17%	227
Growth-100 15% Buffer ETF	November	Growth-100 ETF	3.35%	2.66%	0.69%	12.92%	11.37%	13.17%	-4.03%	197
Growth-100 15% Buffer ETF	October	Growth-100 ETF	5.39%	7.57%	-2.18%	6.21%	7.61%	15.07%	-5.91%	166
Growth-100 15% Buffer ETF	September	Growth-100 ETF	7.80%	13.22%	-5.43%	0.62%	4.89%	16.90%	-8.02%	136
Growth-100 15% Buffer ETF	August	Growth-100 ETF	9.24%	14.30%	-5.06%	0.39%	4.25%	16.38%	-9.25%	105
Growth-100 15% Buffer ETF	July	Growth-100 ETF	10.71%	17.07%	-6.36%	-2.11%	2.72%	16.93%	-10.47%	74
Growth-100 15% Buffer ETF	June	Growth-100 ETF	13.37%	24.41%	-11.04%	-7.26%	0.98%	19.09%	-12.58%	44
Growth-100 15% Buffer ETF	May	Growth-100 ETF	16.16%	35.83%	-19.66%	-13.86%	0.00%	22.71%	-14.71%	13

As of 4/17/26

Educational content provided by Innovator

Courtesy of Innovator

FIGURE 8-1: Intra-outcome parameters for a partial list of Innovator ETFs on April 17, 2026.

OUTCOME PERIOD VALUES (CURRENT/NET) **AS OF 3/31/2026**

Fund Price	Fund Return	SPY Return	Remaining Cap	Remaining Buffer	Downside Before Buffer	Remaining Outcome Period
$53.36	-2.99%	-4.69%	19.86%/19.26%	7.42%/6.82%	0.00%/0.00%	275 days

OUTCOME PERIOD VALUES (CURRENT/NET) **AS OF 12/31/2025**

Fund Price	Fund Return	SPY Return	Cap	Buffer	Downside Before Buffer	Outcome Period
$55.01	0.00%	0.00%	16.46%/15.67%	9.00%/8.21%	0.00%/-0.79%	365 days

Educational content provided by Innovator

Courtesy of Innovator

FIGURE 8-2: Intra-outcome parameters for Innovator U.S. Equity Buffer ETF — January (BJAN) on March 31, 2026.

Which intra-outcome parameters are highlighted and what they're called may differ slightly among issuers. Click the ticker symbol for a buffer ETF to compare the current outcome parameters with the starting outcome parameters. (See Chapter 5 for a list of issuer website addresses.)

Carefully evaluate intra-outcome parameters whenever you're deciding to buy or sell between reset dates. Table 8-1 shows intra-outcome parameters for three Innovator U.S. Equity Power Buffer ETFs — July, August, and September (PJUL, PAUG, and PSEP) — on November 22, 2023. The reference asset is the SPDR S&P 500 ETF Trust (SPY), and all three funds have a starting buffer of 15 percent (not shown in the table).

TABLE 8-1 Intra-Outcome Parameters (November 22, 2023)

Ticker	Reference Asset	ETF Return	Asset Return	Return Difference	Asset Return to Cap	Remaining Cap	Downside Before Buffer	Remaining Days
PAUG	SPY	0.57%	-0.34%	0.91%	15.61%	13.66%	-1.36%	252
PSEP	SPY	1.52%	1.31%	0.21%	13.48%	12.36%	-2.29%	283
PJUL	SPY	2.60%	2.93%	-0.32%	11.03%	10.50%	-3.33%	221

When comparing the potential outcome parameters for these three ETFs, PAUG is probably the most attractive. It has 252 days remaining in the outcome period, which is much less than a newly reset buffer that has 365 days remaining until the next reset date. Its remaining upside cap (13.66 percent) is the highest of the three buffer ETFs, and it has the lowest percentage of downside-before-buffer risk at −1.36 percent (compared to −2.29 and −3.33 percent). Overall, PAUG offers an attractive risk-reward profile with a relatively short outcome period, which could make it a compelling intra-outcome purchase.

Checking Out Potential Outcomes

Buffer ETF issuers may also provide access to *potential outcomes*, which show how a particular fund will perform over the outcome period depending on the return of the reference asset, as shown in Figure 8-3. For example, you can see that if the reference asset (SPY), shown as "Asset" in the figure, gains 15 percent, BJAN will gain 14.29 percent, and BOCT will gain 10.80 percent, net of fees.

These values are important because buffer ETFs don't move in lockstep with their underlying reference asset. They typically lag the reference asset and then catch up to some degree as the options contracts near expiration. In a rapidly rising or declining market, the performance difference can be amplified.

NAME	SERIES	ASSET -50%	ASSET -40%	ASSET -30%	ASSET -20%	ASSET -10%	ASSET -5%	ASSET FLAT	ASSET +5%	ASSET +10%	ASSET +15%	ASSET +20%	ASSET +30%
U.S. Large Cap 9% Buffer ETF	January	-41.61%	-31.55%	-21.49%	-11.43%	-1.97%	-1.97%	-0.21%	4.82%	9.85%	14.29%	14.29%	14.29%
U.S. Large Cap 9% Buffer ETF	December	-42.01%	-32.02%	-22.04%	-12.06%	-2.47%	-2.47%	-0.93%	4.06%	9.05%	14.04%	14.66%	14.66%
U.S. Large Cap 9% Buffer ETF	November	-42.11%	-32.13%	-22.16%	-12.19%	-2.79%	-2.79%	-1.06%	3.92%	8.91%	13.90%	14.46%	14.46%
U.S. Large Cap 9% Buffer ETF	October	-41.70%	-31.62%	-21.55%	-11.47%	-4.07%	-4.07%	-0.02%	5.02%	10.06%	10.80%	10.80%	10.80%
U.S. Large Cap 9% Buffer ETF	September	-41.37%	-31.19%	-21.01%	-10.83%	-6.17%	-4.07%	1.02%	6.11%	8.35%	8.35%	8.35%	8.35%
U.S. Large Cap 9% Buffer ETF	August	-41.24%	-31.00%	-20.77%	-10.53%	-7.59%	-3.57%	1.54%	6.66%	7.13%	7.13%	7.13%	7.13%
U.S. Large Cap 9% Buffer ETF	July	-40.95%	-30.64%	-20.32%	-10.01%	-7.96%	-2.80%	2.36%	5.72%	5.72%	5.72%	5.72%	5.72%
U.S. Large Cap 9% Buffer ETF	June	-39.82%	-29.24%	-18.66%	-10.96%	-5.59%	-0.30%	3.64%	3.64%	3.64%	3.64%	3.64%	3.64%
U.S. Large Cap 9% Buffer ETF	May	-38.37%	-27.45%	-16.54%	-13.47%	-2.55%	2.23%	2.23%	2.23%	2.23%	2.23%	2.23%	2.23%
U.S. Large Cap 9% Buffer ETF	April	-38.25%	-27.32%	-16.40%	-12.74%	-2.47%	1.45%	1.45%	1.45%	1.45%	1.45%	1.45%	1.45%
U.S. Large Cap 9% Buffer ETF	March	-41.22%	-30.90%	-20.58%	-12.42%	-7.89%	-2.72%	1.59%	1.59%	1.59%	1.59%	1.59%	1.59%
U.S. Large Cap 9% Buffer ETF	February	-41.92%	-31.73%	-21.55%	-12.47%	-9.12%	-4.03%	0.94%	0.94%	0.94%	0.94%	0.94%	0.94%

As of 4/17/26

Educational content provided by Innovator

FIGURE 8-3: Potential outcome parameters for Innovator 9 percent buffer ETFs on April 17, 2026.

Courtesy of Innovator

REMEMBER

Generally, in a rising market, a buffer ETF will somewhat lag the return of the reference asset, at least from the beginning to the middle of the outcome period. And, the more protection provided by the ETF, the greater the percentage lag. Price changes in buffer ETFs with minimal protection are more closely correlated with the reference asset's return than those with moderate or deep protection.

In a declining market, buffer ETFs typically hold up better and lose less than the reference asset. This is not always the case, but generally speaking, with conventional buffer ETFs, volatility is decreased in both rising and declining markets, which means a performance lag in up markets and a performance advantage (smaller percentage losses) in declining markets.

Checking the potential outcomes can help shape realistic expectations and formulate better buy-sell decisions. For example, as shown in Figure 8-3, you can see that even if the reference asset (SPY), shown as "Asset" in the figure, remains flat for the remainder of the outcome period, a shareholder would earn an additional 2.36 percent in BJUL. And, if SPY rises 5 percent from current levels, BJUL will gain 5.72 percent.

Unfortunately, not all buffer ETF issuers provide easy access to detailed current potential outcomes. For example, Innovator and FT Vest provide this information only to financial professionals who sign up for access on their websites. You need to create a user ID and password and log in to gain access. Then, after selecting a buffer ETF from the product table, you can scroll down and click the Show Potential Outcomes button to view the table. The good news is that all issuers provide, at least daily, enough information about the current potential outcome parameters (including remaining cap, remaining buffer, and downside before buffer) for you to make well-informed buy-sell decisions.

Using Intra-Outcome Parameters to Your Advantage

TIP

You can use potential outcome parameter information to spot opportunities to lock in profits, reset protection, harvest losses (for tax purposes), or improve your positions (obtain more downside protection with a potentially higher cap). For example, if your buffer ETF is showing a gain midperiod, the entire unrealized gain is at risk over the remainder of the outcome period. So, you may want to lock in your profits and swap into a buffer ETF with a fresh buffer and a higher cap. (See Chapter 9 for additional guidance on spotting opportunities to improve your buffer ETF positions.)

REMEMBER

Keep in mind that swapping out of a buffer ETF position to obtain more downside protection or a higher cap may not always work in your favor. For example, suppose your buffer ETF is close to being capped out with a few months remaining in the outcome period. Suppose it has 2 percent upside remaining to the cap, but perhaps it has lagged the reference asset considerably, and you'll make the 2 percent, even if the reference asset declines 10 percent (or is flat) over the remainder of the outcome period. (Yes, I've seen this scenario quite often after the reference asset has surged over a short period of time.)

Well, if you sell and swap into a buffer ETF with fresh protection and a new upside cap on its reset date, but the reference asset subsequently declines 7 percent, for example, over the next few months, you will show a loss on your new position, *and* you would have missed out on the extra 2 percent you would have made in the buffer ETF you sold. In short, selling before the end of the outcome period, for whatever reason, may not be the best decision, and it could backfire on you. See Chapter 9 for additional guidance on buying and selling buffer ETFs during the intra-outcome period.

PASSIVE VERSUS ACTIVE INVESTING

I asked Bruce Bond, co-founder and CEO of Innovator Capital Management LLC, whether most investors and advisors use Innovator buffer ETFs in a passive manner or whether they trade more actively, looking for opportunities during the intra-outcome period. Here's what he had to say:

> "A large majority of investors are using them to replace equity exposures over a full outcome period, but we do have significant interest from investors who are looking for unique intra-period opportunities."

Actively trading buffer ETFs has a couple of additional potential downsides:

- **Increased costs:** Whenever you buy or sell a buffer ETF, you're paying the bid-ask spread (the difference between the most a buyer will pay and the least a seller will accept). A 0.20 percent spread paid six times during a 12-month outcome period (three swaps) results in a 1.20 percent drag on your investment performance.
- **Reduced tax efficiency:** Whenever you sell a fund that's held in a taxable account, you're creating a taxable event, which could result in taxes owed and a loss of the tax efficiency that's built into ETFs. However, if you're holding a buffer ETF in a tax-deferred account, such as an IRA, there is no tax reporting of realized gains and losses, so you needn't be concerned about the tax consequences of selling during the intra-outcome period.

IN THIS CHAPTER

» Trading buffer ETFs in rising and declining markets

» Preserving your gains

» Navigating short outcome periods

Chapter 9

Exploring Intra-Outcome Strategies

Being able to buy and sell buffer ETFs throughout the outcome period introduces some attractive applications, including the ability to do the following:

- Raise the cap
- Refresh the buffer
- Lock in profits
- Eliminate downside-before-buffer risk

This chapter presents several strategies for buying and selling buffer ETFs during the intra-outcome period while highlighting the potential benefits of each strategy.

Buying and Selling during the Intra-Outcome Period

Rotating buffer ETFs (selling one and buying another that has more attractive outcome parameters) can work to your advantage in both up-market and down-market scenarios, as explained in the following sections.

Up-market scenario

In rising markets, "stepping up" into a new buffer series may be a beneficial approach to locking in gains, expanding upside potential, and resetting the buffer level at the same time.

This step-up strategy is made possible by the monthly issuance of buffer ETFs. Figure 9-1 shows how you can employ a step-up strategy using buffer ETFs that have outcome periods starting in January, April, August, and December. In this example, the January series could have been held for three months to achieve an approximate 10 percent return, then it could be sold, and the proceeds rolled into the April series. This approach raises the cap (7 percent up from the original cap) and resets the buffer at a new, higher price level for the reference asset. Swapping from the April to the August series raised the cap by only 0.10 percent, but because the April series had appreciated approximately 5 percent, the fresh buffer protects that gain. This type of rotation, which is possible due to the liquidity of buffer ETFs, gives you the potential to expand upside caps while protecting your gains.

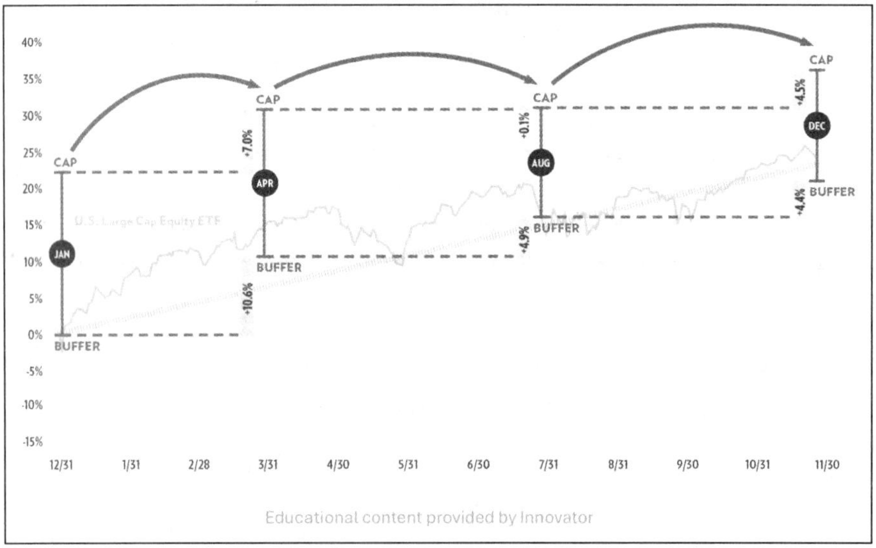

FIGURE 9-1: Step-up strategy.

Courtesy of Innovator

Down-market scenario

A price decline in the underlying reference asset may provide an opportunity to implement a "step-down strategy." For example, if the reference asset, the SPDR S&P 500 ETF Trust (SPY), has declined, and the buffer ETF has outperformed (lost less than the reference asset), you can rotate into a buffer ETF with less protection (for example, from a 15 percent buffer to a 9 percent buffer). By rotating into a fund with a smaller buffer, you typically get a higher cap, which will benefit you in the event the reference asset rallies.

Figure 9-2 shows how a step-down strategy can work in your favor. In this example, at the beginning of a new calendar year, you purchase PJAN (U.S. Large Cap Equity 15% Buffer ETF), with a reset date of December 31, 2021, that has a 15 percent buffer and a 15 percent cap. By October, the reference asset (SPY), shown as "U.S. Large Cap Equity ETF" in the figure, has declined a whopping 24.80 percent, but your buffer ETF experienced a decline of *only* 11.20 percent. This scenario provides a potential opportunity to implement a step-down strategy. You have two options:

- Rotate into a buffer ETF with a fresh buffer of 15 percent (effectively deepening your downside protection from 15 to 26.20 percent), as shown in Figure 9-2.
- Rotate into a buffer ETF with less protection (9 percent, for example) but a higher cap. The thinking here is that because SPY has already suffered a deep loss, it's unlikely to lose another 15 percent, so a smaller 9 percent buffer should hopefully be sufficient. With less downside protection, you get a higher cap, which is an advantage if the reference asset is poised to rebound.

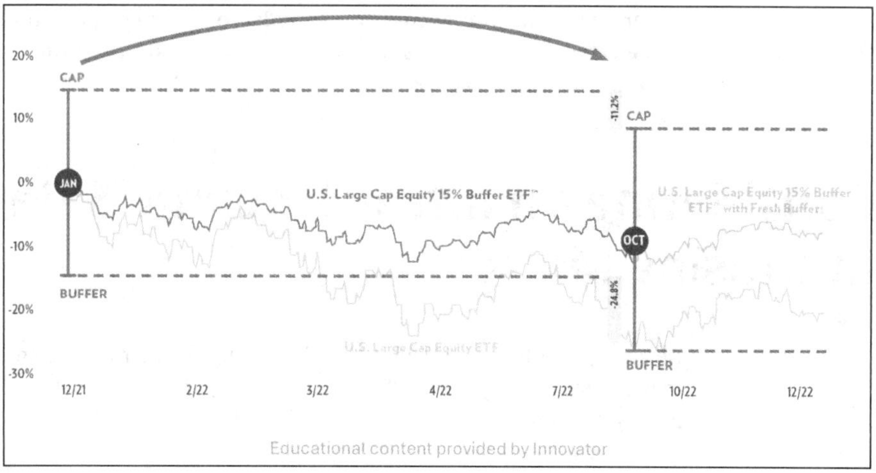

FIGURE 9-2: Step-down strategy.

Courtesy of Innovator

DESIGNED FOR BUY-AND-HOLD INVESTORS

Buffer ETFs were not initially intended to be traded midperiod, as Karan Sood, CEO of Vest Financial LLC, pointed out during a recent interview:

> "Our initial expectation was that investors would buy and hold the investments for a one-year period. And so, our original design contemplated that investors would purchase them on the roll date and hold them to the next roll date. Over the years, the majority of investors in our buffer strategies have adopted the practice of passively holding their buffer funds for longer periods of time, but in the early days, there was a lot of active trading within the target outcome period. Note, we came from a structured note background where liquidity did not meaningfully exist, so everyone held notes until the expiry. So, trading during the target outcome period was novel to us, and it became important to build tools designed to inform investors as to the daily potential outcome parameters."

In 2022, market volatility pushed caps higher, and POCT offered a very high gross cap of 20.70 percent on its reset date (September 30). Stepping down at that point would have been an attractive strategy because you wouldn't be sacrificing much upside potential to obtain more downside protection.

Ultimately, your choice of which buffer ETF to rotate into depends on the level of downside risk you think remains in the reference asset to the next reset date, and how much upside potential remains (upside cap). If you think the reference asset will very likely continue to decline, you might opt for the additional 15 percent protection. If you think the reference asset will likely rally after a steep loss, you may find the 9 percent buffer and a higher cap more attractive. Or, if you're unsure, you can simply continue to hold your current position that shows a loss. If the reference asset finishes the outcome period inside the buffer, you stand to recoup any temporary losses.

Considering an Intra-Outcome Sale in a Rising Market

Deciding whether to sell a buffer ETF during the intra-outcome period in a rising market isn't always easy. To make a well-informed decision, consider the following factors:

- **The current intra-outcome parameters for the buffer ETF you own:** Focus on the remaining buffer, downside before buffer, reference asset return to cap, and the remaining cap. These values can help you gauge how much of your current gains you could possibly lose if you continue to hold the buffer ETF and how much upside you're giving up if you decide to sell.
- **The starting outcome parameters for buffer ETFs you can rotate into:** What you're looking for here is whether you can improve your position with a buffer ETF that has a more attractive buffer and cap. You may also want to consider simply parking the proceeds of the sale of your buffer ETF in cash or Treasury bills and then reinvesting in the same buffer ETF on its next reset date (see the later section "Converting your buffer ETF to cash and back" for details about this strategy).
- **Your temperament:** If you're a passive investor, you can stay invested in the buffer ETF and let it function as designed. If you're more active, you may want to sell during the intra-outcome period to protect your gains (a conservative approach), increase the cap (an aggressive approach), or both.
- **Your investment objectives:** Think about how much profit is sufficient to meet your investment goals. If your buffer ETF has already achieved a satisfactory return during the current outcome period, you may want to sell during the intra-outcome period to protect your gain.

  REMEMBER

  Keep in mind that any gain from the most recent reset date is unrealized and at risk up until the next reset date.
- **Tax consequences:** If your buffer ETF is held in a tax-deferred account, such as a traditional or Roth IRA, you needn't concern yourself with tax consequences. However, if it's in a taxable account, consider the difference you'll pay in short-term versus long-term capital gains taxes — assuming you will sell at some point. Short-term capital gains are taxed as ordinary income (at federal rates up to 37 percent plus possible state and local taxes). Federal taxes on long-term capital gains range from 0 to 20 percent, plus state and local taxes.
- **Your opinion of the short-term direction of the reference asset:** Do you fear a correction (drop of 10 percent), or a deeper decline? Your opinion as to the short-term direction of the reference asset could greatly influence your decision to sell during the intra-outcome period. And if you foresee a potential rebound of the reference asset in the near term, you may decide to sell and swap into a buffer ETF with minimal protection, but more upside potential (higher cap).

For example, suppose you bought PNOV on its reset date of October 31, 2023. PNOV is a 12-month buffer ETF that tracks the SPDR S&P 500 ETF Trust (SPY). It had a starting buffer of 15 percent on its last reset date and a cap of 14.35 percent.

In a few short months, SPY skyrocketed and was up 18.06 percent by February 2, as shown in the table below. PNOV's return lagged SPY by a significant amount (−9.68 percent) but still showed a healthy return of 8.38 percent in the three months since its reset date (when you bought it). Should you consider a sale of PNOV to lock in profits? The unrealized gains are unprotected during the remainder of the outcome period (272 days), so if the reference asset declines and remains down by a significant amount when the next reset date comes around, you could lose your profits.

ETF Ticker	ETF Return	Reference Asset Return	Return Difference	Index Return to Cap	Remaining Cap	Downside Before Buffer	Remaining Days
PNOV	8.38%	18.06%	-9.68%	1.94%	5.97%	-8.53%	272

Consider the factors highlighted at the start of this section:

- **The current intra-outcome parameters:** The current intra-outcome parameters make deciding to sell difficult. Sure, you have a nice unrealized gain of 8.38 percent in a very short period, but the fact that PNOV has lagged the return of SPY by 9.68 percent makes a sale problematic. Even if SPY remains flat to the end of the outcome period or declines slightly, your buffer ETF stands to gain another 5.97 percent.

  TECHNICAL STUFF

  In very fast-rising markets, the combination of the prices of the option contracts within the buffer ETF tends to cause the buffer ETF to significantly lag the performance of the reference asset early in the outcome period. The buffer ETF's performance tends to catch up near the end of the outcome period as the options near expiration. On some issuer websites, you can access each buffer ETF's potential outcomes, which indicate the approximate return you can expect based on the reference asset's return to its next reset date, as shown in the following table. This information can be very useful in helping you decide whether to sell. For example, this table shows that if SPY (the reference asset) were to decline 5 percent from its current level, PNOV would still earn an additional 2.67 percent at the end of the outcome period.

Ticker	Asset -15%	Asset -10%	Asset -5%	Asset Flat	Asset 5%	Asset 10%	Asset 15%
PNOV	-8.14%	-2.74%	2.67%	5.97%	5.97%	5.97%	5.97%

- **Your temperament:** PNOV's downside-before-buffer risk of -8.53 percent indicates that your entire unrealized gain is at risk. If you feel that you can't afford to lose that much, or you think you can improve your position by swapping into a different buffer ETF, you'd be more inclined to sell.

- **Your investment objectives:** Compare your buffer ETF's current return to what you expected on the date of purchase. Would you have been happy with a gain of 8.38 percent in just three months? Are you content with that return? What's more important to you — protecting your gains or trying to capture another 5.97 percent?
- **Tax consequences:** If you hold PNOV in a taxable account, and the position shows a short-term gain, you'll likely want to hold it to avoid paying the short-term capital gains tax. Holding the buffer ETF for more than a year ensures that any gain is taxed at the favorable long-term capital gains rate. I'd lean toward holding the position to get to long-term tax status. Obviously, if you hold PNOV in a tax-deferred account, this consideration is moot.
- **Your opinion of the short-term direction of the reference asset:** Your opinion as to the direction of the reference asset in the coming months could influence your decision to hold or sell PNOV. If you fear a significant decline, for whatever reason, you may be inclined to sell and lock in your profits now. Yes, your gain may be subject to short-term capital gains tax, but if you're worried about a decline of 8.53 percent or more in PNOV (downside before buffer), and it happens, then your profits will erode and perhaps turn into unrealized losses, and you'll likely regret not selling while you were ahead. If, on the other hand, you expect SPY to be relatively stable (range-bound sideways action) or even move higher in the coming months, then you'll likely want to hold your position and hopefully capture an additional 5.97 percent gain over the remainder of the outcome period.

Here's another example: Suppose you bought POCT on its reset date of September 30, 2023. Seven months later (on April 30, 2024), POCT's intra-outcome parameters are as shown in the table below:

ETF Ticker	ETF Return	Reference Asset Return	Return Difference	Index Return to Cap	Remaining Cap	Downside Before Buffer	Remaining Days
POCT	10.49%	19.32%	–8.82%	–3.20%	3.71%	–10.29%	154

Its potential outcomes are as follows:

Ticker	Asset -20%	Asset -15%	Asset -10%	Asset -5%	Asset Flat	Asset 5% or More
POCT	–10.21%	–8.94%	–3.58%	1.78%	3.71%	3.71%

The reference asset (SPY) is up 19.32 percent since you bought it. POCT has lagged SPY by a significant amount (–8.82 percent) but is still showing a nice profit of

10.49 percent in the seven months since the last reset date. Should you consider a sale of POCT to lock in profits? As you know, the unrealized gains are unprotected during the remainder of the outcome period (154 days), so if the reference asset suffers a significant decline, you could lose your profits and some of your principal, too. So, does a sale of POCT make sense?

A primary consideration in this hypothetical case is the percentage shown in the column titled "Downside Before Buffer." The buffer doesn't protect the unrealized gains in your position since your purchase on the last reset date. The ETF could decline 10.29 percent before the buffer would provide protection. And, during the remainder of the outcome period, if SPY declines by 20 percent or more, you'll lose your profits (as shown in the "Asset –20%" column). Does the potential upside of 3.71 percent ("Remaining Cap") over the remaining five months of the outcome period warrant taking the risk of potentially losing your profits?

If you hold POCT in a tax-deferred account (for example, an IRA), the gains are not subject to capital gains tax. If that's the case, selling POCT at this point likely makes sense. Your upside potential over the next five months is only 3.71 percent, but you'd be risking nearly three times that much by not selling, given that you could lose all your profits. Furthermore, if you take your profits and invest the proceeds in Treasury bills, you could earn approximately 2.25 percent (the annualized T-bill rate in late April 2024), with no risk, over the remaining five months of the outcome period. So, if you decide to hold POCT to the next reset date, the net upside potential in POCT is only 1.46 percent more than what you could earn in Treasury bills. Is a gain of only 1.46 percent beyond what Treasury bills will pay you over the next five months worth the risk of losing your 10 percent profit? I think not.

Another potentially attractive strategy would be to sell POCT and rotate into PMAY, which resets the same day (April 30) you'd be selling POCT. Instead of buying Treasury bills, you could rotate (step up) into PMAY and get a fresh buffer at the current price level of the reference asset, with a new upside cap. The upside cap for PMAY is 14.30 percent (before fees), with 15 percent downside protection, so this could be a compelling investment over the 12-month outcome period.

If you own POCT in a taxable account, then you have a much more difficult decision. If you held the position for only seven months before selling, you could owe short-term capital gains taxes, which are typically taxed at a higher rate than long-term capital gains. So, this gives you an incentive to hold the position for another five months. Of course, by holding POCT to get to the next reset date and long-term tax status, you risk losing your profits. Still, I'd lean toward holding POCT to get to long-term tax status, with fresh protection on the next reset date.

Considering an Intra-Outcome Sale in a Declining Market

Deciding whether to sell during the intra-outcome period in a declining market is no easier than making such a decision in a rising market. To make a well-informed decision, consider the following factors:

- **The current intra-outcome parameters for the buffer ETF you own:** Focus on the remaining buffer, the number of days remaining in the outcome period, how far the reference asset has declined, and how your buffer ETF has performed relative to the reference asset. If you're running out of buffer and fear an additional decline, you may prefer to step down into a fund with a new buffer.

  REMEMBER

  In a declining market, a buffer ETF typically outperforms its reference asset. In other words, it loses less.

- **The starting outcome parameters for buffer ETFs you can rotate into:** What you're looking for here is whether you can improve your position with a buffer ETF that has a more attractive buffer and cap. You may also want to consider simply parking your investment capital after the sale in cash or Treasury bills and then reinvesting in the same buffer ETF on its next reset date (see the later section "Converting your buffer ETF to cash and back" for details about this strategy).

  REMEMBER

  Getting a new buffer doesn't necessarily mean accepting a much lower cap. For example, if you're thinking of selling a fund that has a 13 percent cap because its 15 percent buffer is nearly exhausted, you may be able to find a fund with a 10 percent buffer that has a 15 percent or higher cap.

- **The time remaining in the outcome period:** In a declining market, consider how much time the reference asset has to recover from any loss deeper than the buffer. For example, if the reference asset would need to recover 20 percent or more in a matter of 90 days just for your buffer ETF to break even, rotating into a different buffer ETF with a more attractive buffer and cap might make sense.
- **Your temperament:** If you're a passive investor, you can leave your money in the buffer ETF and let it function as designed. Barring a dramatic market reversal, your buffer ETF will likely outperform the reference asset to the next reset date. If you're a conservative investor and you're willing to actively manage your portfolio, you may want to sell during the intra-outcome period to protect against a potentially deeper loss. If you're more aggressive, you may consider rotating into a fund with a minimal buffer and a higher cap.

» **Your investment objectives:** If the reference asset has suffered a loss deep enough to exhaust or nearly exhaust your buffer, and you can't afford to suffer a deeper loss, you may have a compelling reason to sell during the intra-outcome period.

» **Tax consequences:** If your buffer ETF is in a tax-deferred account, such as a traditional or Roth IRA, you needn't concern yourself with tax consequences. However, if it's in a taxable account, you may benefit by selling prior to the end of the outcome period, so you can harvest a short-term capital loss, which can help offset realized capital gains indefinitely, or reduce your taxable income. Typically, you can use a net capital loss (after offsetting any capital gains) to deduct up to $3,000 of ordinary income (like wages) per year, with any remaining loss carried forward to future tax years.

» **Your opinion of the short-term direction of the reference asset:** If you think the reference asset is likely to decline further than the downside protection remaining, you may lean toward selling and rotating into a fund with a new buffer. However, if you think the reference asset will bounce back, you'll probably lean toward staying the course. If you're an aggressive investor, you may look for an opportunity to swap into a buffer ETF with a higher cap.

Suppose you purchased BJAN, PJAN, and UJAN on the last trading day of 2021. The following table lists their starting outcome parameters:

ETF Ticker	Reference Asset	Buffer	Cap	Outcome Period
BJAN	SPY	0 to -9%	13.50%	362
PJAN	SPY	0 to -15%	8.99%	362
UJAN	SPY	-5 to -35%	6.89%	362

Nine months later, on September 30, 2022, stocks were in a bear market, and the S&P 500 had lost nearly 25 percent. The intra-outcome parameters for these funds at that time are shown in the table below:

ETF Ticker	ETF Return	Reference Asset Return	Return Difference	Remaining Cap	Remaining Buffer	Downside Before Buffer	Remaining Days
BJAN	-16.89%	-24.80%	7.91%	35.81%	-1.28%	0.0%	92
PJAN	-11.47%	-24.80%	13.33%	22.36%	-0.69%	0.0%	92
UJAN	-7.49%	-24.80%	17.31%	14.98%	15.77%	0.0%	92

The reference asset (SPY) was crushed, having lost 24.80 percent. All three buffer ETFs held up better than SPY, as they should during a bear market. Nevertheless, all three positions lost money since their most recent reset date (as shown in the column "ETF Return"). So, should you step down, realize the losses (tax-loss harvest), and rotate into a new buffer series with additional downside protection and a new upside cap?

Consider the factors I highlighted at the beginning of this section:

- **The current intra-outcome parameters for the buffer ETF you own:** The current outcome parameters make a sale of all the holdings in the January series potentially attractive. All three buffer ETFs have outperformed their reference asset. UJAN presents the most attractive opportunity, losing only 7.59 percent compared to SPY's decline of 24.80 percent.

  REMEMBER

  By selling BJAN or PJAN, you're locking in a loss, but by not selling, you risk deeper losses because these ETFs are no longer buffered against losses — the reference asset has breached their buffer levels. Note, UJAN still has plenty of downside protection remaining.

  REMEMBER

  Whenever you're thinking of rotating into a different buffer ETF, be mindful of where the reference asset is trading relative to the buffer level. For example, if the reference asset is only slightly below your downside buffer level, all it needs to do is recover into the buffer zone by the end of the outcome period, and your ETF will recoup all its losses. However, if the reference asset is trading significantly below the buffer level, as is the case for BJAN in this example, it would have to recover quickly to finish the outcome period inside the buffer for you to recoup your losses. SPY would have to surge over 20 percent in three months for BJAN to get back in its buffer zone by the end of the outcome period, and that's unlikely.

- **The starting outcome parameters for buffer ETFs you can swap into:** On September 30, the most obvious buffer ETFs to swap into would be BOCT, POCT, and UOCT from the same issuer. The starting outcome parameters for these buffer ETFs on September 30, 2022, are shown in the table below:

ETF Ticker	Reference Asset	Buffer	Cap	Outcome Period
BOCT	SPY	0 to -9%	28.45%	362
POCT	SPY	0 to -15%	20.72%	362
UOCT	SPY	-5 to -35%	17.08%	362

You could swap out of UJAN, take the tax loss, and purchase BOCT. This move would give you a new 9 percent buffer and a starting cap of 28.45 percent, which is considerably higher than the remaining upside cap of UJAN (14.98 percent).

You're also in a good position to swap out of PJAN, harvest a tax loss, create a new buffer, and increase the upside cap. You could swap into BOCT (with a 9 percent buffer and a 28.45 percent cap) or POCT (15 percent buffer and a 20.72 percent cap).

A sale of BJAN is perhaps more difficult. With an upside cap of 35.81 percent, you may be able to recover from the loss and see a positive return if SPY experiences a dramatic rebound. However, with only 92 days remaining in its outcome period, the fund is unlikely to recoup a significant portion of its losses, and if SPY continues to decline, you will suffer deeper losses. Rotating from BJAN to BOCT would give you a fresh 9 percent buffer and a super-attractive 28.45 percent cap. So, if SPY were to recover over the next 12 months, you could recoup all of your losses and potentially have a positive return.

TIP

A swap out of all three holdings and into one of the October series buffer ETFs would likely make the most sense for conservative or moderate risk investors. This move would provide some additional downside protection, but still allow the potential to recoup losses over the coming 12 months. POCT might be the sweet spot for a moderate risk investor. It offers 15 percent downside protection, in case the reference asset continues to decline, but it also offers a very attractive upside cap of 20.72 percent, which would enable you to recoup losses if SPY rebounds strongly over the next 12 months.

Another alternative is to sell all three buffer ETFs and buy an index-based ETF without a buffer, for example, SPY, in the hope the index rebounds. This move would provide you with uncapped potential but no downside protection. You could also consider a purchase of an uncapped buffer ETF that offers additional downside protection but with uncapped upside above the "spread." (Chapter 14 covers uncapped buffer ETFs in detail.)

- **The time remaining in the outcome period:** You have only 92 days remaining in the outcome period for the January series you own, so the reference asset has little time to recoup its losses. You need the reference asset to rally quickly to get back into the buffer zones of your current holdings. For your funds that have depleted their buffers, BJAN and PJAN, you may decide they're unlikely to recover enough in three months to return to the buffer zone, which would make stepping down and rotating into the October series an easier decision, at least for those two funds. UJAN still has plenty of downside protection, so you could decide to hold it. But again, UJAN has also significantly outperformed the reference asset, so it provides you with the best potential to outperform (assuming SPY recovers) if you rotate now to a new buffer ETF series with a higher cap.

- **Your temperament:** If you have a very low risk tolerance, you're likely not comfortable with the losses you're seeing in two of your three buffer ETFs. BJAN and PJAN have both lost quite a bit on a percentage basis, but have still nicely outperformed the reference asset. UJAN is showing a much smaller loss and still offers more downside protection (–5 to –35 percent), so this position is probably not a big concern for you. If you're a conservative investor, you'll likely want to rotate out of BJAN and PJAN to get some additional downside protection from current levels, just in case SPY declines further before the next reset date.

  If you're a moderate risk investor, you may want to capture the outperformance you've had and rotate into the new October series that offers higher caps and more time to recover your losses (12 months).

  If you're somewhat aggressive, you could swap into a buffer ETF that offers the least amount of additional downside protection but the highest cap. Or you could swap into a non-buffered ETF that tracks SPY but provides unlimited upside potential.

- **Tax consequences:** If your buffer ETFs are held in a taxable account, selling them now enables you to harvest losses, which you can use to offset gains or reduce your taxable ordinary income in the current tax year or indefinitely (excess losses can be carried forward to future tax years). However, if your buffer ETFs are in a tax-deferred account, selling at a loss provides no tax advantage.

- **Your opinion of the short-term direction of the reference asset:** If you fear a further decline in the reference asset, you'll probably be inclined to sell BJAN and PJAN and rotate into funds with a fresh buffer. UJAN still provides more downside protection, but your other two holdings have exhausted their buffers.

  On the other hand, if you think SPY has hit bottom and is poised to recover quickly, selling PJAN and UJAN and rotating into BOCT (the October series with the least downside protection but highest cap) would make sense.

  Your choice on how to proceed depends largely on your temperament and your confidence in where the reference asset is heading.

REMEMBER

DON'T WORRY

Despite the higher caps for the October series, staying put in the JAN ETFs wouldn't necessarily be a bad move. In a down market, your buffer ETF will outperform the reference asset. You don't need to rotate or step down in a declining market, but if you're looking to capitalize on a potential opportunity, and it fits your outlook and time horizon, then an intra-outcome trade could indeed be attractive.

As Bruce Bond, co-founder and CEO of Innovator Capital Management, pointed out during our interview:

> "The beauty of buffer strategies is that investors don't have to worry about whether the market goes up or down. If the market goes up, a buffer strategy will participate to a predetermined maximum level, and if it goes down, the strategy offers the chosen level of protection. The smaller buffers that have higher caps tend to perform better in positive markets, while the bigger buffers tend to perform better during bear markets."

Locking In Profits during the Intra-Outcome Period

In rising markets, stepping up into a different buffer ETF or cashing out and keeping your money on the sidelines to reinvest in the same or different buffer ETF with a new buffer and cap enables you to lock in gains and possibly increase your upside potential.

The following table shows the intra-outcome parameters of PNOV (which has a starting buffer of 15 percent) as of June 16, 2023 — about seven months and two weeks into its 12-month outcome period:

ETF Ticker	ETF Return	Reference Asset Return	Return Difference	Index Return to Cap	Remaining Cap	Downside Before Buffer	Remaining Days
PNOV	12.04%	13.79%	-1.75%	5.91%	7.03%	-11.2%	137

This table presents a compelling case for selling PNOV 137 days before the end of its outcome period. Here's why:

- PNOV has already gained 12.04 percent from its most recent reset date, which is a healthy return in only seven months.
- The current gain is unrealized, placing it at risk for the remainder of the outcome period.
- The downside before buffer is –11.2 percent, meaning PNOV could lose 11.2 percent before any of your investment would be protected.
- The upside is capped at 7.03 percent over the remaining 137 days. Although this may seem attractive, it's not as high as the upside cap of PJUL on its upcoming reset date. By selling PNOV and rotating into PJUL (which resets in two weeks on June 30), you could lock in profits and create fresh downside protection with a new upside cap (14.28 percent) over the next 12-month outcome period.

Of course, you can't reliably predict the performance of the reference asset over a short period, but you do know that you have a very attractive unrealized gain that's at risk. Unrealized gains can quickly turn into losses in volatile markets. Selling PNOV at this point would protect the 12.04 percent profit and remove the uncertainty of remaining invested for the balance of the outcome period. Rotating into PJUL would increase your potential upside.

Converting your buffer ETF to cash and back

A more conservative strategy for locking in profits in a rapidly rising market is to sell your buffer ETF during the intra-outcome period, park the proceeds in Treasury bills for the remainder of the outcome period, and then repurchase the buffer ETF on its next reset date.

With the benefit of hindsight, a hypothetical move from PNOV (U.S. Large Cap 15% Buffer) to cash (Treasury bills) on June 16, 2023, and then back to PNOV on October 31, 2023 (the next reset date) would have significantly improved the cumulative percentage gain from October 31, 2022, to December 31, 2023, as compared to keeping the money in PNOV for the duration of this 14-month investment period (see Figure 9-3).

Holding PNOV throughout the 14-month investment period (October 31, 2022, to December 31, 2023) would have produced a return of 14.77 percent. Selling it on June 16, 2023, and repurchasing it on October 31, 2023, would have delivered a return of 21.45 percent, representing a significant performance increase.

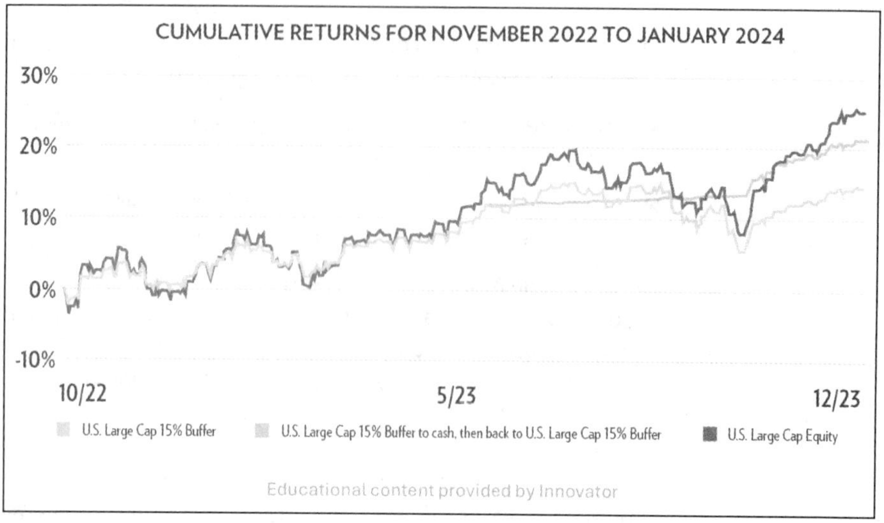

Courtesy of Innovator

FIGURE 9-3: Hypothetical moves from PNOV to cash and back outperformed PNOV by about 7 percent during the 14-month investment period.

REMEMBER

Both strategies (buy-and-hold and buffer-to-cash-and-back) lagged the performance of the SPDR S&P 500 ETF Trust (SPY), shown as "U.S. Large Cap Equity" in the figure, which delivered a return of 25.66 percent. SPY will always at least slightly outperform conventional buffer ETFs in a rising market (fee drag), but it offers no downside protection. The buffer-to-cash-and-back strategy enables you to raise the cap without relinquishing downside protection.

Obviously, in taxable accounts, you must consider the potential tax hit for realizing a short-term taxable gain compared to passively holding PNOV and potentially losing profits during the remainder of the outcome period. Intra-outcome active strategies are much easier to implement in tax-deferred accounts (no IRS reporting of capital gains).

Stepping up late in the outcome period

The step-up strategy can be effective for locking in profits, even late in the outcome period, as shown in Figure 9-4. In this case, the investor purchased PJAN (U.S. Large Cap 15% Buffer) on December 31, 2020, its reset date. During the subsequent 12-month outcome period, the investor saw an opportunity to take profits on August 31, 2021, and simultaneously purchased PSEP, thereby creating a fresh 15 percent downside buffer and new upside cap. The improved performance through the end of the year was minimal, but the real advantage was locking in profits early (four months before the reset date) and receiving a new buffer and higher cap by simultaneously swapping into PSEP.

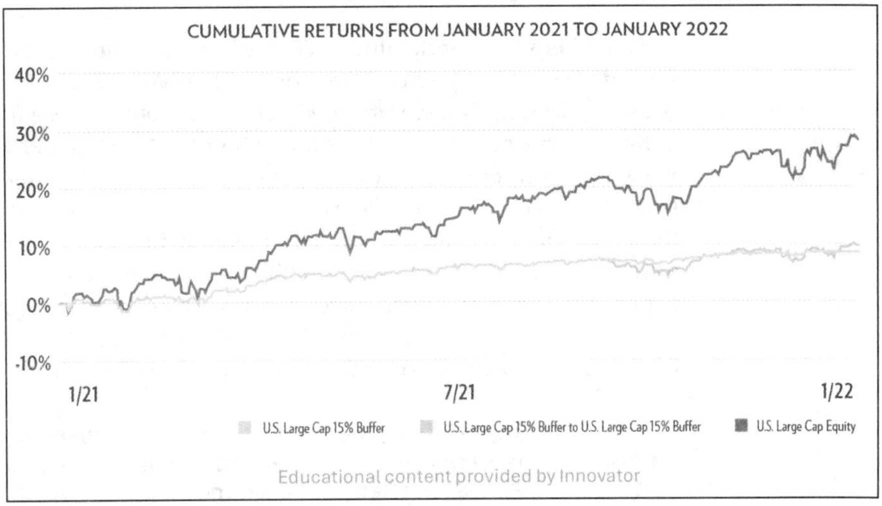

Courtesy of Innovator

FIGURE 9-4: Hypothetical cumulative returns (January 2021 – January 2022).

Bottom line: By paying attention to the ever-changing outcome parameters of Buffer ETFs, you will undoubtedly find some opportunities to lock in profits and potentially improve performance.

Investing during a Stub Outcome Period of an ETF launch

A *stub period* is a shortened outcome period. The term is often used in place of "intra-outcome period" to indicate a timespan shorter than the full outcome period. It's also used to describe an outcome period that an issuer shortens to accelerate the process of issuing a new series of buffer ETFs with varying launch and reset dates.

On October 1, 2025, BlackRock bolstered its buffer ETF suite with the launch of iShares Large Cap 10% Target Buffer ETFs:

- iShares Large Cap 10% Target Buffer — September (STEN)
- iShares Large Cap 10% Target Buffer — December (TEND)
- iShares Large Cap 10% Target Buffer — March (TENM)
- iShares Large Cap 10% Target Buffer — June (TENJ)

Each fund is a 12-month buffer ETF. Their annual outcome period start dates are staggered over four quarters: January 1 (TEND), April 1 (TENM), July 1 (TENJ), and October 1 (STEN). However, to accelerate the rollout of these funds, BlackRock set initial outcome period start dates for all four funds in October 2025. The first ETF, STEN, began trading on October 1, while the remaining three funds were listed later in the month. As you can see in the table below, accelerating the rollout of these four funds resulted in three of them having stub periods in the year they were launched. STEN is the only fund that began with a full 12-month outcome period. TEND had an initial outcome period of about three months, TENM's was about five months, and TENJ's was about eight months. Note, the starting cap for the three funds with shortened outcome periods is reduced.

Buffer ETF Ticker	Fund Launch Date (First Outcome Period Start Date)	Annual Outcome Period End Date	First Outcome Period Duration (in Days)	Starting Cap
STEN	October 1, 2025	September 30, 2026	364	17.30%
TEND	October 7, 2025	December 31, 2025	84	3.33%
TENM	October 21, 2025	March 31, 2026	160	6.99%
TENJ	October 21, 2025	June 30, 2026	251	11.40%

A stub outcome period of an ETF launch provides a unique opportunity for investors. For example, TENM debuted on October 22, 2025, with a 160-day stub period and an upside cap of about 7 percent net. This is the equivalent of an approximate annualized cap of 16 percent with 10 percent protection in place to the end of the stub period, March 31, 2026. If an investor was worried about a correction in Q1 2026, but still wanted to participate in the upside potential of the reference asset (IVV), a purchase of TENM could have been made on October 22, 2025. The investor would have had 10 percent protection over the 160-day stub period with plenty of annualized upside potential remaining, thanks to the net cap of nearly 7 percent.

Investing during an initial launch stub period can allow for various creative applications to help investors reach their short-term investment objectives.

TIP

To find out about upcoming launches of new buffer ETFs, visit issuers' websites regularly. Any new launches will be in the press and will likely be highlighted on the issuer's website.

IN THIS CHAPTER

» Observing buffer ETF performance in a bear market

» Seeing how buffer ETFs perform in a bull market

» Knowing what to expect in a bear-to-bull market scenario

Chapter 10
Observing Buffer ETFs in Action: Case Studies

Examining the historical performance of buffer ETFs in different market environments can help you develop a better sense of how they're likely to respond in different market scenarios, such as a bear or bull market. By increasing your understanding of the price behavior of buffer ETFs, you'll be better equipped to manage your expectations and make well-informed investment decisions.

In this chapter, I show you how buffer ETFs performed in three recent market scenarios — a volatile bear market, a positive-trending bull market, and a bear-to-bull market shift.

REMEMBER

Spoiler alert! What's critical to note is that all the buffer ETFs covered in this chapter performed as expected, given the defined outcome parameters provided by the issuing companies at the start of their respective outcome periods.

Tracking Buffer ETF Performance in a Bear Market

In 2022, unprecedented market dynamics created challenges for all investors. Soaring inflation, along with a rapid tightening of U.S. monetary policy, resulted in significant market volatility. Both stocks and bonds had negative double-digit returns, leading to one of the worst years in history for a traditional 60/40 stock/bond portfolio allocation. And, unfortunately, the traditional move to reduce risk by investing in bonds didn't help in 2022.

Buffer ETFs performed as expected in 2022 and helped protect portfolios from deep losses. As a result, buffer ETFs experienced unprecedented growth, making them one of the fastest-growing corners of the ETF marketplace.

In this section, I present several examples to show how various buffer ETFs performed in the 2022 bear market.

TIP

To see how Innovator buffer ETFs performed relative to their respective reference assets during their previous outcome periods, use Innovator's Previous Outcome Period Tool (see Figure 10-1). To access this valuable tool, take the following steps:

1. **Go to** `www.innovatoretfs.com`.
2. **Open the Tools menu (near the top of the page) and select Previous Outcome Period.**
3. **Open the dropdown menu near the top of the page and select the buffer ETF whose previous outcome period you want to view.**

   TIP

   Press the View Video Tutorial button (upper right) for additional guidance on how to use this tool.

Innovator U.S. Equity Buffer — January (BJAN)

Innovator U.S. Equity Buffer – January (BJAN) is a 12-month buffer ETF with a starting 9 percent buffer that tracks the SPDR S&P 500 ETF Trust (SPY). In the outcome period from January 1, 2022, to December 31, 2022, BJAN (U.S. Large Cap 9% Buffer) mostly tracked SPY (U.S. Large Cap Equity) lower but with some performance enhancements as shown in Figure 10-2 and Table 10-1.

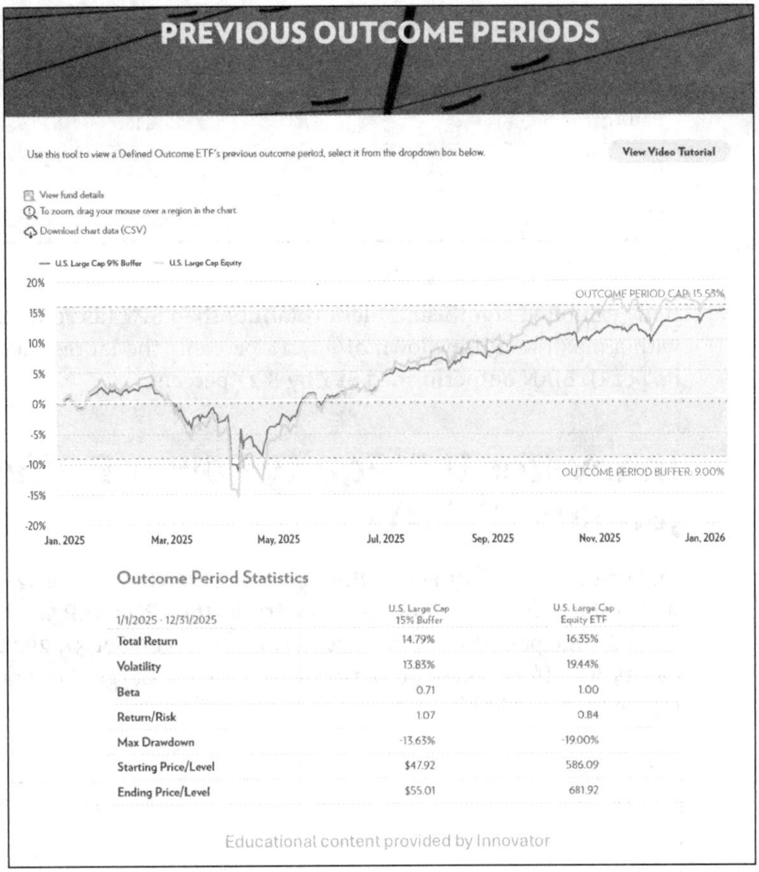

FIGURE 10-1: Innovator's Previous Outcome Period Tool.

Courtesy of Innovator

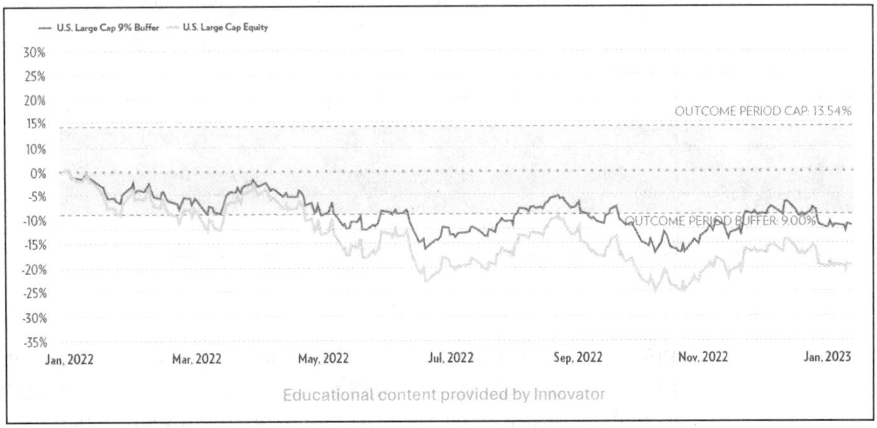

FIGURE 10-2: BJAN versus SPY (2022).

Courtesy of Innovator

TABLE 10-1 BJAN versus SPY 2022

January 1, 2022 – December 31, 2022	BJAN	SPY
Return	-11.21%	-19.48%
Beta	0.77	1.00
Max Drawdown	-17.26%	-25.36%

BJAN exhibited significantly less volatility than SPY (as reflected in its 0.77 beta) with a maximum drawdown of −17.26 percent (the largest decline in value from its peak). BJAN outperformed SPY by 8.27 percent.

Innovator U.S. Equity Power Buffer — January (PJAN)

Innovator U.S. Equity Power Buffer — January (PJAN) is a 12-month buffer ETF with a starting 15 percent buffer that tracks the SPDR S&P 500 ETF Trust (SPY). In the outcome period from January 1, 2022, to December 31, 2022, PJAN (U.S. Large Cap 15% Buffer) nicely outperformed SPY (U.S. Large Cap Equity), as shown in Figure 10-3 and Table 10-2.

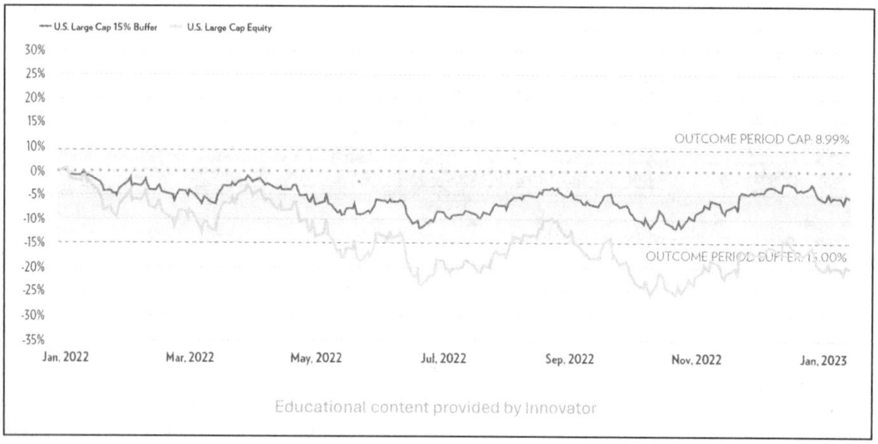

FIGURE 10-3: PJAN versus SPY (2022).

Courtesy of Innovator

PJAN exhibited much less volatility than SPY (as reflected in its 0.57 beta) with a maximum drawdown of −11.88 percent. PJAN outperformed SPY by 14.26 percent. The result was a more comfortable investment experience for shareholders compared to holding SPY without any downside protection.

TABLE 10-2 PJAN versus SPY 2022

January 1, 2022 – December 31, 2022	PJAN	SPY
Return	-5.22%	-19.48%
Beta	0.57	1.00
Max Drawdown	-11.88%	-25.36%

Innovator U.S. Equity Ultra Buffer — January (UJAN)

Innovator U.S. Equity Ultra Buffer — January (UJAN) is a 12-month buffer ETF with a starting 30 percent buffer (−5 to −35 percent) that tracks the SPDR S&P 500 ETF Trust (SPY). In the outcome period from January 1, 2022, to December 31, 2022, UJAN (U.S. Large Cap 30% Buffer) provided a significantly better return than SPY (U.S. Large Cap Equity), with reduced volatility (see Figure 10-4 and Table 10-3).

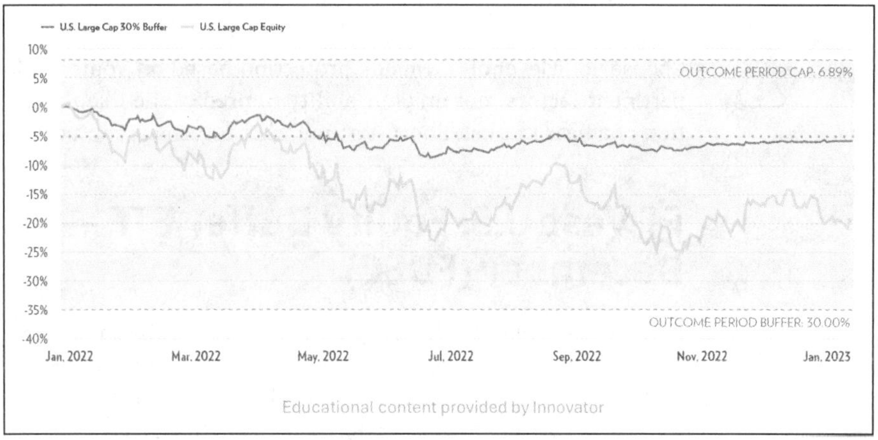

FIGURE 10-4: UJAN versus SPY (2022).

Courtesy of Innovator

UJAN exhibited significantly less volatility than SPY (as reflected in its 0.25 beta). Its return hugged the −5 percent level for most of the outcome period. The result was a much better investment experience for shareholders compared to holding SPY without any downside protection.

TABLE 10-3

UJAN versus SPY 2022

January 1, 2022 - December 31, 2022	UJAN	SPY
Return	-5.73%	-19.48%
Beta	0.25	1.00
Max Drawdown	-8.82%	-25.36%

TIP

A comparison of PJAN and UJAN during this relatively shallow bear market reveals an interesting insight. PJAN outperformed UJAN but only slightly (−5.22 percent versus −5.73 percent) for two reasons:

- PJAN protected against the first 5 percent loss. However, with UJAN, investors absorbed the first 5 percent loss.
- While PJAN protected against the first 15 percent loss, UJAN protected against the loss from -5 percent down to -19.48 percent — which represents 14.48 percent protection (not much different from 15 percent). If SPY had finished the outcome period down another 10 percent or so, UJAN would have significantly outperformed PJAN.

WARNING

Choose your level of downside protection based on your risk tolerance and other pertinent factors, not on your ability to predict the likelihood, severity, or duration of a bear market. Short-term market returns are impossible to predict.

FT Vest U.S. Equity Buffer ETF — December (FDEC)

FT Vest U.S. Equity Buffer ETF — December (FDEC) is a 12-month buffer ETF with a starting 10 percent buffer that tracks the SPDR S&P 500 ETF Trust (SPY). In the outcome period from December 20, 2021, to December 16, 2022, FDEC mostly tracked SPY lower but with performance benefits. (*Source:* `www.ftportfolios.com`.)

As shown in Table 10-4, FDEC displayed less volatility (as reflected in its 0.72 beta) with a maximum drawdown of −15.24 percent, outperforming SPY by 9.3 percent.

TABLE 10-4

FDEC versus SPY (December 20, 2021 - December 16, 2022)

December 20, 2021 - December 16, 2022	FDEC	SPY
Return	-7.4%	-16.7%
Beta	0.72	1.00
Max Drawdown	-15.24%	-23.93%

Note, the tables comparing FDEC, DDEC, and SPY reflect price returns only for SPY, excluding dividends. Including SPY's annual dividend would increase its performance by approximately 1.5 percent.

FT Vest U.S. Equity Deep Buffer ETF — December (DDEC)

FT Vest U.S. Equity Deep Buffer ETF – December (DDEC) is a 12-month buffer ETF with a starting 25 percent buffer (–5 to –30 percent) that tracks the SPDR S&P 500 ETF Trust (SPY). In the outcome period from December 20, 2021, to December 16, 2022, DDEC greatly outperformed SPY and had much less volatility. (*Source:* `www.ftportfolios.com`.)

As shown in Table 10-5, DDEC outperformed SPY by 11 percent and exhibited significantly less volatility (as reflected in its 0.28 beta). Its return mostly hugged the –5 percent level for most of the outcome period. The result was a much better investment experience for shareholders compared to owning the S&P 500 without any downside protection.

TABLE 10-5 DDEC versus SPY 2022 (December 20, 2021 - December 16, 2022)

December 20, 2021 - December 16, 2022	DDEC	SPY
Return	-5.7%	-16.7%
Beta	0.28	1.00
Max Drawdown	-8.81%	-23.93%

Seeing How Buffer ETFs Respond in a Bull Market

In a bull market, buffer ETFs generally underperform compared to their reference assets. The question is whether they perform well enough to meet your investment objectives and justify the upside potential you're sacrificing to obtain the peace of mind they provide.

In this section, I show you how the same buffer ETFs covered in the previous section performed during the 2023 bull market.

Innovator U.S. Equity Buffer — January (BJAN)

At the start of its outcome period (January 1, 2023), BJAN had a 9 percent buffer and a 25.06 percent cap. In hindsight, the buffer was unnecessary because the reference asset finished the outcome period in positive territory.

During the outcome period, BJAN (U.S. Large Cap 9% Buffer) tracked its reference asset SPY (U.S. Large Cap Equity) higher, but with less volatility (0.80 beta), as shown in Figure 10-5 and Table 10-6. By the end of the outcome period, BJAN provided a return of 23.48 percent, only slightly below SPY's return of 24.28 percent. BJAN had a maximum drawdown of −8.22 percent compared to −10.29 percent for SPY, which helped make investors a little more comfortable.

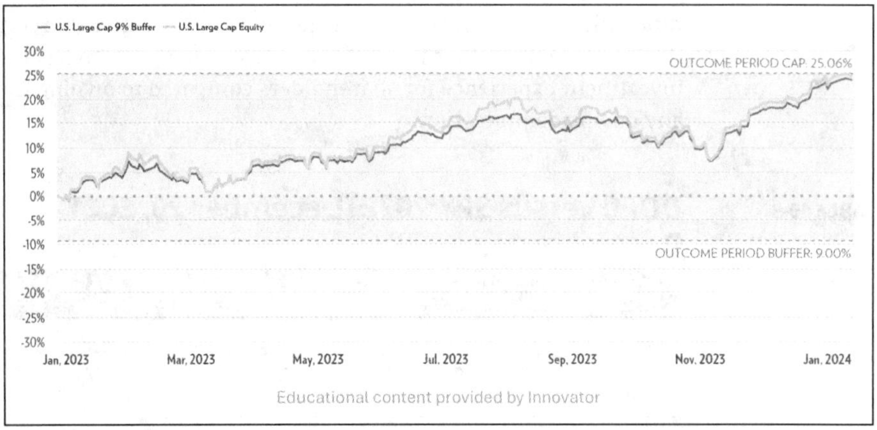

FIGURE 10-5: BJAN versus SPY (2023).

Courtesy of Innovator

TABLE 10-6 BJAN versus SPY 2023

January 1, 2023 – December 31, 2023	BJAN	SPY
Return	23.48%	24.28%
Beta	0.80	1.00
Max Drawdown	-8.22%	-10.29%

Innovator U.S. Equity Power Buffer — January (PJAN)

PJAN (U.S. Large Cap 15% Buffer) provided 15 percent protection at the start of the outcome period in 2023. Its starting cap was 18.84 percent. Given the strong bull market throughout 2023, PJAN's return lagged the return of SPY (U.S. Large Cap Equity) by 6.24 percent, as shown in Figure 10-6 and Table 10-7.

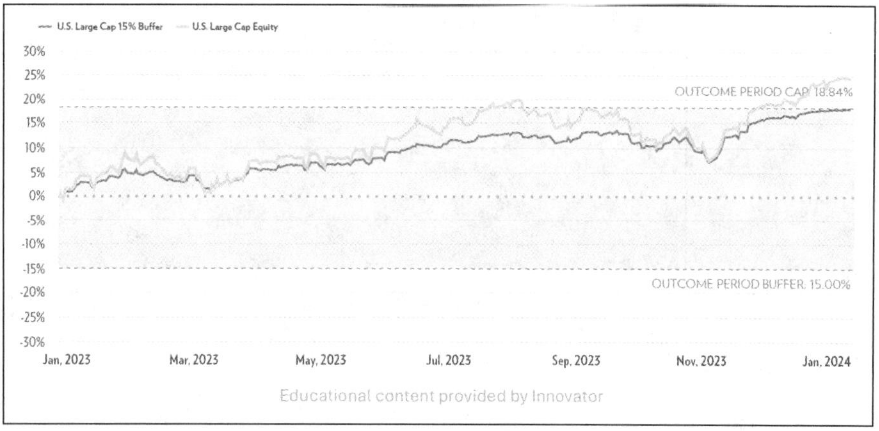

FIGURE 10-6: PJAN versus SPY (2023).

Courtesy of Innovator

TABLE 10-7 PJAN versus SPY 2023

January 1, 2023 – December 31, 2023	PJAN	SPY
Return	18.05%	24.28%
Beta	0.54	1.00
Max Drawdown	-5.75%	-10.29%

PJAN's major advantage during this period was that it provided significant downside protection and reduced volatility (as reflected in its low beta), resulting in a more comfortable investment experience for shareholders.

Innovator U.S. Equity Ultra Buffer — January (UJAN)

UJAN's 30 percent buffer (−5 to −35 percent) came at a slightly higher cost than PJAN's 15 percent buffer in the form of a lower starting cap (16.4 percent).

Obviously, the buffer was unnecessary in 2023, which caused UJAN (U.S. Large Cap 30% Buffer) to underperform its reference asset SPY (U.S. Large Cap Equity) by 8.68 percent. However, UJAN delivered a respectable 15.6 percent return, while providing significant downside protection, reduced volatility (0.46 beta), and a lower maximum drawdown (–4.87 percent compared to SPY's –10.29 percent). The result was a smooth ride and a positive investment experience for shareholders (see Figure 10-7 and Table 10-8).

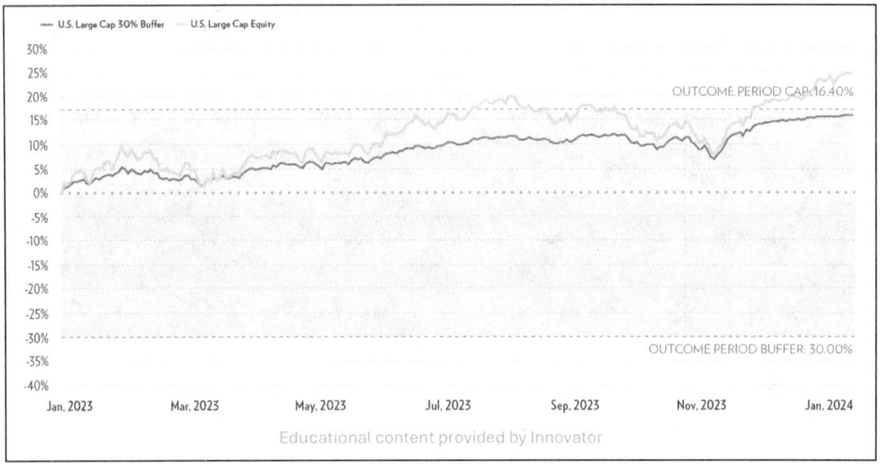

FIGURE 10-7: UJAN versus SPY (2023).

Courtesy of Innovator

TABLE 10-8 UJAN versus SPY 2023

January 1, 2023 - December 31, 2023	UJAN	SPY
Return	15.60%	24.28%
Beta	0.46	1.00
Max Drawdown	-4.87%	-10.29%

FT Vest U.S. Equity Buffer ETF — December (FDEC)

FDEC had a starting buffer of 10 percent. Its upside cap at the beginning of its outcome period (December 19, 2022) was 22.25 percent net. As a result, FDEC mostly tracked its reference asset (SPY) higher but with less volatility (0.83 beta) and a lower maximum drawdown (–6.2 percent compared to SPY's –8.3 percent). The result was a worry-free investment experience for shareholders, but with slight underperformance (fee drag) relative to its reference asset (see Table 10-9). (*Source:* `www.ftportfolios.com`.)

TABLE 10-9 FDEC versus SPY (December 19, 2022 - December 15, 2023)

December 19, 2022 - December 15, 2023	FDEC	SPY
Return	21.7%	22.5%
Beta	0.83	1.00
Max Drawdown	-6.20%	-8.30%

Note, the tables comparing FDEC, DDEC, and SPY reflect price returns only for SPY, excluding dividends. Including SPY's annual dividend would increase its performance by approximately 1.50 percent.

FT Vest U.S. Equity Deep Buffer ETF — December (DDEC)

DDEC had a starting buffer of 25 percent (–5 to –30 percent). DDEC mostly tracked its reference asset (SPY) higher but with less volatility (0.56 beta) and a lower maximum drawdown (–3.41 percent compared to SPY's –8.32 percent). The result was a pleasant investment experience for shareholders, but with some underperformance, which is expected with a relatively deep buffer in a strong market, as shown in Table 10-10. (Source: `www.ftportfolios.com`.)

TABLE 10-10 DDEC versus SPY 2023 (December 19, 2022 - December 15, 2023)

December 19, 2022 - December 15, 2023	DDEC	SPY
Return	15.9%	22.5%
Beta	0.56	1.00
Max Drawdown	-3.41%	-8.32%

REMEMBER

DDEC underperformed SPY by 6.6 percent (providing a return of 15.9 percent compared to SPY's 22.5 percent), but 15.9 percent is still an attractive return in most markets, especially given that the fund provides significant downside protection (25 percent) for risk-averse investors.

With the benefit of hindsight, obviously, you would have wanted the least amount of downside protection in 2023, which would have allowed for the highest cap and subsequently a better return. However, if the bear market of 2022 had you spooked into wanting more downside protection, deeper buffer ETFs enabled you to remain comfortably invested in the stock market in 2023 and still earn a respectable return.

Seeing How Buffer ETFs Behave in a Bear-to-Bull Market Scenario

The bear-to-bull market period of 2022-2023 provides an excellent case study for highlighting how buffer ETFs can preserve wealth in a declining market while enabling investors to participate nicely during a rebound at the start of a new bull market.

In this section, I show you how buffer ETFs from Innovator and FT Vest performed over the two-year, bear-to-bull market period (2022-2023) relative to the SPDR S&P 500 ETF Trust (SPY). The returns of all five of these buffer ETFs prove the value of having a buffer in a difficult year like 2022 and, perhaps surprisingly, how they have the potential to outperform their reference asset in a volatile bear-to-bull market.

Innovator U.S. Equity Buffer — January (BJAN)

Over the two-year period 2022–2023, BJAN (U.S. Large Cap 9% Buffer) mostly tracked its reference asset SPY (U.S. Large Cap Equity) but with slightly less volatility (0.78 beta). It outperformed SPY by 6.39 percent, providing a return of 9.65 percent compared to SPY's 3.26 percent (including dividends) (see Figure 10-8 and Table 10-11).

REMEMBER

BJAN not only outperformed SPY over this bear-to-bull market transition period, but it did so while providing 9 percent downside protection each year, reduced volatility, and a lower maximum drawdown (−17.26 percent compared to SPY's −24.5 percent). In other words, BJAN shareholders worried less during this volatile period and still came out on top.

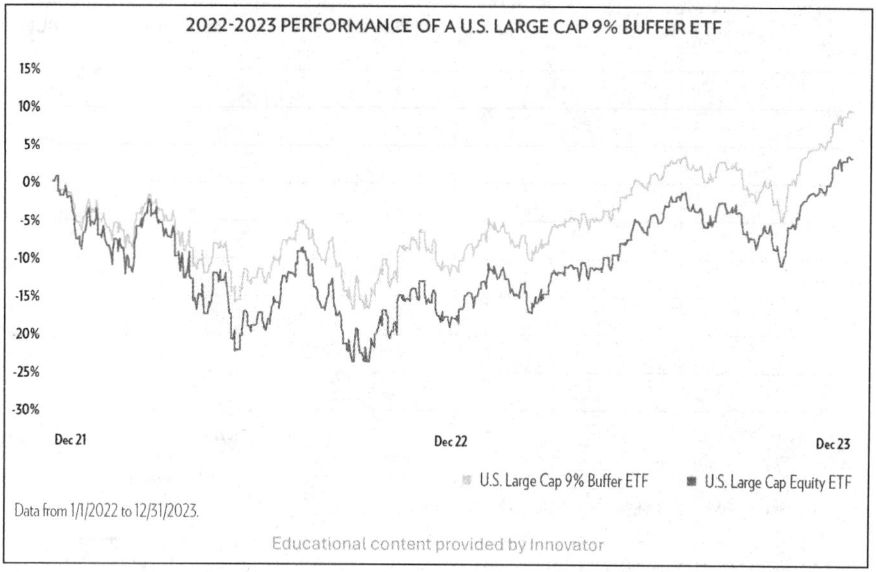

FIGURE 10-8: BJAN versus SPY (2022–2023).

Courtesy of Innovator

TABLE 10-11

BJAN versus SPY 2022–2023

January 1, 2022 – December 31, 2023	BJAN	SPY
Return	9.65%	3.26%
Beta	0.78	1.00
Max Drawdown	–17.26 %	-24.50%

Innovator U.S. Equity Power Buffer — January (PJAN)

PJAN's performance over the bear-to-bull market of 2022–2023 serves as a good example of why losing less matters (see Chapter 3). PJAN (U.S. Large Cap 15% Buffer) had a 15 percent buffer (compared to BJAN's 9 percent) and had lower starting caps than BJAN for both years, yet it outperformed BJAN by more than 2 percent, and it outperformed SPY (U.S. Large Cap Equity) by 8.63 percent (see Figure 10-9 and Table 10-12).

PJAN mostly tracked its reference asset during the two-year period, but with much less volatility (0.56 beta). With its reduced volatility and lower maximum drawdown (–11.88 percent compared to SPY's –24.5 percent), PJAN gave investors a smoother ride, while still outperforming SPY.

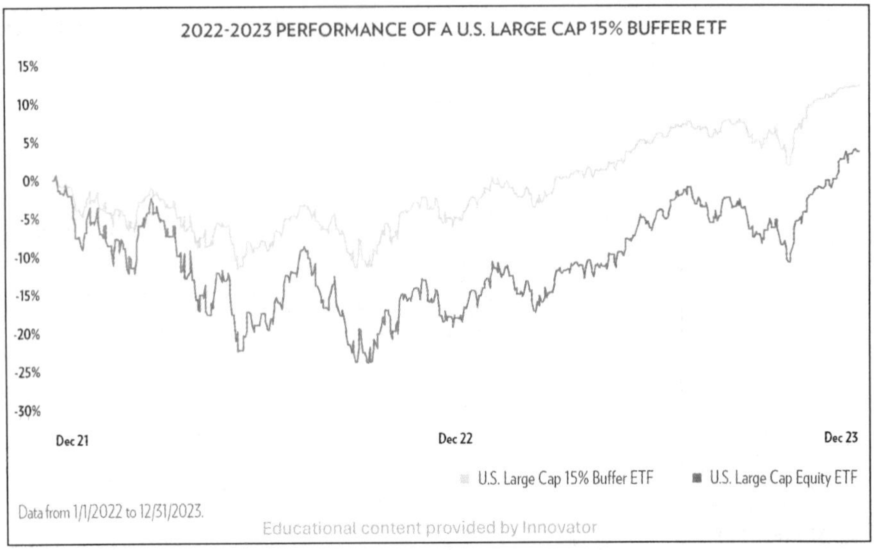

FIGURE 10-9: PJAN versus SPY (2022–2023).

Courtesy of Innovator

TABLE 10-12 PJAN versus SPY 2022–2023

January 1, 2022 – December 31, 2023	PJAN	SPY
Return	11.89%	3.26%
Beta	0.56	1.00
Max Drawdown	−11.88%	−24.5%

Innovator U.S. Equity Ultra Buffer — January (UJAN)

Due to UJAN's deep buffer of 30 percent, it had a lower cap than either BJAN or PJAN at the beginning of each outcome period, yet UJAN (U.S. Large Cap 30% Buffer) still outperformed its reference asset SPY (U.S. Large Cap Equity) by 5.72 percent over the two-year period from January 1, 2022, to December 31, 2023 (see Figure 10-10 and Table 10-13). And it accomplished this feat while providing 30 percent downside protection, reduced volatility (0.30 beta), and a significantly lower maximum drawdown (−8.82 percent compared to SPY's −24.5 percent).

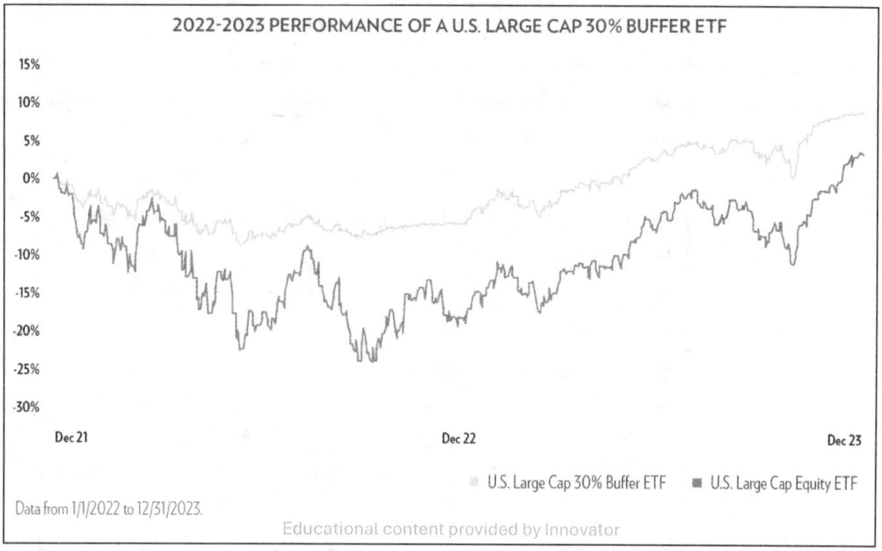

FIGURE 10-10: UJAN versus SPY (2022–2023).

Courtesy of Innovator

TABLE 10-13 **UJAN versus SPY 2022–2023**

January 1, 2022 – December 31, 2023	UJAN	SPY
Return	8.98%	3.26%
Beta	0.30	1.00
Max Drawdown	-8.82%	-24.5%

REMEMBER

All three Innovator January buffer ETFs, with their various levels of downside protection and upside caps, outperformed SPY during the two-year, bear-to-bull market period (see Figure 10-11). The data provide evidence of the value of losing less during a bear market (2022), thanks to the downside protection provided by Buffer ETFs. The data also stress the importance of remaining invested so you can participate in the upside whenever the market recovers (as it did in 2023).

FT Vest U.S. Equity Buffer ETF — December (FDEC)

During the two-year bear-to-bull market of 2022–2023 (December 20, 2021, to December 15, 2023), FDEC mostly tracked its reference asset, but with less volatility, and it ended the two-year period outperforming its reference asset (SPY) by 10.6 percent, delivering a total return of 12.70 percent compared to SPY's 2.1 percent (see Table 10-14). FDEC also had a lower maximum drawdown of −15.2 percent compared to SPY's −23.9 percent. (*Source:* `www.ftportfolios.com`.)

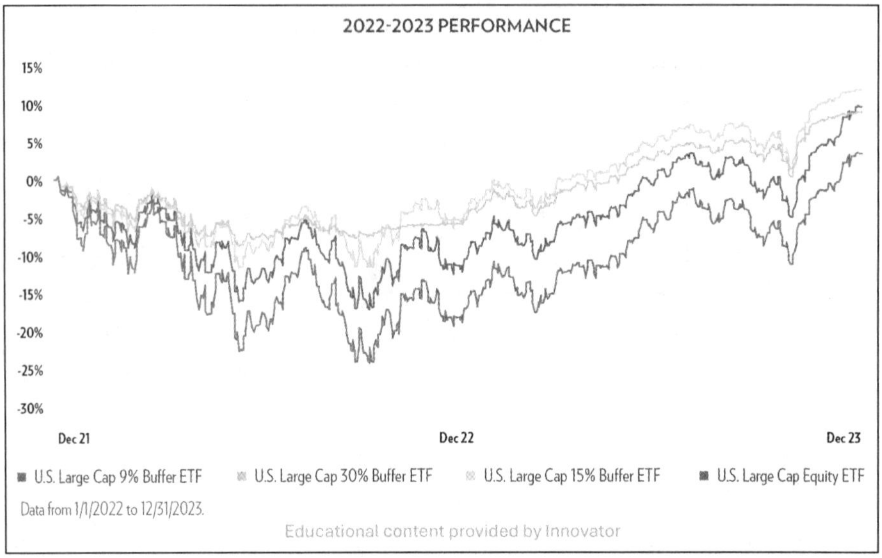

FIGURE 10-11: BJAN, PJAN, and UJAN versus SPY (2022–2023).

Courtesy of Innovator

TABLE 10-14 FDEC versus SPY (December 20, 2021 – December 15, 2023)

December 20, 2021 – December 15, 2023	FDEC	SPY
Return	12.7%	2.1%
Beta	0.74	1.00
Max Drawdown	–15.20%	–23.90%

Note, the tables comparing FDEC, DDEC, and SPY reflect price returns only for SPY, excluding dividends. Including SPY's annual dividend would increase its two-year performance by approximately 3.0 percent.

FT Vest U.S. Equity Deep Buffer ETF — December (DDEC)

DDEC mostly tracked its reference asset during the two-year period, but with much less volatility (0.37 beta) and a far lower maximum drawdown (–8.81 percent compared to SPY's –23.93 percent). The result was a very comfortable investment experience for shareholders compared to holding SPY without any downside protection (see Table 10-15). (*Source:* www.ftportfolios.com.)

TABLE 10-15 **DDEC versus SPY (December 20, 2021 – December 15, 2023)**

December 20, 2021 – December 15, 2023	DDEC	SPY
Return	9.2%	3.3%
Beta	0.37	1.00
Max Drawdown	–8.81%	–23.93%

REMEMBER

DDEC provided an important buffer against most of the losses during the 2022 bear market, reinforcing the value of losing less in a down market.

4 Exploring More Buffer ETF Offerings

IN THIS PART . . .

Decide whether a buffer step-up strategy ETF is the way to go.

Simplify the process of staggering your investments over time with laddered buffer ETFs.

Understand when an uncapped buffer ETF might be a good choice.

Earn a positive return, whether the market rises or falls, with dual-directional buffer ETFs.

Set your maximum loss limit with a floor ETF.

Take some of the risk out of investing in gold or bitcoin.

Use buffer and barrier income ETFs to implement an income-investing strategy.

IN THIS CHAPTER

» Understanding what a buffer step-up strategy ETF is and how it works

» Deciding whether a buffer step-up strategy ETF is right for you

» Exploring available buffer step-up strategy funds

Chapter 11

Graduating to Buffer Step-Up Strategy ETFs

Thanks to their liquidity, buffer ETFs provide the opportunity to implement a *step-up strategy* — swapping one fund for another that has a higher cap as markets rise — or a *step-down strategy* — swapping one fund for another that has a fresh buffer when the current buffer is partially depleted. Perhaps you find this approach appealing, but you don't have the time to actively manage your buffer ETF portfolio. The solution? Buffer step-up strategy ETFs — ETFs that implement a step-up or step-down strategy for you, on schedule and in response to market conditions.

In this chapter, you discover what buffer step-up strategy ETFs are, how they work, their pros and cons, and how to use them to meet your investment objectives. I also introduce you to buffer step-up strategy ETFs you may want to consider.

Wrapping Your Brain around the Concept

Buffer step-up strategy ETFs seek to outperform a static buffer strategy by evaluating each month for opportunities to "step up" to a higher cap or "step down" to a new buffer and then taking advantage of any such opportunities. These funds allow investors to employ step-up and step-down strategies without having to actively manage a buffer ETF portfolio. (See Chapter 1 for step-up and step-down strategy basics.)

Figure 11-1 shows a hypothetical buffer ETF step-up strategy in action:

1. **The June series buffer ETF had a starting cap of 11.3 percent.** Halfway through its outcome period, its value had increased by 7 percent, leaving a remaining upside potential of 4.3 percent.
2. **The investor sold the June series, locking in the 7 percent gain and stepping up to the December series with a cap of 9.68 percent.**
3. **In the first half of its outcome period, the December series' return exceeded that of the June series by 3.3 percent.**

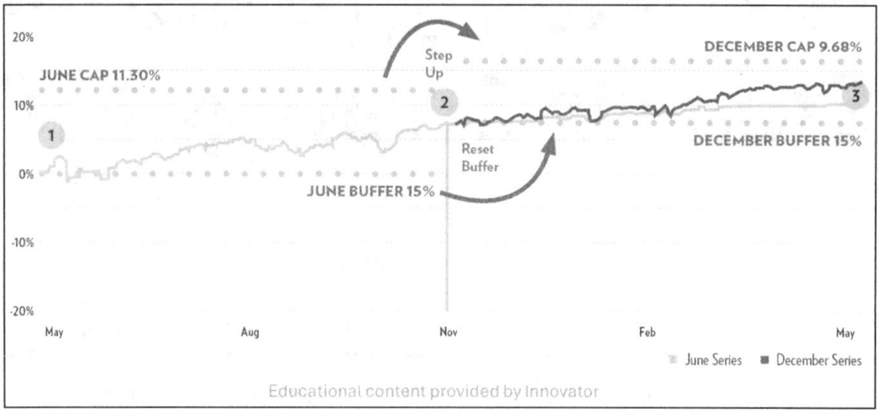

FIGURE 11-1: A hypothetical buffer ETF step-up strategy in action.

Courtesy of Innovator

REMEMBER

Technically, managed funds have a reset date, but that date doesn't play a significant role in the fund's overall behavior. A step up or step down is typically triggered before the fund's reset date, making that date insignificant.

Understanding how buffer step-up strategy ETFs work

TECHNICAL STUFF

Buffer step-up strategy ETFs begin with a one-year options portfolio and are actively managed from that point forward (see Figure 11-2):

1. **Two business days before the end of the month, the portfolio is evaluated to determine whether it meets a predetermined step-up or step-down threshold.**
2. **On the last business day of the month,**
   - If a step-up threshold has *not* been met, the portfolio remains unchanged.
   - If a step-up threshold *has* been met, the fund manager sells the current options portfolio and purchases a new one-year options package.
3. **On the first business day of the next month,**
   - If the portfolio is unchanged, the remaining buffer and cap stay in place.
   - If the fund has a new options package, it enters a new one-year outcome period with a new buffer and cap.

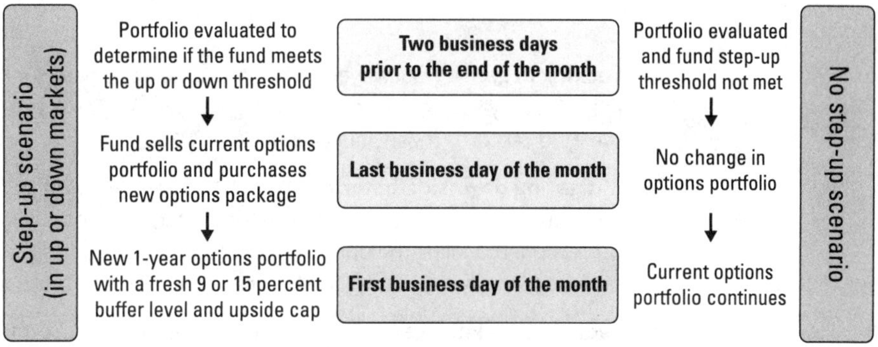

FIGURE 11-2: How buffer step-up strategy ETFs work.

Courtesy of Innovator

REMEMBER

As an investor, you never have to swap one fund for another; all transactions occur within the fund and are triggered according to a pre-established schedule and threshold.

Step-up and step-down thresholds are predetermined percentages. For example, as of this writing, Innovator's Buffer Step-Up Strategy ETF (BSTP) had a monthly 5 percent threshold for positive markets and a monthly -2 percent threshold for negative markets. Whenever a threshold is met on evaluation day, it triggers a step-up or step-down reset, as shown in Figure 11-3.

WARNING

I'm not a big fan of buffer step-up strategy ETFs because I can't tell an investor, "You have a defined level of protection in place against X percent of initial losses." I feel the same about laddered buffer ETFs, although I know many investment advisors and retail investors prefer managed buffer ETFs. I favor conventional buffer ETFs that have a defined level of protection and a cap.

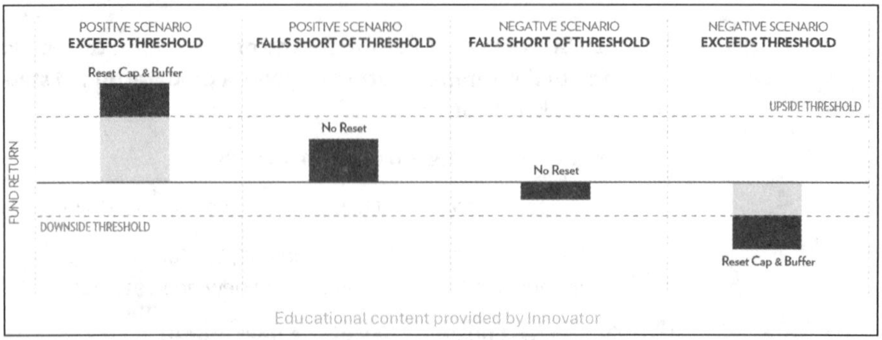

FIGURE 11-3: Buffer step-up strategy ETFs reset whenever pre-established thresholds are crossed.

Courtesy of Innovator

Improving your position

Buffer step-up strategy ETFs may improve your investment return by doing the following:

- **Locking in gains:** Until the end of an outcome period, any unrealized gains are at risk. By selling the options package when the fund's return is positive, the fund captures those gains early.
- **Mitigating downside-before-buffer risk:** *Downside before buffer* is the percentage you stand to lose before the buffer provides any downside protection. By selling the options package when the fund's return is in positive territory, any downside-before-buffer risk is reduced or eliminated.
- **Seeking to take advantage of return dispersions:** As a buffer ETF nears its cap, it has less upside potential and becomes less sensitive to increases in the value of the reference asset. A buffer step-up strategy ETF has the potential to create increased upside by providing a higher cap, which also increases the portfolio's sensitivity to upward moves in the reference asset.

TECHNICAL STUFF

Return dispersions are variations in returns that funds can experience over a defined period (see Figure 11-4). Although each ETF tracks the same reference asset (SPY) and has the same 15 percent buffer, it has its own level of sensitivity to the reference asset. Buffer step-up strategy ETFs seek to take advantage of these dispersions to optimize the fund's upside potential.

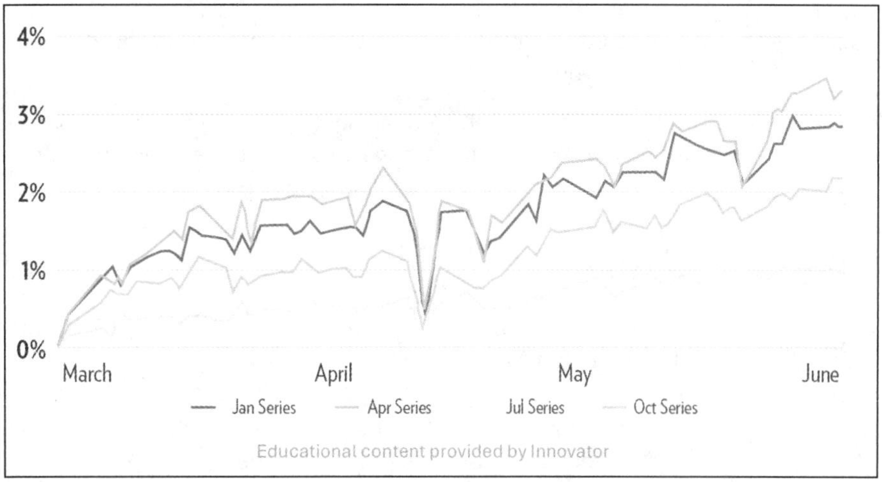

FIGURE 11-4: Return dispersions among buffer ETFs with different outcome periods.

Courtesy of Innovator

Weighing the Pros and Cons of Buffer Step-Up Strategy ETFs

To determine whether a buffer step-up strategy ETF is the right solution for you, weigh the pros and cons highlighted in this section.

Pros

Buffer step-up strategy ETFs have several potential benefits to consider, including the following:

- Built-in buffers to protect against some reference asset losses while allowing participation in the upside.
- A single-ticker solution that implements step-up and step-down strategies for you.
- Reduced cap-timing risk: Any adjustments are automatic (based on predetermined thresholds).
- Smoother overall investment experience (less volatility).
- Potential for outperformance of the reference asset due to the ability to step up to a higher cap or step down to a new buffer.
- Tax-efficient rotation: All transactions occur within the fund without triggering a taxable event (until you sell).

- Ease of implementation: The fund is actively managed, doing all the work for you.
- Automatic resets: You can hold the fund indefinitely, and it will continue to roll into new outcome periods according to pre-established conditions.

Cons

Before deciding to invest in a buffer step-up strategy ETF, consider the following potential drawbacks:

- You don't control when the step-up or step-down occurs; the fund's management team makes that determination.
- Slow markets may not move far enough or fast enough to trigger resets, which could result in a restrictive cap or insufficient buffer.
- Total cost of ownership (TCO) is generally higher than that of conventional buffer ETFs. Expense ratios tend to be slightly higher, and you'll be paying a bid-ask spread every time the fund resets. (See Chapter 5 for more about TCO.)
- Downside protection can be depleted faster than expected. For example, if the reference asset has a strong rally, and the fund resets, the new buffer may be insufficient to protect against a subsequent steep pullback in the reference asset.

Checking Out Two Buffer Step-Up Strategy ETFs

As of this writing, Innovator has two managed Buffer Step-Up Strategy ETFs:

- **Innovator Buffer Step-Up Strategy ETF (BSTP)** is an actively managed fund that seeks to provide risk-managed exposure to the SPDR S&P 500 ETF Trust (SPY). It offers a starting buffer of 9 percent and a monthly evaluation frequency.
- **Innovator Power Buffer Step-Up Strategy ETF (PSTP)** is an actively managed fund that seeks to provide risk-managed exposure to the SPDR S&P 500 ETF Trust (SPY). It offers a starting buffer of 15 percent and a monthly evaluation frequency.

The difference between these two funds boils down to the buffer. PSTP offers a deeper buffer, so more downside protection and less upside participation (a lower cap) than BSTP. PSTP also has tighter thresholds — 4 percent in positive markets and 1 percent in negative markets — so it could reset more frequently. As shown in Figures 11-5 and 11-6, from 2022 through 2025, PSTP provided a slightly smoother ride but with a lower return compared to BSTP.

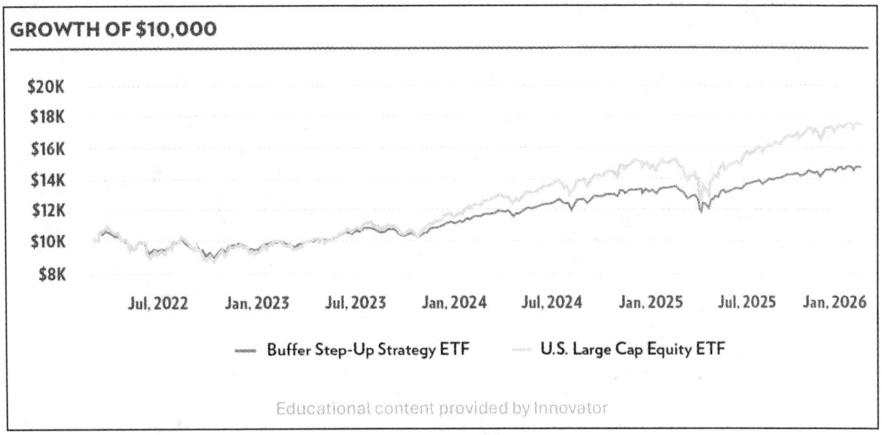

FIGURE 11-5: BSTP (2022–2025).

Courtesy of Innovator

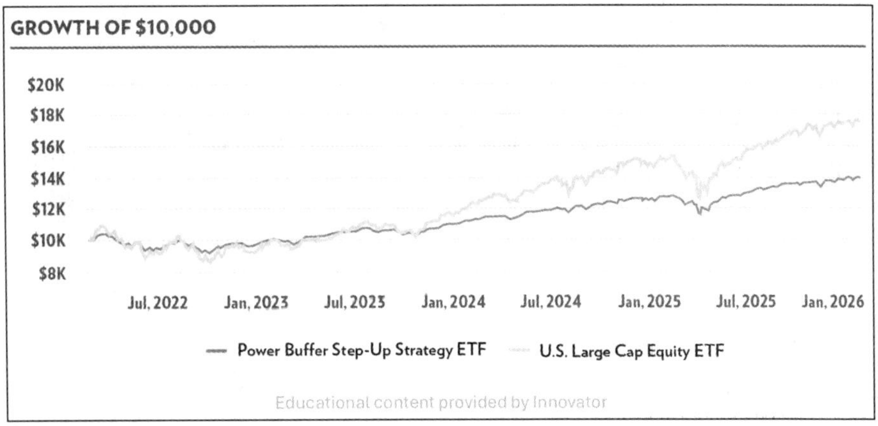

FIGURE 11-6: PSTP (2022–2025).

Courtesy of Innovator

As with any buffer ETF, let your risk tolerance be your guide. If you need a 15 percent buffer to stay comfortably invested, then go with the 15 percent buffer ETF. If you're less risk-averse, go with the 9 percent buffer ETF. And if you're somewhere in between, you could split your allocation between the two.

TIP

To find out more about Innovator's Buffer Step-Up Strategy ETFs, visit `www.innovatoretfs.com` and search for the fund by ticker: BSTP or PSTP.

IN THIS CHAPTER

» Getting up to speed on the laddered buffer ETF concept

» Deciding whether a laddered buffer ETF is right for you

» Seeing what issuers have to offer

Chapter 12

Investing in Laddered Buffer ETFs

A *laddered buffer ETF strategy* involves buying multiple buffer ETFs with different reset dates; for example, instead of purchasing one buffer ETF that has a starting outcome period in January, you buy four buffer ETFs with outcome periods that start in January, April, July, and October. By spreading out your total allocation over time, you avoid being locked into a single 12-month period, and you're not relying on the timing of one single market entry point.

Sounds good? Well, it gets even better. Some issuers offer laddered buffer ETFs that create and manage the ladder for you. The ETF is a "fund of funds," typically twelve 12-month buffer ETFs in a single ETF wrapper with a single ticker symbol. A laddered buffer ETF has no defined outcome period. You can hold your shares indefinitely or sell them whenever you decide to cash out.

In this chapter, you discover more about what laddered buffer ETFs are, how they work, their pros and cons, and how to use them to help meet your investment objectives. I also introduce you to several laddered buffer ETFs you may want to consider.

REMEMBER

Laddered buffer ETFs are designed for investors who don't have the time or interest in monitoring a portfolio of buffer ETFs on an ongoing basis. They provide a potential solution by offering a single-ticker ETF with the benefits of defined outcome investing.

Understanding How Laddered Buffer ETFs Work

A laddered buffer ETF is a fund of funds with reset dates spread over 12 months, four quarters, or some other interval. The ETF is invested in a laddered portfolio — typically twelve 12-month buffer ETFs, each assigned an equal weight. Each month, one of the ETFs resets to a new 12-month outcome period. As a result, when you invest in a laddered buffer ETF, you're getting 12 funds (or four 3-month funds) at different stages in their outcome periods. (See Figure 12-1.)

FIGURE 12-1: How Innovator's Laddered Buffer ETFs work.

Courtesy of Innovator

Weighing the Pros and Cons of Laddered Buffer ETFs

To determine whether a laddered buffer ETF is the right solution for you, weigh the pros and cons highlighted in this section.

Pros

Laddered buffer ETFs have several potential benefits to consider, including the following:

- Built-in buffers to protect against some market losses while enabling participation in potential market upside.
- A single-ticker solution that implements a laddered strategy for you, which means less complexity and less work than investing in and managing multiple buffer ETFs.
- Lower volatility relative to the reference asset and potentially lower volatility than a buffer ETF with a single 12-month outcome period.

- Reduced market timing risk, because you're spreading out your allocation over multiple buffer ETFs in different stages of their respective outcome periods.
- Tax-efficient rotation: All transactions occur within the ETF wrapper without triggering a taxable event (until you sell).
- Automatic resets: You can hold the fund indefinitely, and the underlying ETFs will continue to automatically roll into new outcome periods.

Cons

Before deciding to invest in a laddered buffer ETF, consider the following potential drawbacks:

- Your investment is never fully buffered. In a declining market, some funds within the laddered fund may have a partially or fully depleted buffer.
- Your upside gain potential is always capped, so you're not going to fully participate in any strong rallies.
- Predictability and transparency are reduced because the fund has no clearly defined outcome period. Each underlying fund has its own buffer, cap, and outcome period, which can make it difficult to predict outcomes over any given investment time horizon.
- Laddered buffer ETFs may perform poorly in slow or choppy markets due to their capped upside. In addition, if the reference asset is exhibiting sideways price action but not necessarily declining, then the protection provided by the various underlying ETFs may not be helpful.
- Expense ratios tend to be a bit higher than conventional buffer ETFs. For example, both Innovator and FT Vest charge approximately 0.10 percent more annually for their laddered buffer ETF offerings. Note, BlackRock laddered buffer ETFs have the same expense ratios as their conventional buffer ETF offerings.

REMEMBER

Bottom line: With most issuers, you pay a little extra for a laddered buffer ETF (than a fund with a single outcome period), but what you get in return are the benefits of a laddered strategy (reduced timing risk and less volatility) without having to put forth the time and effort required to actively implement the strategy on your own.

Keep in mind, however, that if you employ a laddered strategy on your own, you have more flexibility in buying and selling the underlying buffer ETFs, so you can take a more opportunistic approach — for example, selling a fund midperiod when its buffer is nearly exhausted or it is nearing its cap, and buying a fund with a fresh buffer and a new cap.

Checking Out Available Laddered Buffer ETFs

Innovator and FT Vest offer laddered buffer ETFs that seek to give investors a smoother investment experience. This section covers several popular laddered buffer ETFs from Innovator and FT Vest. I've also included laddered buffer ETFs issued by PGIM, Calamos, and BlackRock (iShares), so you can comparison shop.

REMEMBER

Innovator and FT Vest have a selection of laddered buffer ETFs that track the SPDR S&P 500 ETF Trust (SPY). Innovator's Laddered Buffer ETFs protect against the first 9 percent or 15 percent loss and have a total expense ratio of 0.89 percent. FT Vest's Laddered Buffer ETFs protect against the first 10, 15 or 25 percent loss (from −5 to −30 percent) and have an expense ratio of 0.95 percent. FT Vest also offers a laddered buffer ETF that tracks the Invesco QQQ Trust (QQQ) and protects against the first 10 percent loss; it has an expense ratio of 1.0 percent.

REMEMBER

The buffer in all laddered buffer ETFs is provided only by the underlying ETFs. The funds do not provide any buffer against losses.

Innovator Laddered Allocation 15% Power Buffer ETF (BUFF)

Innovator's BUFF holds equal shares of the 12 underlying Innovator U.S. Equity Power Buffer ETFs, all with a starting buffer of 15 percent. Figure 12-2 shows the 12 ETF holdings and their starting caps and the performance of each ETF relative to its cap, buffer, and reference asset as of February 2, 2026. You can also see the remaining upside potential and downside buffer for each of the underlying funds.

As shown in Figure 12-3, the calendar year returns over the five years from December 31, 2020, to December 31, 2025, show how BUFF performed relative to the S&P 500 (U.S. Large Cap Equity) and U.S. Aggregate Bond ETF. Notice that BUFF lagged the S&P 500 in 2021, but nicely outperformed U.S. Aggregate Bond ETF. In the 2022 bear market, BUFF significantly outperformed both the S&P 500 and

U.S. Aggregate Bond ETF. In 2023, BUFF showed a nice return of 16.4 percent while the S&P 500 surged 26.1 percent (including dividends). BUFF handily beat U.S. Aggregate Bond ETF in all five calendar years, which explains why it could serve as a substitute for part of the bond allocation in a balanced portfolio.

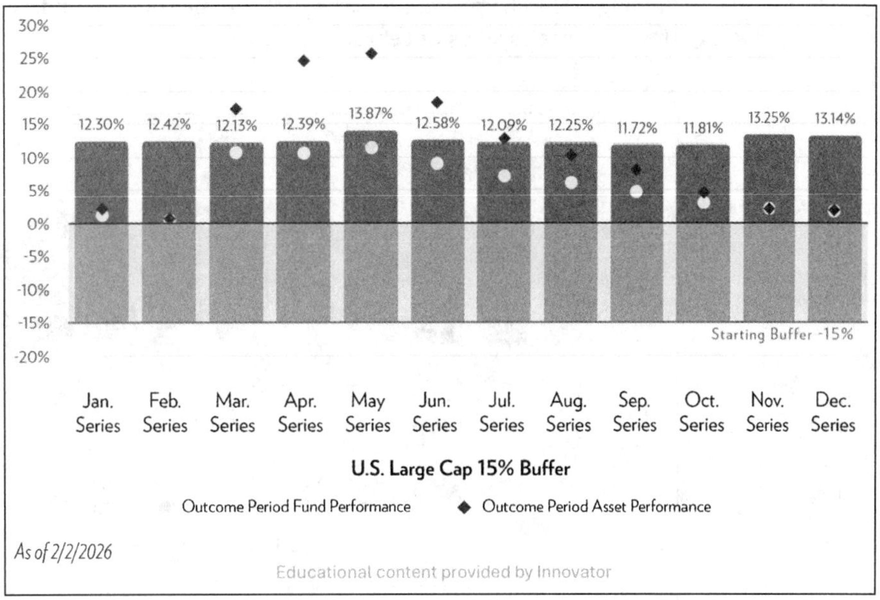

FIGURE 12-2: BUFF's 12 buffer ETFs.

Courtesy of Innovator

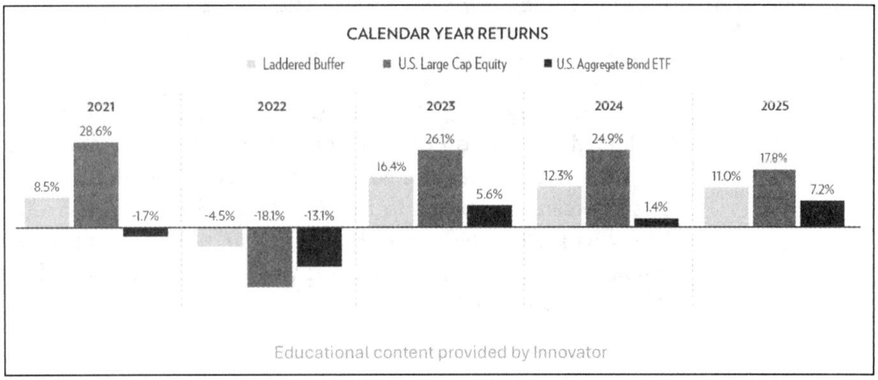

FIGURE 12-3: BUFF versus S&P 500 and Core Bonds (2021–2024).

Courtesy of Innovator

Innovator Laddered Allocation 9% Buffer ETF (BUFB)

Innovator's BUFB holds equal shares of the 12 underlying Innovator U.S. Equity Buffer ETFs, each with a starting buffer of 9 percent. Figure 12-4 shows the 12 ETF holdings. The chart highlights the performance of each underlying ETF relative to the reference asset as of February 2, 2026.

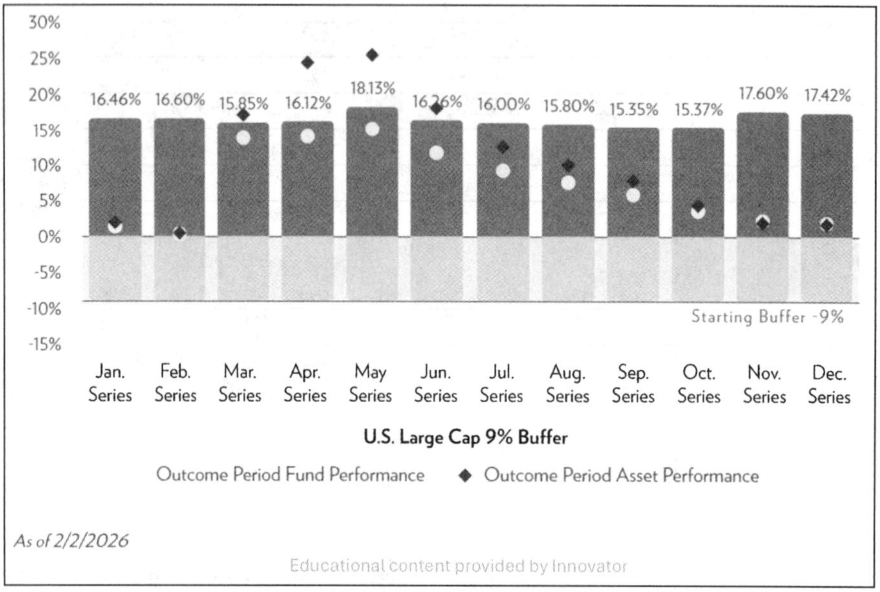

FIGURE 12-4: BUFB's 12 buffer ETFs.

Courtesy of Innovator

As shown in Figure 12-5, from February 8, 2022, through January 3, 2026, BUFB (Laddered Allocation Buffer) offered investors a smoother ride than the S&P 500, although it underperformed the reference asset, delivering a 4-year return of 48.42 percent compared to the S&P 500's 62.18 percent return (a 13.76 percent difference). However, over the four-year period, BUFB delivered a respectable annualized return of 10.44 percent with a defined level of downside protection in each underlying ETF.

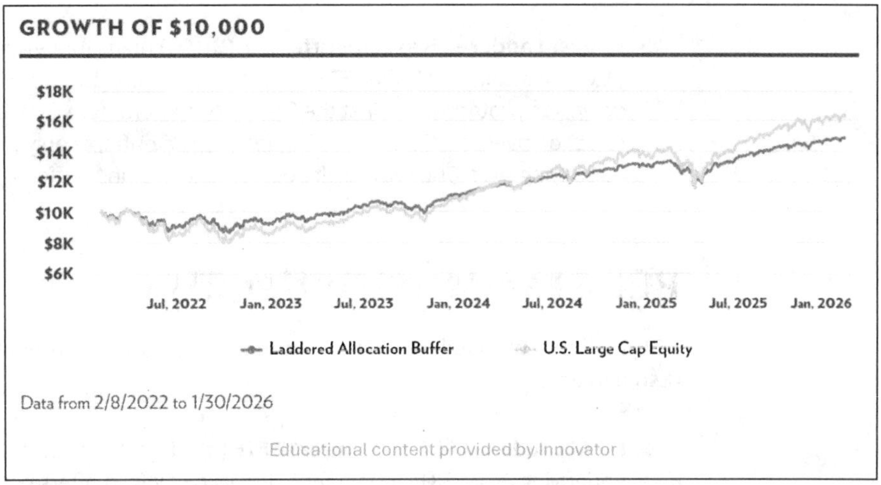

FIGURE 12-5: BUFB versus S&P 500.

Courtesy of Innovator

FT Vest Laddered Buffer ETFs

FT Vest offers four laddered buffer funds with annual expense ratios ranging from 0.95 to 1.0 percent:

- **FT Vest Laddered Buffer ETF (BUFR)** holds 12 equally weighted FT Vest Equity Buffer ETFs that track the SPDR S&P 500 ETF Trust (SPY) and provide a buffer against the first 10 percent (before fees, expenses, and taxes) of SPY losses. The buffer is provided only by the underlying ETFs. The fund itself does not provide any buffer against losses.

  With more than $8.5 billion in assets, FT Vest's BUFR, which debuted on August 10, 2020, is the largest buffer ETF in the options trading category, as defined by *Morningstar*.

- **FT Vest Laddered Moderate Buffer ETF (BUFZ)** holds 12 equally weighted FT Vest U.S. Equity Moderate Buffer ETFs that track the SPDR S&P 500 ETF Trust (SPY) and provide a buffer against the first 15 percent (before fees, expenses, and taxes) of SPY losses. The buffer is only provided by the underlying ETFs. The fund itself does not provide any buffer against losses.
- **FT Vest Laddered Deep Buffer ETF (BUFD)** holds 12 equally weighted FT Vest U.S. Equity Deep Buffer ETFs that track the SPDR S&P 500 ETF Trust (SPY) and provide a buffer against 25 percent (before fees, expenses, and taxes) of SPY losses — from –5 to –30 percent. The buffer is only provided by the underlying ETFs. The fund itself does not provide any buffer against losses.

- **FT Vest Laddered Nasdaq Buffer ETF (BUFQ)** holds four equally weighted FT Vest Nasdaq-100 Buffer ETFs — one resets every quarter. BUFQ provides downside protection against the first 10 percent (before fees, expenses, and taxes) of Invesco QQQ Trust (QQQ) losses. The buffer is only provided by the underlying ETFs. The fund itself does not provide any buffer against losses.

PGIM Laddered Buffer ETFs

PGIM offers two laddered buffer funds, each with an annual expense ratio of 0.50 percent:

- **PGIM Laddered S&P 500 Buffer12 ETF (BUFP)** holds equal shares of 12 underlying PGIM S&P 500 buffer ETFs, each of which offers protection against the first 12 percent loss in the reference asset, SPDR S&P 500 ETF Trust (SPY), during its outcome period. BUFP could be a good option for investors wanting a little bit more protection than is offered by a laddered buffer ETF with 9 or 10 percent protection.
- **PGIM Laddered Nasdaq Buffer12 ETF (PBQQ)** is a laddered portfolio of four PGIM Nasdaq-100 Buffer 12 ETFs, each of which offers protection against the first 12 percent loss in the reference asset, Invesco QQQ Trust (QQQ), during its outcome period.

Calamos Laddered S&P 500 Structured Alt Protection ETF (CPSL)

CPSL holds equal shares of 12 underlying S&P 500 Structured Alt Protection buffer ETFs. Each underlying ETF offers 100 percent protection against losses in the reference asset during the outcome period. CPSL could be an attractive investment vehicle for extremely risk-averse investors wanting full downside protection with outcome period diversification. CPSL's expense ratio is 0.79 percent.

iShares Large Cap Moderate Quarterly Laddered ETF (IVVM)

BlackRock's iShares Large Cap Moderate Quarterly Laddered ETF (IVVM) seeks to provide exposure to large-cap U.S. equities with downside protection through a series of buffers with staggered maturities. Each buffer is designed to protect approximately the first 5 percent of losses in the reference asset, iShares Core S&P 500 ETF (IVV), in exchange for limited upside potential. IVVM owns a series of buffers that expire in consecutive months. When one of the buffers nears its expiration, it is replaced with a new buffer that expires further out in time (for example, 3 months later).

What makes IVVM unique in the laddered buffer ETF category is that it provides quarterly protection, but only on the first 5 percent loss for each buffer. Other ETFs in this category typically offer more protection but with 12-month, instead of quarterly, resets.

iShares Large Cap Deep Quarterly Laddered ETF (IVVB)

BlackRock's iShares Large Cap Deep Quarterly Laddered ETF (IVVB) seeks to provide exposure to large-cap U.S. equities with downside protection through a series of buffers with staggered maturities. Each buffer is designed to protect approximately −5 to −20 percent, in exchange for limited upside potential.

What makes IVVB somewhat unique in the laddered buffer ETF category is that it provides deep quarterly protection, but shareholders absorb the first 5 percent loss in the reference asset, iShares Core S&P 500 ETF (IVV), and then are protected to −20 percent. So, effectively, each underlying buffer in the series offers 15 percent protection, but not on the initial 5 percent loss of each buffer in the ladder.

IN THIS CHAPTER

» Grasping accelerated buffer ETF basics

» Weighing the pros and cons

» Seeing what's available

Chapter 13

Doubling Down on Accelerated Buffer ETFs

If you were told you could double or even triple the return on your investment in a certain type of buffer ETF, you'd probably think it was too good to be true. Well, accelerated buffer ETFs *can* deliver that outcome, but with a cap on gains. And that's the catch — they typically have a lower cap than comparable buffer ETFs that don't offer the "double or triple your return" potential.

In this chapter, you discover more about what accelerated buffer ETFs are, how they work, when they may be a good choice (and when they're not), and how to use them to meet your investment objectives. I also introduce you to a couple of accelerated buffer ETFs you may want to consider.

REMEMBER

Accelerated Buffer ETFs seek to provide double or triple the upside return of the SPDR S&P 500 ETF Trust (SPY) or the Invesco QQQ Trust (QQQ), to a cap. Some accelerated buffer ETFs offer a buffer against the first 9 or 15 percent loss, and some offer no downside protection.

Understanding How Accelerated Buffer ETFs Work

Accelerated buffer ETFs enable investors to reshape the return profile of the reference asset. These funds seek to double or triple the gain of their reference asset to a cap, with approximately *single downside exposure* (meaning potential losses are *not* doubled or tripled).

WARNING

Accelerated buffer ETFs that have the potential to triple the return of the reference asset, to a cap, don't provide downside protection. However, many of the offerings that have the potential to double your return, to a cap, protect against the first 9 or 15 percent loss. Specifically, some Innovator offerings provide double the upside, to a cap, with 9 percent protection, while FT Vest's offerings provide double the upside, to a cap, with 15 percent protection.

As shown in Figure 13-1, any positive movement in the reference asset is accelerated to the cap. Any negative movement tracks the negative return of the reference asset; in other words, losses are *not* accelerated (they're *not* doubled or tripled).

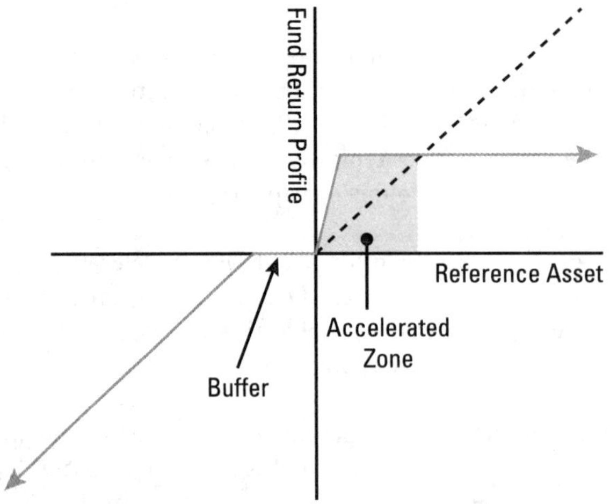

FIGURE 13-1: Accelerated buffer ETFs reshape the return profile of the reference asset.

Figure 13-2 shows the return of Innovator's U.S. Equity Accelerated 9 Buffer ETF (XBJA), shown as "Buffer ETF" in the figure, from January 1, 2024, to December 31, 2024. XBJA offers double the upside participation of its reference asset, SPY, shown as "U.S. Large Cap Equity" in the figure, and includes a 9 percent buffer. During this outcome period, SPY produced a return of 23.31 percent, so XBJA underperformed SPY by 10.61 percent. As I point out in the next section, underperformance like this is expected in a strong market. Accelerated buffer ETFs generally perform better than the reference asset in a low-return (single-digit percentage gain) market. Had SPY produced a return of only 6.35 percent during this period, XBJA would have delivered a return of 12.70 percent, outperforming SPY by 6.35 percent (doubling SPY's return).

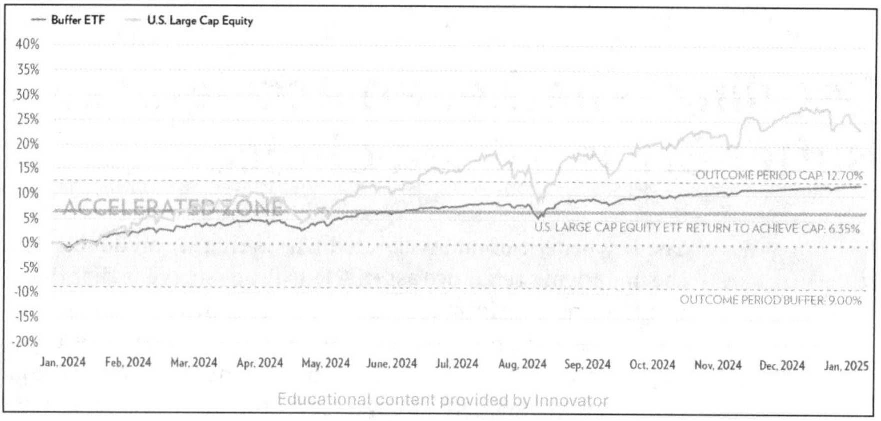

FIGURE 13-2: XBJA versus SPY (2024).

Courtesy of Innovator

Innovator also offers an *unbuffered* accelerated ETF that seeks to provide triple the positive return of the Invesco QQQ Trust (QQQ) to a cap. Figure 13-3 shows how U.S. Equity Accelerated Plus — April (QTAP), shown as "Accelerated ETF" in the figure, performed from April 1, 2023, to March 31, 2024, compared to its reference asset, QQQ, shown as "Growth-100 ETF" in the figure. Since QTAP was capped at 21.75 percent in a period when QQQ produced a whopping 38.35 percent return, QTAP underperformed its reference asset. However, in a low-return market — for example, if QQQ had produced a return of only 7.25 percent — QTAP would have delivered a return of 21.75 percent (triple that of QQQ).

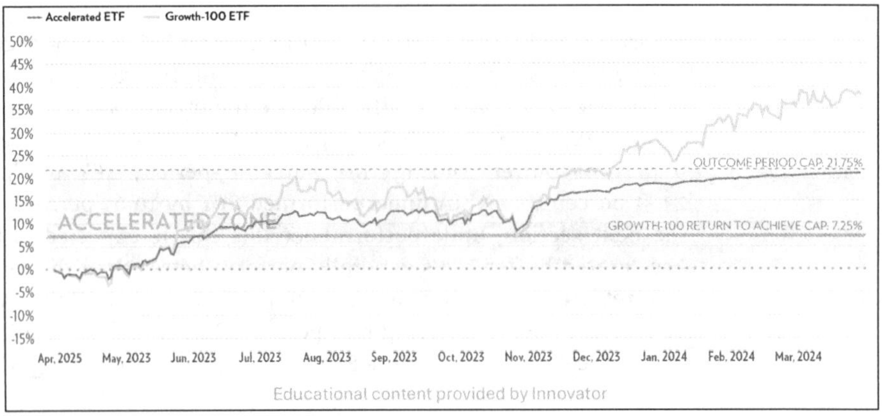

FIGURE 13-3: QTAP versus QQQ (April 1, 2023, to March 31, 2024).

Courtesy of Innovator

Deciding Whether an Accelerated Buffer ETF Is a Good Choice

The key benefit of an accelerated ETF is that it can double or triple the return of the underlying reference asset. A key disadvantage is that the cap can lead to substantial underperformance during strong markets. Figure 13-4 shows how an accelerated buffer ETF with two times the acceleration, a 15 percent buffer, and a 12 percent cap would typically perform in different market conditions — a major sell-off, a market correction, a slow growth market, and a high growth market. The chart assumes the investor purchased the ETF on the first day of the outcome period and held until the end of the period. Here are the highlights:

- **In a major market sell-off of –30 percent, the ETF would lose 15 percent (before fees).** By losing less, the ETF would outperform its reference asset by 15 percent.
- **In a normal market correction of –10 percent, the ETF would break even (no gain, no loss).** By breaking even (thanks to the buffer), the ETF would outperform its reference asset by 10 percent.
- **If SPY finished the outcome period in positive territory, the ETF's return would double, up to the 12 percent cap.** For example, if SPY returned 5 percent, the ETF would show an approximate return of 10 percent. If SPY returned 7 percent, the ETF would show an approximate return of 12 percent, at its cap.
- **If SPY showed a high return and finished the outcome period up 20 percent, the ETF would be capped out with a return of 12 percent.**

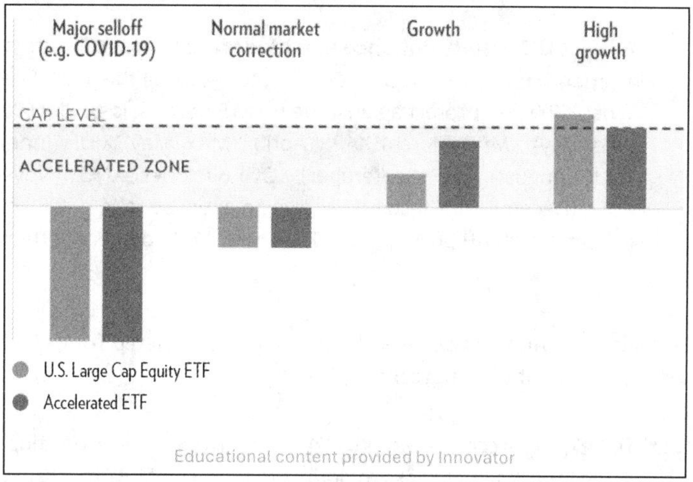

FIGURE 13-4: An accelerated buffer ETF is likely to outperform its reference asset in all but a strong bull market.

Courtesy of Innovator

As you can see, an accelerated buffer ETF is likely to match or outperform the reference asset except during a period of high growth.

REMEMBER

Accelerated Buffer ETFs should appeal to conservative or moderate risk investors who think the market will be experiencing slow growth (single-digit gains) over the outcome period. If, on the other hand, you think the underlying reference asset has a good chance of outperforming the cap, then an accelerated buffer ETF probably isn't the best choice. You'd probably be better off investing in a buffer ETF without acceleration, or a traditional ETF that tracks the same reference asset but without an upside cap.

Checking Out Available Accelerated Buffer ETFs

Innovator and FT Vest both offer accelerated buffer ETFs. As of this writing, the following funds are available:

- **Innovator's U.S. Equity Accelerated 9 ETF** offers four 12-month funds that seek to double the return of the SPDR S&P 500 ETF Trust (SPY) and protect against the first 9 percent loss: XBJA (January), XBAP (April), XBJL (July), and XBOC (October). These funds have an expense ratio of 0.79 percent. The net cap for XBAP on March 31, 2026, clocked in at 14.25 percent at the start of its outcome period.

» **FT Vest U.S. Equity Enhance and Moderate Buffer ETF** offers twelve 12-month funds that seek to double the return of the SPDR S&P 500 ETF Trust (SPY) and protect against the first 15 percent loss: XJAN (January), XFEB (February), XMAR (March), XAPR (April), XMAY (May), XJUN (June), XJUL (July), XAUG (August), XSEP (September), XOCT (October), XNOV (November), and XDEC (December). These funds have an expense ratio of 0.85 percent. The net cap for XMAR on March 23, 2026, was 11.37 percent at the start of its outcome period.

In addition, Innovator offers the following *unbuffered* funds, all of which have an expense ratio of 0.79 percent:

» **U.S. Equity Accelerated (XDSQ)** is a quarterly series (resetting every three months) that seeks to double the return of SPY to a cap.

» **Growth Accelerated ETF (XDQQ)** is a quarterly series (resetting every three months) that seeks to double the return of QQQ to a cap.

» **U.S. Equity Accelerated Plus** offers four 12-month funds that seek to triple the return of SPY to a cap: XTJA (January), XTAP (April), XTJL (July), and XTOC (October).

» **Growth Accelerated Plus** offers four 12-month funds that seek to triple the return of QQQ to a cap: QTJA (January), QTAP (April), QTJL (July), and QTOC (October).

WARNING

These last four accelerated ETFs are *unbuffered*. They do not protect against downside risk.

For additional details about these funds, visit the issuer websites:

» **Innovator:** `www.innovatoretfs.com`

» **FT Vest:** `www.ftportfolios.com`

IN THIS CHAPTER

» Going behind the scenes with uncapped buffer ETFs

» Seeing how an uncapped buffer ETF behaves in the real world

» Knowing when uncapped buffer ETFs are a good fit and when they're not

» Highlighting some funds to consider

Chapter 14

The Sky's the Limit with Uncapped Buffer ETFs

What's the biggest potential drawback of buffer ETFs? If you answered, "The cap!" you are correct. The price you pay for downside protection is having a capped return. Now, what if you could remove the cap altogether? That's crazy talk, right? Well, some issuers of buffer ETFs have done just that, delivering what investors in the past could only dream of — uncapped buffer ETFs.

What's the catch? For investors to earn a profit, the return at the end of the outcome period must exceed a predetermined *spread* (a certain percentage gain), which varies depending on the same factors that influence the upside caps of conventional buffer ETFs (volatility and interest rates). For example, if the spread is 4 percent (after fees), and the reference asset shows a return of 4 percent at the end of the ETF's outcome period, your return is zero. However, if the reference asset shows a return of 30 percent, you get the full upside minus the 4 percent net spread — 26 percent. The moral of the story is that you probably want to invest in an uncapped buffer ETF only if you expect the return of the reference asset to far exceed the upside caps on conventional buffer ETFs (which can happen, particularly coming out of bear markets and crashes).

This chapter presents details about uncapped buffer ETFs and provides guidance on how to decide when this ETF type might be a good addition to your portfolio. I also point you in the direction of some uncapped buffer ETFs you may want to consider.

REMEMBER

Uncapped buffer ETFs blend the best of both worlds — downside protection and potential for unlimited growth above the spread.

Understanding How Uncapped Buffer ETFs Work

Uncapped buffer ETFs, like their capped counterparts, track the price of a reference asset (for example, S&P 500), and they provide downside protection against the first X-percent loss the reference asset might suffer. Where uncapped buffer ETFs differ is that they don't limit the upside, beyond the *spread* (the first X-percent gain of the reference asset). Figure 14-1 shows the payoff profile of an uncapped buffer ETF, highlighting its four key components:

- **Downside buffer:** The buffer protects the first X-percent loss (before fees) during the outcome period.
- **Spread:** For investors purchasing an uncapped buffer ETF on the reset date, the spread represents the minimum percentage return the reference asset must achieve, at the end of the outcome period, before the investor participates in any gains.
- **Uncapped upside:** Upside potential above the spread is unlimited.
- **Reference asset:** The ETF tracks the price of a reference asset, such as SPDR S&P 500 ETF Trust (SPY).

TECHNICAL STUFF

A conventional buffer ETF holds four different option contracts: two put options create a put spread, which defines the downside protection; a purchase of a call option establishes exposure to the reference asset, and the sale of a call option defines the upside cap (see Chapter 2 for details). An uncapped buffer ETF holds only three option contracts: two put options create a put spread, which defines the downside protection, and a deep-in-the-money call option establishes exposure to the reference asset. The ETF doesn't sell a call option, so the upside is uncapped.

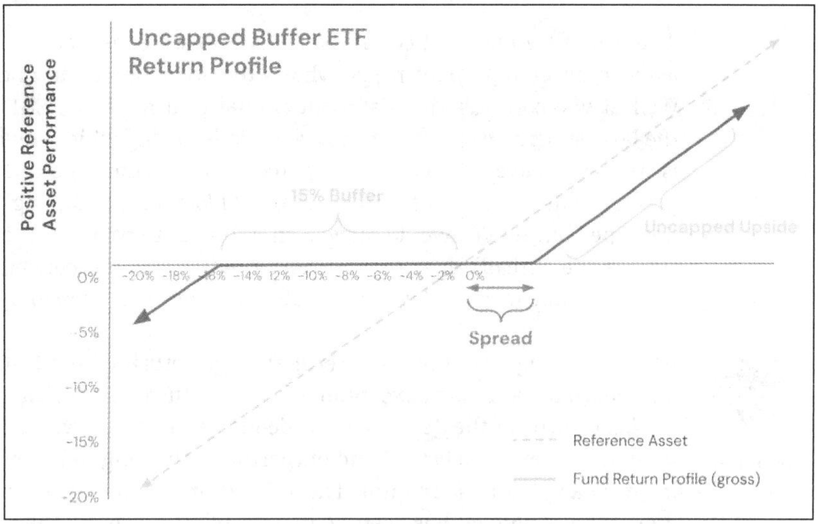

FIGURE 14-1: The return profile for an uncapped buffer ETF.

The spread percentage is influenced primarily by the following two factors:

- **Volatility:** Increased volatility can drive up the cost of put options, increasing the spread. Decreased volatility typically reduces the spread.
- **Interest rates:** In a declining rate environment, spreads are likely to widen, and in a rising rate environment, spreads should narrow.

The spread percentage is likely to be more heavily influenced by changes in interest rates than by changes in volatility, but volatility can offset rate movements one way or the other.

Observing an Uncapped Buffer ETF in Action

AllianzIM is a leading issuer of uncapped buffer ETFs. It launched its first uncapped buffer ETF, U.S. Equity Buffer 15 Uncapped ETF — April (ARLU) on April 1, 2024, with a gross spread of 2.96 percent (3.70 percent net) and downside protection against the first 15 percent loss. At the end of its first outcome period on March 31, 2025, its reference asset (SPY) produced a return of 6.94 percent. After subtracting the spread of 3.70 percent, ARLU's return, net of fees, was 3.20 percent. If SPY produced a return of anything less than 3.70 percent, investors would have walked away with nothing. And, if SPY had declined more than 15 percent at the end of the outcome period, ARLU would have shown a loss.

A return of 3.20 percent certainly isn't impressive, especially when the reference asset returned 6.94 percent, so what's the attraction of an uncapped buffer ETF? Well, if you consider the historical annual returns of the S&P 500 (1960–2023), the largest percentage of returns are periods during which the index performance is well above average. Forty-one percent of the time, the S&P 500 has achieved greater than 15 percent gains (source: *Bloomberg*). During these periods, an uncapped buffer ETF would allow a shareholder to participate in unlimited upside (minus the spread), likely significantly outperforming conventional buffer ETFs with the same level of downside protection, but with capped upside.

TECHNICAL STUFF

It's fascinating how the long-term average return of the S&P 500 is so heavily influenced by periods of exceptionally high returns. Historically, 41 percent of the annual returns of the S&P 500 exceeded 15 percent, and when the index does well, it often does extremely well and outperforms the long-term average return of the index by a significant amount. The average annual return when the S&P 500 is up more than 15 percent has been 24.10 percent. That's more than double the historical average annual return of the index! The take-home lesson here is that uncapped buffer ETFs perform best in strong markets, enabling you to ride the wave. And if the market doesn't perform as well as you anticipated, at least you have some downside protection to soften the landing.

Consider how an uncapped buffer ETF, with a 4 percent spread and 15 percent buffer, would have performed in the following scenarios (based on historical data for the S&P 500 from 1960 to 2023):

- **Scenario 1:** If the S&P 500 were to lose 15 percent or more in a calendar year, the 15 percent buffer would help mitigate losses. The average annual return for the S&P 500 when losses were worse than –15 percent was –25.70 percent, which means the average loss to an investor with a 15 percent buffer would have been –10.70 percent (before fees).
- **Scenario 2:** Since 1960, 19 percent of annual returns resulted in a loss between zero and –15 percent. In this scenario, before fees and expenses, an investor with a 15 percent buffer would not have incurred a loss. (See Chapter 5 for more about why losing less matters.)
- **Scenario 3:** In years when the S&P 500 had returns between zero and 15 percent, an investor would participate in the upside only above the spread. For example, if the net spread was 4 percent and the reference asset (SPY) finished the outcome period up 14 percent, the investor's return would be 10 percent (14 – 4 percent).
- **Scenario 4:** Perhaps surprisingly, the most common return-period scenario is when returns exceed 15 percent. Throughout history, when the S&P 500's annual return was greater than 15 percent, its average return was well over 20 percent. The uncapped nature of these buffer ETFs would allow an investor

to have unlimited participation in the gains, above the spread. For example, if the net spread was 4 percent and the reference asset (SPY) returned 28 percent during the outcome period, the investor would earn 24 percent (28 – 4 percent).

Deciding Whether an Uncapped Buffer ETF Is Right for You

Deciding whether an uncapped buffer ETF is right for you depends on multiple factors, including your personal financial situation, investment objectives, investor temperament, and market conditions. In this section, I provide guidance to help you decide.

Weighing the pros and cons of uncapped buffer ETFs

Uncapped buffer ETFs offer many of the same advantages as their capped counterparts: a buffer against the first X-percent loss, automatic resets with fresh buffers, transparency (a known outcome range prior to investing), liquidity, tax efficiency, and no credit risk. (See Chapter 1 for a more detailed explanation of these benefits.) In addition, uncapped buffer ETFs offer the following advantages over capped buffer ETFs:

- Unlimited upside participation in the reference asset above the spread, resulting in potentially higher returns than conventional buffer ETFs during years when the returns of the S&P 500 far exceed the long-term average
- Potentially higher returns for buy-and-hold investors
- An attractive core long-term holding with high upside potential and moderate downside protection

The big disadvantage of uncapped buffer ETFs is related to the spread, which makes them a poor investment choice in low-return markets. If the reference asset delivers a single-digit return, the spread can take a considerable chunk out of your return. In such markets, accelerated buffer ETFs may be the better choice (see Chapter 13 for details).

Evaluating your temperament

Uncapped buffer ETFs may appeal to all investors — conservative, moderate, or aggressive. The downside buffer gives the risk-averse investor some comfort, and the unlimited upside potential, above the spread, is attractive for all investors.

TIP

Make sure the buffer provides a level of downside protection that aligns with your risk profile. If it doesn't, you may need to go with a capped buffer ETF that offers more protection.

Gauging market conditions

Uncapped buffer ETFs are best to own in strong markets. The challenge comes in predicting when the absence of a cap is likely to be advantageous and when the cost of the spread is likely to be too high.

TIP

In my opinion, the ideal time to buy an uncapped buffer ETF is when stock prices are depressed, sentiment is extremely negative, and stock valuations are attractive. These conditions typically exist during deep corrections or bear markets. History has shown that markets can often post outsized gains coming out of bear markets, so an uncapped buffer ETF could be super attractive under these conditions. And, because it's impossible to know the trough of a bear market in advance, the 15 percent buffer may give you the courage to step in and buy when you might otherwise be too uncomfortable to enter the market.

REMEMBER

Obviously, knowing when markets are poised to deliver above-average returns is extremely difficult, if not impossible, but you can certainly increase your odds of success by buying an uncapped buffer ETF when stock prices are already depressed and trading well below their all-time highs.

REMEMBER

Returns have often been strongest after the sharpest declines, bouncing back quickly from market bottoms. Research by the *Capital Group* tracked the 18 biggest market declines since the Great Depression, and in each case, the S&P 500 was higher five years later. And, the first year return following the five biggest bear markets since 1929 averaged an astonishing 70.9 percent! If you own a capped buffer ETF coming out of a deep bear market, and stocks recover strongly, you could be capped out early in the recovery. On the other hand, an uncapped buffer ETF would allow you to capture most of the outsized gains, given its unlimited upside above the spread.

Perhaps the worst time to own an uncapped buffer ETF is in a single-digit, low-return stock market environment, when returns are below average. Why? Because if stock returns are positive, but below 10 percent, you're forfeiting a significant portion of your return. For example, if the S&P 500 provides an average annual return of 7 percent in the coming years, and the spread averages 3.5 percent net, you could make as little as 3.5 percent annually (spreads will vary during each outcome period). In this hypothetical return scenario, you would forgo half the gain of the reference asset.

TIP

For a long-term growth strategy, consider maintaining an allocation in an uncapped buffer ETF instead of trying to predict when forward returns will be below average and when markets will recover after a decline.

Consider the spread

Before investing in any uncapped buffer ETF, check its current spread. Deciding whether a spread is attractive or not is somewhat subjective and depends on your opinion of the market environment and the forward return potential of the reference asset. If the reference asset is deep in bear market territory and the upside potential is very high — as is usually the case when stock prices are very depressed — a spread of 4 percent or more can still make for an attractive investment opportunity. On the other hand, in a low-return market, a 4 percent spread may seem too high.

REMEMBER

A spread of 4 or even 6 percent may be acceptable for a long-term allocation. Historical data (1970–2023) from *Morningstar*, using various spread percentages, showed that a 4 percent spread still allowed for upside capture of 78 percent of the S&P 500's gains, and a 6 percent spread showed upside capture of 68 percent (excluding the impact of fees), as shown in Table 14-1.

TABLE 14-1 Uncapped Buffer 15 Historical Upside/Downside Capture (1970–2023)

	2% Spread	3% Spread	4% Spread	6% Spread
Up Market Capture	88%	83%	78%	68%

WARNING

Never buy an uncapped buffer ETF expecting it to outperform the reference asset. While it might outperform in certain periods, over multiple years, it's unlikely to do so.

Comparing capped and uncapped buffer ETF performance

When comparing capped and uncapped buffer ETFs, the key differences show up in how they perform relative to each other and to the underlying reference asset they track. For example, suppose you're comparing an uncapped buffer ETF to a capped version of a similar fund, and they both track the S&P 500. Both ETFs provide a 15 percent buffer at the start of each outcome period. The capped buffer ETF has an upside potential of 12 percent (before fees), and the uncapped buffer ETF has a spread of 4 percent (before fees). Assume the S&P 500 pays an annual dividend of 1.10 percent. Consider the following scenarios:

- **Scenario 1:** S&P 500 finishes inside the spread with a return of 2 percent.

Index/ETF	Price Return	Income Return	Total Return
S&P 500	2%	1.10%	3.10%
Capped Buffer ETF	2%	0%	2%
Uncapped Buffer ETF	0%	0%	0%

- **Scenario 2:** S&P 500 finishes below the spread, but inside the buffer, losing 14 percent.

Index/ETF	Price Return	Income Return	Total Return
S&P 500	-14%	1.10%	-12.90%
Capped Buffer ETF	0%	0%	0%
Uncapped Buffer ETF	0%	0%	0%

- **Scenario 3:** S&P 500 finishes below the spread and below the buffer, losing 20 percent.

Index/ETF	Price Return	Income Return	Total Return
S&P 500	-20%	1.10%	-18.90%
Capped Buffer ETF	-5%	0%	-5%
Uncapped Buffer ETF	-5%	0%	-5%

- **Scenario 4:** S&P 500 finishes above the spread, but below the cap, with a return of 10 percent.

Index/ETF	Price Return	Income Return	Total Return
S&P 500	10%	1.10%	11.10%
Capped Buffer ETF	10%	0%	10%
Uncapped Buffer ETF	6%	0%	6%

- **Scenario 5:** S&P 500 finishes above the spread and above the cap, with a return of 30 percent.

Index/ETF	Price Return	Income Return	Total Return
S&P 500	30%	1.10%	31.10%
Capped Buffer ETF	12%	0%	12%
Uncapped Buffer ETF	26%	0%	26%

REMEMBER

Uncapped buffer ETFs have one of the most intriguing payoff profiles in the buffer ETF space. Consider investing in an uncapped buffer ETF, particularly when spreads are reasonable, stock prices are depressed, and valuations are attractive.

Checking Out Some Uncapped Buffer ETFs

If the concept of an uncapped buffer ETF appeals to you, the next step is to check out what's available. As of this writing, here's a sampling of current choices that are available for purchase:

- **AllianzIM U.S. Equity Buffer15 Uncapped ETFs** are 12-month funds with a 15 percent buffer and a 0.74 percent expense ratio that track the SPDR S&P 500 ETF Trust (SPY). AllianzIM offers a series that resets every month of the year.
- **AllianzIM International Equity Buffer15 Uncapped ETFs** are 12-month funds with a 15 percent buffer and a 0.79 percent expense ratio that track the iShares MSCI EAFE ETF (EFA). During this writing, AllianzIM was in the process of rolling out a series of four ETFs with reset dates for each calendar quarter of the year. Note, because of the high dividend yield provided by the reference asset (EFA) and other factors, the international uncapped ETFs have a much lower spread than the equivalent that tracks the SPDR S&P 500 ETF Trust (SPY). Currently, this is a nice advantage for investors wanting exposure to international markets, with a level of downside protection and unlimited upside potential. The net spread differential on the two AllianzIM January 2026 series (JANU and JANI) was 1.24 percent (4.47 percent versus 3.23 percent).
- **AllianzIM Buffer15 Uncapped Allocation ETF (SPBU)** is a fund-of-funds solution that ladders the entire lineup of all 12 AllianzIM Buffer15 Uncapped ETFs in one ticker, so you don't have to monitor individual funds. Each month, one of the underlying ETFs resets its full 15 percent buffer for the new

12-month outcome period, with an adjusted spread. Its expense ratio is 0.79 percent.

- **Innovator Uncapped Bitcoin 20 Floor ETF** is a quarterly (3-month) fund with a 20 percent floor (investors absorb initial losses to –20 percent but are protected against deeper losses). It's important to stress that this is a quarterly floor ETF, and it doesn't really provide much protection unless bitcoin crashes below –20 percent during the outcome period. The fund has a 0.79 percent expense ratio.
- **TrueShares Structured Outcome ETFs** are 12-month funds with an 8 to 12 percent buffer (targeting a 10 percent buffer) and a 0.79 percent expense ratio that track the S&P 500.

REMEMBER

Keep in mind that you always have the option of investing in traditional (uncapped, unbuffered) ETFs, which may be the better choice for a long-term growth strategy.

IN THIS CHAPTER

» Understanding what dual-directional buffer ETFs are

» Looking into how these funds work

» Knowing when dual-directional buffer ETFs are and aren't a good choice

» Finding dual-directional buffer ETFs to invest in

Chapter 15
Having It Both Ways with Dual-Directional Buffer ETFs

Is it possible to get a positive return investing in the stock market regardless of whether the market rises or falls? Such a scenario may strike you as too good to be true, but that's exactly what dual-directional buffer ETFs seek to accomplish. What's the catch? You sacrifice significant potential gains, and in a booming market, this may leave you feeling frustrated.

Maybe that's all you need to know to convince you *not* to invest in dual-directional buffer ETFs, but if that brief description of them has piqued your interest, you've come to the right place. This chapter explains what they are, how they work, and under what conditions they can be a good addition to your portfolio. It also introduces you to some dual-directional buffer ETFs you may want to consider.

REMEMBER

What makes dual-directional buffer ETFs unique is they have the potential to produce positive returns in both up and down markets.

Getting Up To Speed on Dual-Directional Buffer ETFs

Dual-directional buffer ETFs seek to do exactly what their name suggests — deliver a positive return whether the reference asset's value increases or decreases, within a specific range, and provide downside protection within a defined buffer zone. These funds have the following characteristics:

- **Reference asset:** Dual-directional buffer ETFs typically track a reference asset such as SPDR S&P 500 ETF Trust (SPY).
- **Outcome period:** The predefined timeframe (typically 12 months) during which the ETF's defined buffer and cap limits apply.
- **Buffer:** The buffer defines the level of downside protection and the range of reference asset loss over which the inverse cap comes into play.
- **Caps:** Dual-directional buffer ETFs have essentially two caps:
  - **Upside cap:** The maximum positive return the fund can produce when the reference asset posts a gain at the end of the outcome period.
  - **Inverse cap:** The maximum positive return the fund can produce when the reference asset posts a loss at the end of the outcome period.

  The two caps have the potential to create a condition in which the fund gains more when the reference asset produces a negative return than when it produces a positive return. For example, if the upside cap is 9 percent, and the inverse cap is 15 percent, the fund has the potential to earn up to 15 percent if the reference asset declines, but only up to 9 percent if it shows a positive return. However, the upside cap may be higher than the inverse cap depending on the fund.

Figure 15-1 shows the expected outcomes for a dual-directional 15 percent buffer ETF with a 9 percent upside cap and a 15 percent inverse cap in the following four market scenarios:

- **Negative scenario (buffer is breached):** If the reference asset posts a loss that exceeds the buffer, the investor absorbs the excess loss. As shown in Figure 15-1, if the SPDR S&P 500 ETF Trust (SPY) loses 20 percent, the fund loses 5 percent (before fees).
- **Inverse performance scenario:** If the reference asset loses 0 to 15 percent, the fund gains the same percentage (before fees) up to the inverse cap.
- **Positive scenario (up to the cap):** The fund's value increases the same percentage as the reference asset increases up to the cap.

» **Positive scenario (beyond the cap):** If the value of the reference asset increases beyond the upside cap, the fund's return is limited to the cap. As shown in Figure 15-1, the reference asset has exceeded both caps, but the fund's return is limited to the upside cap.

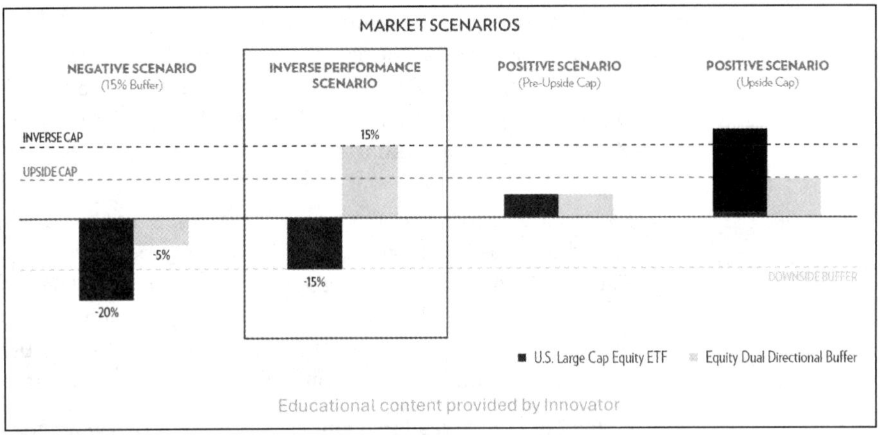

FIGURE 15-1: Dual-directional buffer ETFs seek to deliver positive returns in up and down markets.

Courtesy of Innovator

As shown in Figure 15-2, dual-directional buffer ETFs expand the "gain zone" by stretching it back into negative-return territory. These funds deliver a positive return not only when the reference asset shows a positive return but also when it shows a negative return within the buffer. Research conducted by Innovator shows that dual-directional funds with a 15 percent buffer create a "gain zone" that covers approximately 95 percent of historical returns.

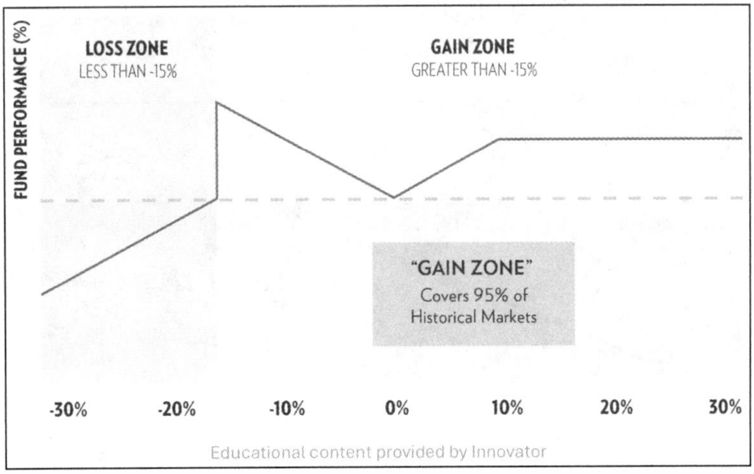

FIGURE 15-2: Dual-directional buffer ETFs expand the gain zone.

Courtesy of Innovator

Understanding How Dual-Directional Buffer ETFs Work

TECHNICAL STUFF

All buffer ETFs are structured using options contracts, which allow but don't obligate the purchase or sale of an asset, such as shares of a stock market reference asset (see Chapter 2 for more about options). A buffer ETF's options positions are all established at the same time — usually at the beginning of its outcome period. However, visualizing the options contracts as layers sheds light on how dual-directional buffer ETFs work. Here's what the four layers look like, using a dual-directional 15 percent buffer ETF as an example:

- **Layer 1** is a deep-in-the-money call option that simulates owning the underlying asset, thereby enabling the fund to track its reference asset (see Figure 15-3). A *deep-in-the-money call option* means the *strike price* (the fixed price at which the holder of the option can buy the underlying asset) is much lower than the reference asset's price. Nearly all buffer ETFs use a deep-in-the-money call option to replicate the performance of the reference asset.
- **Layer 2** is a put spread that enables the fund to gain when the reference asset declines in value within the specified buffer (see Figure 15-4). A *put* is an option to sell an asset on a specified date. A *put spread* is an options strategy that involves buying one put option and selling another one with a different strike price but the same expiration date on the same underlying asset.
- **Layer 3** is a bullish put spread that transitions the fund to a 15 percent buffer if the reference asset's value breaches the buffer (see Figure 15-5). A *bullish put spread* is an options strategy that involves selling a put at a higher strike and buying a put with the same expiration date at a lower strike. These transactions result in a net credit that helps pay for downside protection while the fund transitions to a buffered profile in deeper drawdowns.

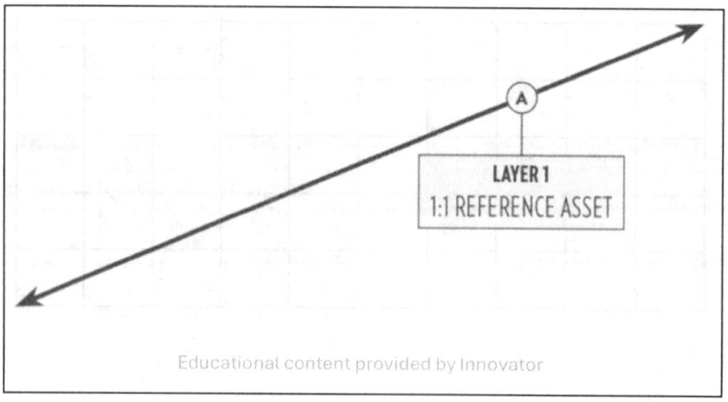

FIGURE 15-3: Layer 1 uses option contracts to track the reference asset.

Courtesy of Innovator

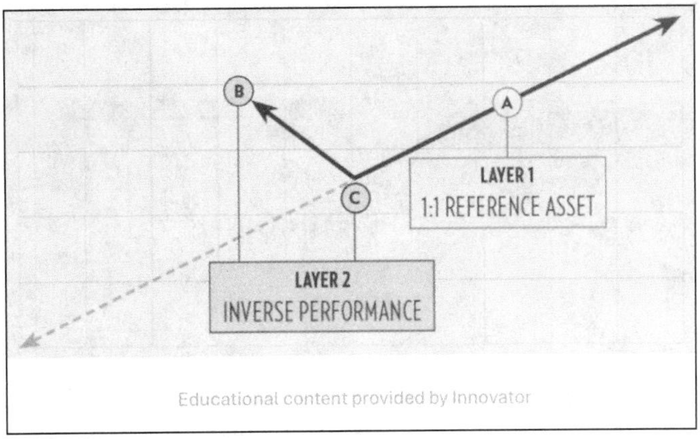

FIGURE 15-4: Layer 2 enables the fund to gain value when the reference asset loses value.

Courtesy of Innovator

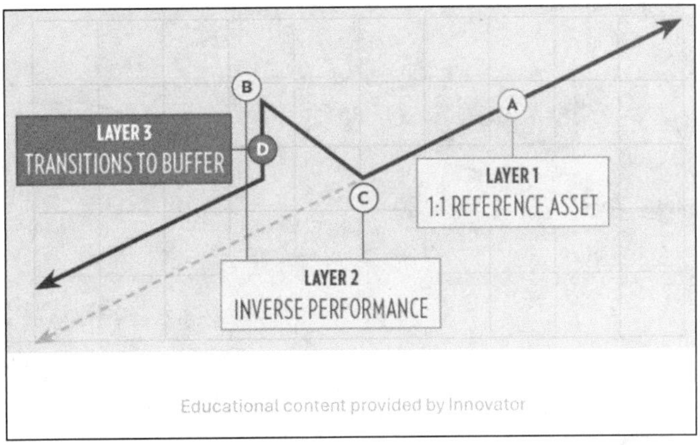

FIGURE 15-5: Layer 3 transitions the portfolio to a 15 percent buffered profile.

Courtesy of Innovator

- **Layer 4** consists of selling a call option as far *out of the money* (above the reference asset's price) as possible while still generating enough premium to cover the cost of the buffer. The sale of this call creates the upside cap (see Figure 15-6).

The resulting payoff profile seeks a one-to-one upside return (A) to a cap (E) and one-to-one inverse return (C-B) when the reference asset suffers a loss of 0 to −15 percent, as shown in Figure 15-7.

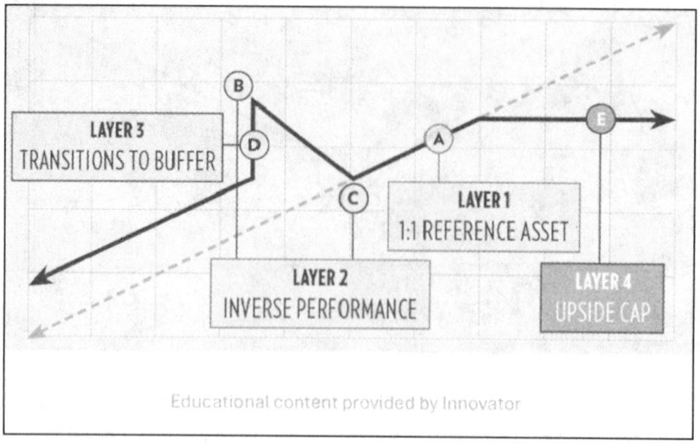

FIGURE 15-6: Layer 4 creates the upside cap.

Courtesy of Innovator

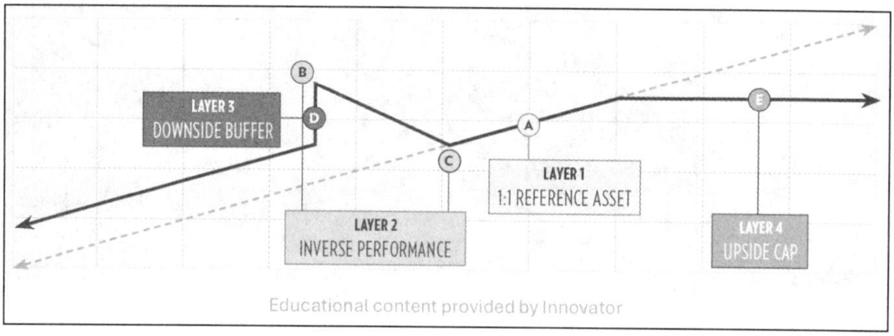

FIGURE 15-7: Dual-directional buffer ETFs use options strategies to produce positive returns in up or down markets.

Courtesy of Innovator

Deciding When to Consider a Dual-Directional Buffer ETF

Dual-directional buffer ETFs should be considered for purchase only if your outlook for the reference asset is somewhat negative. Why? Two reasons:

- You have more upside if the reference asset loses value, as long as it doesn't breach the buffer.
- The upside cap for dual-directional buffer ETFs is lower than that of comparable conventional buffer ETFs (see Table 15-1).

  Bottom line, you may be getting 25 to 30 percent less upside potential in a positive market with a dual-directional buffer ETF compared to a conventional buffer ETF. The only good time to forfeit that much upside is when you think there's not much upside to forfeit.

TABLE 15-1 **Upside Caps — Dual-Directional versus Conventional Buffer ETFs**

Fund	Upside Cap (before fees)
Innovator Equity Dual Directional 15 Buffer — February (DDFF)	9.34%
Innovator U.S. Equity Power Buffer — February (PFEB)	12.4%
Innovator Equity Dual Directional 10 Buffer — February (DDTF)	13.23%
Innovator U.S. Equity Buffer — February (BFEB)	16.6%

Note: BFEB offers protection on the first 9 percent decline in the reference asset, while DDTF offers protection on the first 10 percent loss of the same reference asset, so the comparison isn't exactly "apples-to-apples." Upside caps are as of February 2026.

REMEMBER

Consider buying a dual-directional buffer ETF only if you think the probability of a negative return of the reference asset is highly likely and, obviously, you're hoping that any decline in the reference asset doesn't breach the buffer at the end of the outcome period.

Checking Out Available Dual-Directional Buffer ETFs

As of this writing, only two issuers offer dual-directional buffer ETFs — Innovator and FT Vest. Innovator offers the following four products:

- **Equity Dual Directional 10 Buffer ETFs:** These are 12-month funds that track the SPDR S&P 500 ETF Trust (SPY) and have a starting buffer and starting inverse cap of 10 percent. The starting upside cap is calculated at the beginning of the outcome period. They have an expense ratio of 0.79 percent.
- **Equity Dual Directional 15 Buffer ETFs:** These are 12-month funds that track the SPDR S&P 500 ETF Trust (SPY) and have a starting buffer and starting inverse cap of 15 percent. The starting upside cap is calculated at the beginning of the outcome period. They have an expense ratio of 0.79 percent.
- **Equity Dual Directional 5 Buffer ETF:** This is a 3-month (quarterly) fund that tracks the SPDR S&P 500 ETF Trust (SPY) and has a starting buffer and starting inverse cap of 5 percent. The starting upside cap is calculated at the beginning of the outcome period. It has an expense ratio of 0.79 percent.

» **Growth-100 Dual Directional 5 Buffer ETF:** This is a 3-month (quarterly) fund that tracks the Invesco QQQ Trust (QQQ) and has a starting buffer and starting inverse cap of 5 percent. The starting upside cap is calculated at the beginning of the outcome period. It has an expense ratio of 0.79 percent.

First Trust (FT) Vest offers the following series:

U.S. Equity Dual Directional Buffer ETFs: These are 12-month funds that track the SPDR S&P 500 ETF Trust (SPY) and have a starting buffer and starting inverse cap of 10 percent. The starting upside cap is calculated at the beginning of the outcome period. They have an expense ratio of 0.85 percent.

TIP

When you're deciding which dual-directional buffer ETF to purchase, compare potential outcomes for different funds based on their starting parameters (buffer, upside cap, and inverse cap). As shown in Figure 15-8, the fund with a shallower 10 percent buffer and inverse cap has greater profit potential if the reference asset increases in value. The fund with the deeper 15 percent buffer has more profit potential if the reference asset's value declines. Their performance is identical in the range from where the reference asset loses 10 percent or less to where it gains up to 5 percent.

FIGURE 15-8: Potential outcomes can differ considerably between dual-directional ETFs with different buffers and caps.

STARTING PARAMETERS FOR THE FEBRUARY 2026 DUAL DIRECTIONAL ETFs

TICKER	ASSET -20%	ASSET -15%	ASSET -10%	ASSET -5%	ASSET FLAT	ASSET +5%	ASSET +10%	ASSET +15%	ASSET +20%
10% Dual Directional ETF *Net Return** *(Net Upside Cap: 12.44%)*	-10.79%	-5.79%	9.21%	4.21%	-0.79%	4.21%	9.21%	12.44%	12.44%
15% Dual Directional ETF *Net Return** *(Net Upside Cap: 8.55%)*	-5.79%	14.21%	9.21%	4.21%	-0.79%	4.21%	8.55%	8.55%	8.55%

Educational content provided by Innovator

Courtesy of Innovator

You can access Innovator's Potential Outcome Analyzer via its website at `www.innovatoretfs.com`. Open the Tools menu and select Potential Outcome Analyzer. You can also access it by choosing the fund you're interested in, which gets you to its ETF Summary page; scroll down, and select Show Potential Outcomes. You will need to register and log in to access the tool.

IN THIS CHAPTER

» Understanding floor ETFs and how they work

» Distinguishing between conventional and managed floor ETFs

» Considering ways to use floor ETFs in your portfolio

» Researching floor ETFs

Chapter 16

Limiting Your Downside with Floor ETFs

Investing in the stock market can be scary, even when you have a buffer to provide some downside protection. You may worry about what would happen to your nest egg if the U.S. were to experience another Great Depression, when the stock market dropped nearly 90 percent from its peak. A moderate 15 percent buffer would be little consolation, especially if you were really counting on that money for retirement.

Well, the developers of buffer ETFs have recognized that concern and developed unique ETFs to address it. Commonly referred to as *floor ETFs*, instead of buffering against an initial loss (say the first 10 or 20 percent loss), these funds have investors absorbing the initial loss (usually no more than 5 or 10 percent), and then they protect against any further loss.

REMEMBER

If you're a risk-averse investor wanting to participate in the stock market's upside while minimizing the risk of larger losses, and you can tolerate a small loss, a floor ETF may be the perfect solution.

This chapter brings you up to speed on the basics of floor ETFs and how they work, introduces you to two types of floor products — conventional and managed, helps you weigh their pros and cons, and reveals various ways you can use floor ETFs to help meet your investment objectives. It also introduces you to a variety of floor products you may want to consider.

Getting Up To Speed on Floor ETF Basics

A *floor ETF* is an exchange-traded fund that provides downside protection below a specified level (the floor) and some participation in market gains over a specified outcome period. If the floor is −5 percent, the most you stand to lose is 5 percent (before fees). Figure 16-1 illustrates the overall behavior of Innovator's 20+ Year Treasury Bond 5 Floor ETF in both positive and negative markets, highlighting the fund's deepest possible loss (floor) and maximum potential upside (cap).

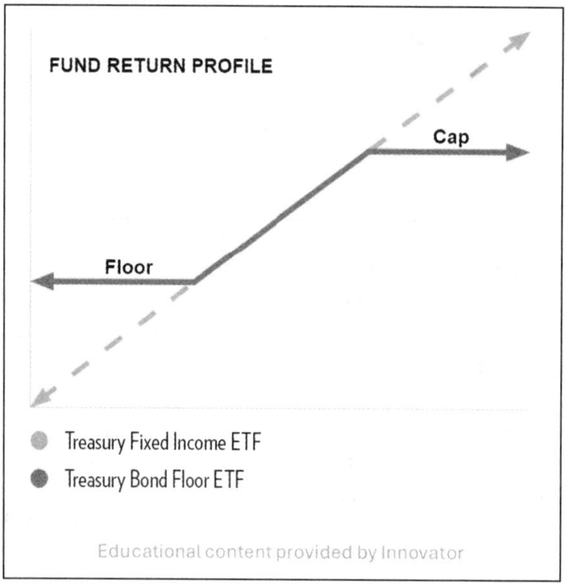

FIGURE 16-1: With a floor ETF, you absorb the initial loss and are protected against any further loss.

Courtesy of Innovator

The following sections take a deeper dive into floor ETFs, explaining how they work, the difference between conventional and managed floor ETFs, and the potential advantages and disadvantages of these products.

Understanding how floor ETFs work

TECHNICAL STUFF

Managed Floor ETFs combine traditional equity exposure with a structured options-based risk management overlay. The strategy typically consists of the following three components:

- **Equity basket (to track the reference asset):** Each fund holds a broad mix of stocks from a specific market index (for example, S&P 500, Nasdaq-100). The carefully selected sample enables the fund to follow the index's performance and creates opportunities for *tax-loss harvesting*.

TIP

Tax-loss harvesting means selling stocks that have declined in value to realize losses that can help reduce taxable gains.

- **Put protection (for downside protection):** The fund buys put options, which are contracts that increase in value when the market falls. Specifically, the fund buys put options that are 10 percent *out of the money*, meaning the options start to pay off only after the market has dropped about 10 percent. The puts establish the floor, which helps to mitigate losses during deep market declines. In this example, the options protect approximately 90 percent of the investor's capital.
- **Call writing (to generate income):** To help pay for the cost of the downside protection, the fund sells call options, which establish the cap. A *call option* gives the buyer the right to purchase stocks from the fund at a fixed price. When the fund sells calls, it receives cash (a *premium*). The fund sells short-term calls (often expiring every two weeks) and chooses strike prices that have a low probability of being reached. (The *strike price* is the fixed price at which the owner of the option can purchase the stock.) With this strategy, if the market rises moderately, the fund keeps the premium paid for the options and participates in the gain. However, if the market rises sharply above the strike price, gains are limited because the fund must sell the stock at the agreed-upon strike price.

Comparing conventional floor ETFs to managed floor ETFs

Floor ETFs come in two varieties:

- **Conventional floor ETFs** have a hard floor (for downside protection) and ceiling (cap), as illustrated in Figure 16-1. Gains are limited to the cap, and losses are limited to the floor.

- **Managed floor ETFs** have no ceiling and a softer floor. They don't cap upside performance, but upside participation may be limited to about 70 to 80 percent of the reference asset's upside performance. And instead of using a fixed percentage for the maximum loss, these funds have a range, such as –8 to –12 percent. Figure 16-2 illustrates how managed floor ETFs behave compared to conventional floor ETFs. This structure is designed to better preserve accumulated gains and provide a more durable defense during deep market sell-offs.

TECHNICAL STUFF

Managed floor ETFs use put options laddered quarterly to create a more gradual transition to the floor, helping to mitigate losses during deep market declines.

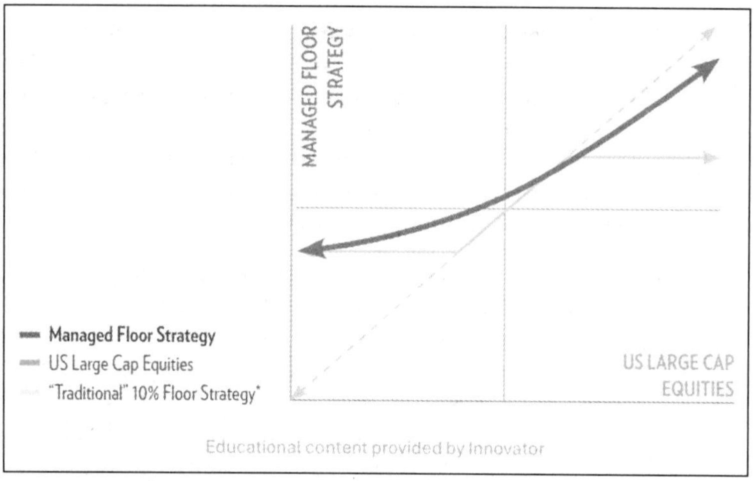

FIGURE 16-2: A managed floor ETF has a softer floor and more upside potential.

Courtesy of Innovator

Figure 16-3 illustrates the loss-dampening profile of the Innovator Equity Managed Floor ETF (SFLR) from January 1 through April 30, 2025 — a period that included a sharp equity market sell-off beginning on February 20.

Over this period of decline, SFLR began to decouple from the broader equity index as market losses intensified, with downside participation becoming increasingly limited. This pattern of resilience during sharp drawdowns — where losses are meaningfully reduced relative to the benchmark — is referred to as *crisis alpha*.

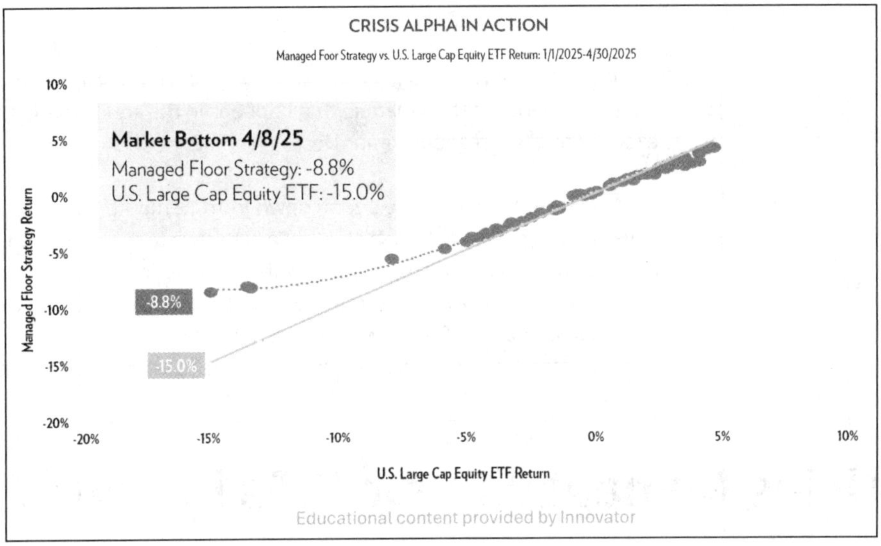

FIGURE 16-3: Managed floor ETFs improve downside protection during deep drawdowns.

Courtesy of Innovator

Weighing floor ETF pros and cons

Floor ETFs have many of the same benefits of buffer ETFs — downside protection, upside participation (to a cap or not), liquidity, transparency, tax-efficiency, and no credit risk, and they can be held indefinitely, rebalancing at the beginning of each outcome period. The big advantage they offer over most conventional buffer ETFs is that they seek to provide downside protection against deeper losses.

One disadvantage of floor ETFs, compared to conventional buffer ETFs, is that initial losses are absorbed by the shareholder. And, with managed floor ETFs, "initial losses" aren't clearly defined — it's a range, typically about 5 to 12 percent, depending on the fund.

WHY A FLOOR ETF?

I interviewed Johan Grahn, former Head ETF Strategist at Allianz Investment Management LLC, shortly after AllianzIM had launched its first floor ETF. During the interview, I asked him to tell me more about their floor ETF and why investors might find the strategy attractive. His response:

> "The floor strategy is effectively in place so that you can lose no more than 5 percent over the course of the full outcome period (gross of fees). Our fees are 74 basis points [0.74 percent], annualized, which means it's half of that for a 6-month period."

(continued)

(continued)

"So, it can be used as a very conservative allocation for any investor, frankly. It gives them confidence that no matter what happens in the equity market, they're only exposed to a 5 percent maximum loss."

"And we intentionally cut the period down from 12 months to six months so that you have an opportunity to have higher delta exposure to the S&P 500 as it's going up, because in more market environments than not, as you know, the market does go up. [*Delta* is a measure of how much an asset is expected to move when the underlying market moves.] This also allows the floor to be reset at a higher portfolio value every six months without creating a taxable event, since we do this in an ETF."

Using Managed Floor ETFs in Your Portfolio

You can use managed floor ETFs in a variety of ways to meet your investment objectives. Here are a few approaches to consider:

- **Replace a portion of traditional equity exposure:** Substituting a portion of traditional equity holdings with managed floor ETFs may help reduce overall portfolio volatility while maintaining equity exposure.
- **Increase equity exposure with built-in protection:** For investors seeking to modestly increase equity allocations, managed floor ETFs may offer a way to do so with embedded tail-risk protection. (*Tail risk* refers to the probability of an extreme, unexpected market event that results in significant losses.) Protective puts can help cushion severe market losses while keeping the portfolio aligned with long-term investment objectives.
- **Manage drawdown risk for pre-retirees and retirees:** Managed floor ETFs may be particularly well-suited for risk-averse investors or those nearing or in retirement. One of the most significant risks during this stage is *sequence-of-returns risk*, when large losses early in retirement can negatively impact long-term outcomes. By limiting the severity of drawdowns, managed floor ETFs are designed to help mitigate this risk and allow for more stable retirement planning.

Checking Out Some Floor and Managed Floor ETFs

If you're interested in floor or managed floor ETFs, I encourage you to research and compare the following products:

- **AllianzIM Floor ETFs:**
  - **AllianzIM U.S. Equity 6-Month Floor5 — Jan/Jul ETF (FLJJ)** is a 6-month floor ETF that tracks the SPDR S&P 500 ETF Trust (SPY) and limits any loss to 5 percent over the outcome period. At the start of its most recent outcome period on January 1, 2026, FLJJ had a 6-month upside cap of 5.65 percent net of fees. This outcome period will reset on June 30, 2026, at which point the fund will offer the same 5 percent downside floor along with a newly established upside cap for the next 6-month period. FLJJ carries an expense ratio of 0.74 percent annualized (so 0.37 percent for a 6-month period).
  - **AllianzIM U.S. Equity 6-Month Floor5 — Apr/Oct ETF (FLAO)** is a 6-month floor ETF that tracks the SPDR S&P 500 ETF Trust (SPY) and limits any loss to 5 percent over the outcome period. At the start of its most recent outcome period on October 1, 2025, FLAO had a 6-month upside cap of 5.58 net of fees. The fund will reset on March 31, 2026, providing a new upside cap while maintaining the same 5 percent downside floor. FLAO has an expense ratio of 0.74 percent annualized.
- **Innovator Floor and Managed Floor ETFs:**
  - **Innovator 20+ Year Treasury Bond 5 Floor ETF (TFJL)** is a 3-month (quarterly) conventional floor ETF that seeks to provide the upside performance of the price return of the iShares 20+ Year Treasury Bond ETF (TLT), to a cap, with a maximum loss of 5 percent over the outcome period. It has an expense ratio of 0.79 percent.
  - **Innovator Equity Managed Floor ETF (SFLR)** seeks to provide capital appreciation through participation in large-cap U.S. equities while seeking to manage risk through a portfolio of 12-month puts, laddered so that one resets each quarter. It's designed to provide 70 to 80 percent upside participation while limiting the maximum potential loss to 8 to 12 percent with ⅔ of index volatility. It carries an annualized expense ratio of 0.89 percent.

- **Innovator Nasdaq-100 Managed Floor ETF (QFLR)** seeks to provide capital appreciation through participation in Nasdaq-100 equities while seeking to manage risk through a portfolio of 12-month puts, laddered so that one resets each quarter. It's designed to provide 70 to 80 percent upside participation while limiting the maximum potential loss to 7 to 15 percent with ⅔ of index volatility. It carries an expense ratio of 0.89 percent annualized.
- **Innovator U.S. Small Cap Managed Floor ETF (RFLR)** seeks to provide capital appreciation through participation in Russell 2000 equities while seeking to manage risk through a portfolio of 12-month puts, laddered so that one resets each quarter. It's designed to provide 70 to 80 percent upside participation while limiting the maximum potential loss to 8 to 12 percent with ⅔ of index volatility. It carries an expense ratio of 0.89 percent annualized.
- **Innovator International Developed Managed Floor ETF (IFLR)** seeks to provide capital appreciation through participation in international developed equities while seeking to manage risk through a portfolio of 12-month puts, laddered so that one resets each quarter. It's designed to provide 70 to 80 percent upside participation in international equities (EFA) while limiting the maximum potential loss to 8 to 12 percent with ⅔ of index volatility. It carries an expense ratio of 0.89 percent annualized.

Innovator Managed Floor ETFs are sub-advised by Parametric Portfolio Associates, LLC. Parametric has over 30 years of experience in institutional options-based strategies and manages more than $660 billion in assets.

REMEMBER

Calamos and other issuers offer floor ETFs that track bitcoin. See Chapter 17 for more about these funds.

IN THIS CHAPTER

» Recognizing the risk of investing in bitcoin

» Using a buffer or floor ETF to reduce the potential downside

» Adding gold to your portfolio with a buffered gold ETF

» Checking out available bitcoin and gold buffer and floor ETFs

Chapter 17

Investing in Bitcoin and Gold with Downside Protection

If you've ever considered investing in bitcoin or gold but hesitated because of the risk, a bitcoin or gold ETF that provides downside protection can make that idea more appealing. ETFs simplify investing in these assets, buffer ETFs curtail some of the risk, and this chapter provides the guidance you need to decide whether a bitcoin or gold ETF with downside protection might be a good addition to your portfolio.

Getting Up To Speed on Investing in Bitcoin

Bitcoin is a digital currency that operates without a central authority, such as a government or a bank. It runs on a public *blockchain* — a distributed ledger that records transactions. You can use it to pay online for certain products and services.

From an investor's perspective, bitcoin is a digital asset that can serve different roles, such as the following:

- **Speculative asset:** Bitcoin is a high–volatility asset whose value is driven by supply and demand and influenced by sentiment, liquidity, and *macro trends* (large, broad forces, such as inflation and economic growth that affect the overall economy and financial markets).
- **Digital store of value:** Bitcoin is often compared to gold because its supply is capped (at 21 million coins), it can't be printed or devalued by a central authority, and it's portable and globally accessible.
- **Portfolio diversifier:** Bitcoin is a non-traditional asset that has a historically low to moderate correlation with stocks and bonds, although this correlation varies over time.
- **Hedge against monetary instability:** Because bitcoin provides a decentralized financial infrastructure, it can serve as a hedge against sovereign debt risk (such as a government default) or financial system instability.

Even though bitcoin's total market value has fallen from its peak of about $2.4 trillion in October 2025 to roughly $1.3 trillion in April 2026, it's increasingly viewed as a global store of value. However, most investors remain underinvested (or not invested at all) in bitcoin. The issue isn't a lack of belief in bitcoin's long-term potential; rather, it's the difficulty of fitting a highly volatile asset with meaningful downside risk into a traditional portfolio.

In this section, I explain why bitcoin historically has been difficult to own, why it can be beneficial, and how buffer ETFs can make it easier to add bitcoin to your portfolio.

Understanding why bitcoin is hard to own

Bitcoin has a very distinctive return profile that can make it difficult to own even for investors who have a relatively high tolerance for risk:

- Historically strong long-term returns
- Low correlation to stocks, bonds, and gold
- Extremely high volatility
- *Fat-tailed downside risk* — the possibility of large, severe losses occurring more frequently than traditional models would predict

Even a small allocation in bitcoin can meaningfully change a portfolio's risk profile. For many investors, the extreme volatility simply exceeds their comfort level. Investing in bitcoin has often felt like a purely speculative proposition.

Considering a new approach: Bitcoin floor and buffer ETFs

Bitcoin floor and buffer ETFs aim to reshape bitcoin's risk profile. Instead of full exposure to downside losses, these ETFs:

- Retain exposure to a portion of bitcoin's upside
- Limit or eliminate losses beyond a predefined level
- Use defined 12-month outcome periods

By removing most extreme-loss scenarios, bitcoin floor and buffer ETFs allow investors to focus on long-term outcomes, rather than short-term price volatility. Importantly, bitcoin exposure can now be positioned intentionally within a portfolio — alongside fixed income, equities, or gold — rather than treated as a speculative outlier.

WHAT THE DATA SHOW

Calamos evaluated its three Protected Bitcoin Strategies, which provide 100, 90, and 80 percent downside protection, from April 2019 through June 2025, to see how they stacked up against bitcoin, equities, gold, and fixed-income. Here's what they found:

Strategy	Average drawdown	Average loss
Bitcoin	-30.30%	-12.70%
80% Protected Bitcoin	-10.61%	-3.87%
Equities	-11.81%	-4.16%
90% Protected Bitcoin	-5.36%	-2.38%
Gold	-8.66%	-2.54%
100% Protected Bitcoin	-0.45%	-0.27%
Fixed Income	-2.42%	-0.82%

(continued)

(continued)

The findings show that all three of Calamos' Protected Bitcoin Strategies:

- Significantly reduced volatility and drawdowns
- Exhibited low correlation to stocks, bonds, and gold
- Preserved bitcoin's diversification benefits

The key takeaway here, from the perspective of portfolio creation, is that buffered bitcoin strategies enable investors to gain exposure to bitcoin without assuming unlimited downside risk.

Finding a place for bitcoin floor or buffer ETFs in your portfolio

Because bitcoin has a low correlation to stocks, bonds, and gold, it can help diversify your total portfolio. Investing in bitcoin via a floor or buffer ETF can reduce the risk, and even though it limits the upside potential, it provides you with exposure to an asset that may rise when everything else is falling.

Consider adding a small allocation in bitcoin floor or buffer ETFs to your portfolio. You can use the ETF to replace a portion of any existing allocation in bitcoin, equities, gold, or fixed-income:

- **Bitcoin:** If you already have an allocation in bitcoin, consider replacing all or a portion of it with a bitcoin buffer or floor ETF that has 80 percent downside protection. Typically, this level of downside protection still allows for significant upside potential.
- **Equities:** If you're replacing a portion of your allocation in equities with a bitcoin floor or buffer ETF, consider choosing one that has 80 or 90 percent downside protection, so it has more upside potential. Obviously, you have to be willing to absorb a fairly large percentage of initial losses during the outcome period (10 or 20 percent), but these ETFs would give you the highest upside potential.
- **Gold:** If you're replacing a portion of your allocation in gold with a bitcoin floor or buffer ETF, consider choosing one that has 90 percent downside protection.
- **Fixed-income:** If you're replacing a portion of your allocation in fixed-income with a bitcoin floor or buffer ETF, consider choosing one that has 100 percent downside protection.

Using a Buffer ETF to Add Gold to Your Portfolio

Gold can be a valuable addition to any investment portfolio because it offers the following benefits:

- **Diversification:** Gold behaves differently than stocks, bonds, and real estate because its price isn't tied to corporate earnings (like equities) or interest payments (like bonds). Gold's price is typically driven by inflation, currency strength, geopolitical stress, and central bank policy.
- **Hedge against inflation and currency risk:** Gold is a store of value that generally preserves purchasing power better than cash. When the U.S. dollar weakens, the price of gold often rises.
- **Crisis protection:** During periods of financial stress, such as banking crises, geopolitical conflict, and high market volatility, investment capital often flows into gold, elevating its price.
- **Volatility reduction:** Even a modest allocation of 5 to 10 percent in gold can help reduce overall portfolio volatility and potentially improve risk-adjusted returns.

A gold buffer ETF, such as FT Vest Gold Strategy Quarterly Buffer ETF (BGLD), enables you to participate in gold's potential upside with a range of downside protection — from –5 to –15 percent. Compare the hypothetical performance of BGLD to SPDR Gold Trust (GLD) in the following market scenarios:

- **Very negative scenario:** In a very negative scenario (GLD loses more than 15 percent), BGLD loses 10 percent less (minus fees).
- **Negative scenario:** In a negative scenario (GLD loses more than 5 percent up to 15 percent), BGLD loses 5 percent (minus fees).
- **Slightly negative scenario:** If GLD suffers a loss not exceeding 5 percent, BGLD loses the same amount (minus fees).
- **Positive (below-cap) scenario:** BGLD rises the same amount (minus fees) as GLD until GLD reaches the cap.
- **Positive (capped) scenario:** If GLD rises above the cap, BGLD's price is limited to the cap.

REMEMBER

Consider adding a small allocation of BGLD to your portfolio if you'd like some exposure to gold but with a level of downside protection.

WARNING

BGLD issued a taxable distribution of $7.58 per share on December 31, 2025, which represented nearly 30 percent of its value at the time. Because of its structure, BGLD could distribute more taxable gains in the future. You may prefer to own BGLD in a tax-deferred account to avoid having to pay taxes on any future distributions. In addition, if you want to maintain consistent exposure to BGLD over the coming years, it would be a good idea to automatically reinvest any dividends or capital gains distributions. You should be able to set this up for free through your custodian (bank or brokerage firm where your account is held).

Checking Out Bitcoin and Gold Buffer ETFs

If you're interested in adding a buffer or floor bitcoin ETF to your portfolio, you have plenty to choose from. However, only one buffer ETF is available for purchase that tracks the price of gold. This section introduces you to currently available investment options.

Calamos Protected Bitcoin ETFs

Calamos is the leading issuer of bitcoin floor and buffer ETFs. As of this writing, Calamos offers three 12-month series, each with an expense ratio of 0.69 percent:

- **Bitcoin Structured Alt Protection ETFs** are four 12-month ETFs with 100 percent downside protection, and reset dates at 3-month intervals — CBOJ (January), CBOA (April), CBOY (July), and CBOO (October).
- **Bitcoin 90 Series Structured Alt Protection ETFs** are four 12-month ETFs with 90 percent downside protection (from –10 to –100 percent) and reset dates at 3-month intervals — CBXJ (January), CBXA (April), CBXY (July), and CBXO (October).
- **Bitcoin 80 Series Structured Alt Protection ETFs** are four 12-month ETFs with 80 percent downside protection (–20 to –100 percent) and reset dates at 3-month intervals — CBTJ (January), CBTA (April), CBTY (July), and CBTO (October).

REMEMBER

The deeper the buffer, the lower the cap. This rule of thumb is evident in the starting caps of Calamos Bitcoin Structured Alt Protection ETFs on February 2, 2026 (see Table 17-1):

TABLE 17-1 The Deeper the Buffer, the Lower the Cap

Fund	Buffer	Cap
CBOJ	100%	7.67%
CBXJ 90 Series	90%	21.55%
CBTJ 80 Series	80%	36.81%

Calamos also offers laddered versions, which spread exposure across multiple outcome periods to reduce timing risk. Each of the following ETFs comprises four Calamos 12-month buffered bitcoin ETFs with a single ticker symbol that has an expense ratio of 0.79 percent:

- **Laddered Bitcoin Structured Alt Protection ETF (CBOL)** comprises the four ETFs that make up the Calamos Bitcoin Alt Protection ETF series — CBOO, CBOY, CBOA, CBOJ. Each fund in the ladder offers 100 percent downside protection.
- **Laddered Bitcoin 90 Series Structured Alt Protection ETF (CBXL)** comprises the four funds that make up the Calamos Bitcoin 90 Series Structured Alt Protection ETF series — CBXO, CBXY, CBXA, CBXJ. Each fund in the ladder offers 90 percent downside protection (from –10 to –100 percent).
- **Laddered Bitcoin 80 Series Structured Alt Protection ETF (CBTL)** comprises the four funds that make up the Calamos Bitcoin 80 Series Structured Alt Protection ETF series — CBTO, CBTY, CBTA, CBTJ. Each fund in the ladder offers 80 percent downside protection (from –20 to –100 percent).

See Chapter 12 for an explanation of how laddered buffer ETFs work.

Other bitcoin floor ETF options

First Trust (FT) Vest and Innovator also offer bitcoin floor ETFs. With a floor ETF, you absorb any initial loss (for example, the first 0 to –15 percent) and are protected against any further loss. Check out the following offerings:

- **FT Vest Bitcoin Strategy Floor 15 ETFs** are four 12-month funds that provide downside protection beyond the first 15 percent loss (from –15 to –100 percent) — BFJA (January), BFAP (April), BFJL (July), BFOC (October). The expense ratio for each of these funds is 0.90 percent.
- **Innovator Uncapped Bitcoin 20 Floor ETF (QBF)** is a quarterly fund that provides protection beyond the first 20 percent loss (from –20 to –100 percent) and has an annual expense ratio of 0.79 percent (about 0.20 percent per quarter). QBF is somewhat unique in the bitcoin buffer

ETF space because it offers uncapped upside over each quarterly outcome period. However, an investor must be willing to accept a large potential initial loss in the price of bitcoin (–20 percent) every quarter, which makes QBF highly speculative.

FT Vest's Gold Buffer ETF

As of this writing, FT Vest is the only issuer of a buffer ETF that uses gold as its reference asset. FT Vest Gold Strategy Quarterly Buffer ETF (BGLD) is an actively managed ETF that seeks to provide investors with returns (before fees, expenses, and taxes) that match those of the SPDR Gold Trust (GLD), up to a predetermined upside cap, while providing a buffer against GLD losses between −5 and −15 percent over its quarterly outcome period.

IN THIS CHAPTER

» Understanding what buffer and barrier income ETFs are and how they work

» Seeing how buffer and barrier income ETFs stack up against bonds

» Looking into available buffer and barrier income ETFs

» Achieving growth and income by buying during the Intra-outcome period

Chapter 18

Investing for Cash Flow with Buffer and Barrier Income ETFs

If your investment objective is to generate a predictable and stable income stream, consider buffer and barrier income ETFs. They blend downside risk management and income generation into a single rules-based investment strategy. Built on options that track a reference asset (for example, SPDR S&P 500 ETF Trust), these funds are designed to protect against a defined percentage of market losses while generating stable income (monthly or quarterly distributions), typically in exchange for any upside potential. The result is a return profile positioned between stocks and traditional income strategies, potentially offering a smoother ride for investors who prioritize cash flow and risk control over growth.

In this chapter, you discover what buffer and barrier income ETFs are, how they generate income, their pros and cons, how they stack up against each other and against bonds, and how to use them to help meet your investment objectives.

I also introduce you to several buffer and barrier income ETFs you may want to consider.

Brushing Up on Buffer and Barrier Income ETF Basics

Buffer and barrier income ETFs are engineered to generate meaningful income return potential in both positive and negative markets while protecting against initial losses. They're structured around the following four building blocks:

- **Outcome period:** The 12-month period over which the defined outcome is realized.
- **Reference asset:** The underlying asset the fund tracks, typically the SPDR S&P 500 ETF Trust (SPY).
- **Buffer or barrier:** The range of any reference-asset losses the fund protects against. Here's where buffer and barrier income ETFs differ:
  - A *buffer income ETF* protects against the first portion of the reference asset's losses; for example, 0 to –15 percent. The investor absorbs any loss that exceeds the buffer. For example, if the fund has a 15 percent buffer, and the reference asset loses 20 percent, the fund's *net asset value* (*NAV* = the dollar value of its shares) drops 5 percent.
  - A *barrier income ETF* offers *conditional* protection against the first portion of the reference asset's losses; for example, a 30 percent barrier income ETF protects against the first 0 to –30 percent loss but only if the loss is short of the defined barrier. If the barrier is breached, the investor absorbs the *entire* loss. So, if the reference asset loses 30 percent, the fund's NAV loses nothing (except expenses), but if the reference asset loses 31 percent, the NAV drops 31 percent.

  The fund's value may fluctuate during the outcome period and can decline during the intra-outcome period if the reference asset falls, especially as it nears the buffer or barrier threshold. However, a breach occurs only if the reference asset is below the lower protection level at the close of trading on the final day of the outcome period.
- **Income (distribution rate):** The predetermined amount, as a percentage of the fund's value, the fund seeks to distribute over the full outcome period. Buffer and barrier income ETFs seek to provide predictable income regardless of whether the reference asset losses exceed the buffer/barrier.

The fund's *total return* is the increase or decrease in the fund's NAV plus distributions. For example, suppose you own a 15 percent buffer income ETF that pays 8 percent in distributions annually, and its reference asset shows a loss of 20 percent at the end of the fund's outcome period. The fund's total return would be 3 percent (less expenses): −5 percent (the loss exceeding the buffer) plus 8 percent (in the form of annualized monthly distributions).

REMEMBER

Generally, the shallower the buffer, the higher the distribution rate.

Figure 18-1 illustrates how a buffer income ETF with a 15 percent buffer and an 8 percent distribution rate would be expected to perform under the following market conditions (not accounting for expenses, which are typically less than one percent per year):

- **Negative scenario (buffer level is breached):** If the reference asset's losses were to exceed the buffer, the investor would still receive the 8 percent in distributions, but the total return could be negative. For example, if the reference asset (U.S. Large Cap Equity ETF) were to decline by 30 percent, the buffer income ETF would lose 15 percent. The total return would be -7 percent, because the ETF provided distributions totaling 8 percent during the outcome period (-15 percent + 8 percent = -7 percent). The share price would be reduced by 15 percent.

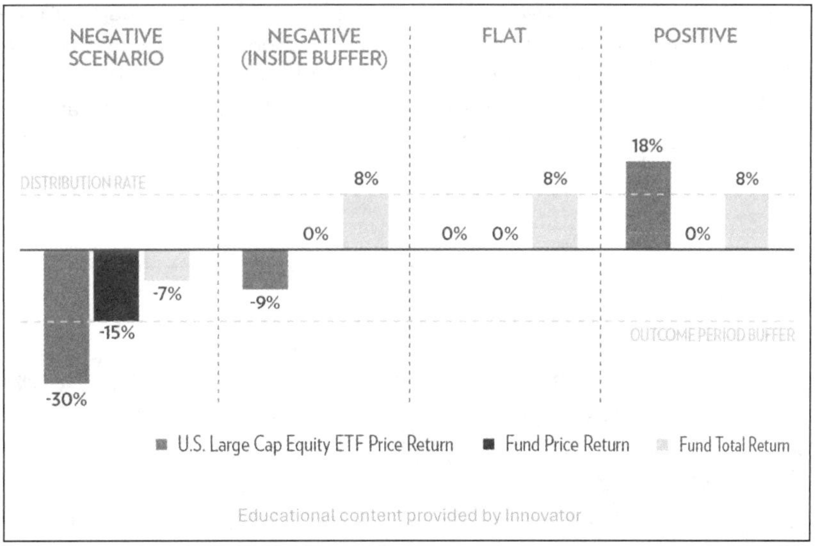

Courtesy of Innovator

FIGURE 18-1: Hypothetical performance of a 15 percent buffer income ETF with an 8 percent distribution rate.

» **Negative scenario (inside the buffer):** If the reference asset were to suffer a 9 percent loss (or any loss up to –15 percent), the share price would stay about the same, and the fund would pay 8 percent in distributions.

» **Flat:** If the reference asset neither gained nor lost value, the share price would stay about the same, and the fund would pay 8 percent in distributions, which would equal the fund's total return.

» **Positive scenario:** If the reference asset produced a positive return, the share price would stay about the same, and the fund would pay 8 percent in distributions, which would equal the fund's total return.

REMEMBER

With buffer and barrier income ETFs, you're getting income along with downside protection in exchange for having no upside participation. Notice that in none of the scenarios is the fund's price return greater than the distribution rate.

Barrier income ETFs behave differently. If the reference asset experiences a loss that breaches the barrier, the fund's NAV absorbs the entire loss. However, the fund would pay all scheduled distributions, thereby reducing the fund's total loss. Figure 18-2 illustrates how a barrier income ETF with a 20 percent barrier and an 8 percent distribution rate would be expected to perform under the following market conditions (not accounting for expenses, which are typically less than one percent per year):

» **Very negative scenario (barrier is breached):** If the reference asset's losses were to breach the barrier, the investor would still receive 8 percent in distributions, but the total return could show a large loss. For example, if the reference asset were to decline by 40 percent, the ETF's NAV would lose 40 percent. The total return would be –32 percent because the ETF provided distributions totaling 8 percent during the outcome period (–40 percent + 8 percent = –32 percent). The share price would be reduced by 40 percent.

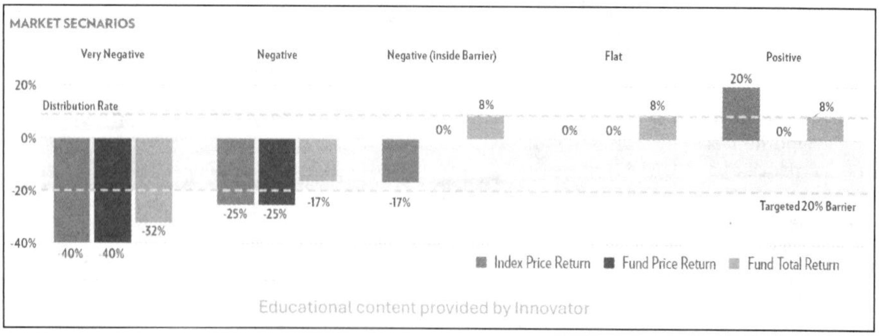

FIGURE 18-2: Hypothetical performance of a 20 percent barrier income ETF with an 8 percent distribution rate.

Courtesy of Innovator

- **Negative scenario (barrier is breached):** If the reference asset were to suffer a 25 percent loss, the fund's NAV would also lose 25 percent. The fund would pay 8 percent in distributions, so the total loss would be 17 percent (–25 percent + 8 percent = –17 percent).
- **Negative (inside barrier):** If the reference asset were to suffer a 17 percent loss (or any loss to –20 percent), the fund's NAV would stay about the same, and the fund would pay 8 percent in distributions, which would equal the fund's total return.
- **Flat:** If the reference asset neither gained nor lost value, the fund's NAV would stay about the same, and the fund would pay 8 percent in distributions, which would equal the fund's total return.
- **Positive scenario:** If the reference asset produced a positive return, the share price would stay about the same, and the fund would pay 8 percent in distributions, which would equal the fund's total return.

WARNING

Barrier income ETFs can be very risky. If the reference asset shows a loss that exceeds the barrier at the end of the outcome period, you absorb all losses. Theoretically, an extreme drop in the reference asset could crush your position.

The following sections take a deeper dive into buffer and barrier income ETFs, explaining how they generate income, revealing their pros and cons, and showing you how to calculate a buffer or barrier income ETF's break-even point.

Understanding how buffer and barrier income ETFs generate income

Buffer and barrier income ETFs seek to generate relatively high rates of income through a combination of option premiums and U.S. Treasury bills. The process goes like this (see Figure 18-3):

1. **Sell a one-year FLEX put option.**
2. **Collect the option premium.**
3. **Invest in short-term U.S. Treasury bills.**
4. **Make regular distributions to investors.**

Typically, distributions are made monthly for buffer income ETFs and quarterly for barrier income ETFs. The final distribution of each outcome period is made the same day the ETF resets its distribution rate and buffer.

HOW DISTRIBUTIONS ARE PAID

Distributions follow a schedule that includes an ex-date, record date, and payment date:

- **Ex-date** is a cutoff date when new owners of the ETF are no longer entitled to the upcoming income distribution. At market open on the ex-date, the NAV of the ETF will drop by the amount of the upcoming distribution.
- **Record date** is the last trading day of the month or quarter, depending on the ETF series. Owners of the ETF on the record date will receive a distribution on the payment date.
- **Payment date** is the first trading day of the next month or quarter, depending on the ETF series.

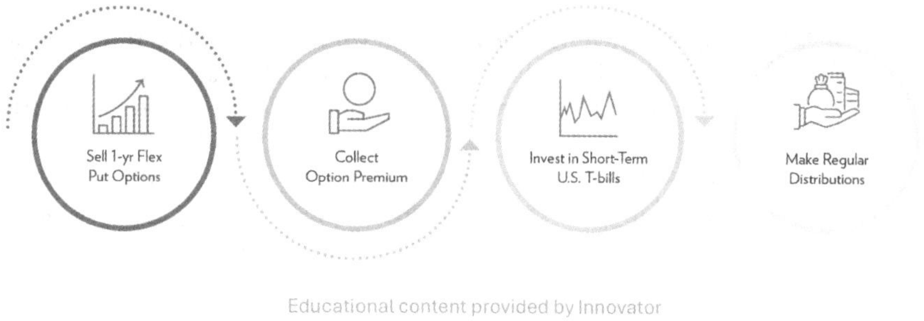

FIGURE 18-3: How buffer income ETFs generate income.

Courtesy of Innovator

WARNING

A fund's distribution rate is not guaranteed. It's set at the start of each outcome period and is based on the premium received from sold option contracts and the fund's investments in U.S. T-bills.

Weighing buffer and barrier income ETF pros and cons

Buffer and barrier income ETFs offer two big benefits:

- Potential downside protection to provide a buffer against losses in the reference asset. Note, with barrier income ETFs, the protection is conditional.
- Predictable monthly or quarterly income.

Buffer and barrier ETFs also rebalance/reset annually, and you can hold them indefinitely.

WARNING

In exchange for downside protection and income, you forfeit all upside participation (growth) in the reference asset. The fund's *net asset value (NAV)*, its dollar value per share, will not appreciate in positive markets.

Considering the break-even point

The *break-even point* is the maximum loss the reference asset could incur over the fund's full 12-month outcome period for the fund to not produce a negative total return after factoring in the distribution rate. To determine the break-even point, add the buffer or barrier percentage to the distribution rate. For example, for a buffer income ETF that has a 15 percent buffer and a 7.5 percent distribution rate, its break-even point is 15 percent plus 7.5 percent for a total of 22.5 percent. In other words, the reference asset would need to lose more than 22.5 percent (before expenses) for the shareholder to suffer a loss.

Consider another example: if a buffer income ETF has 15 percent protection with a 6 percent distribution rate, the break-even point for the reference asset is a loss of 21 percent. A shareholder is protected against the first 15 percent loss, and if SPY (reference asset) declined a total of 21 percent, the shareholder would still break even after factoring in the 6 percent income stream.

Comparing Buffer and Barrier Income ETFs to Bonds

Buffer and barrier income ETFs are often discussed in the context of bonds because they're used for risk management and income generation. However, they are fundamentally different investment vehicles. Understanding how each works and recognizing their respective pros and cons can help you use them together or separately to help achieve your investment objectives.

Grasping bond basics

Bonds are contractual debt instruments, like a mortgage or an IOU. They enable you to loan money to an issuer in exchange for interest payments and the return of *principal* (the amount of the loan) when the bonds reach their maturity date (assuming the issuer hasn't defaulted on the loan).

Bonds are often held in investment portfolios to:

- Preserve capital
- Provide a reliable source of income
- Reduce overall portfolio volatility
- Diversify the portfolio and offset equity risk — when stock prices go down, bond prices generally hold steady (but not always)

Bonds have several characteristics that make them useful for mitigating risk and generating income:

- **Predictable income:** Regular interest payments are defined upfront.
- **Reduced risk:** If the issuer declares bankruptcy, bondholders may be paid before equity shareholders.
- **Defined maturity:** Investors can hold bonds to maturity to reduce price risk. Assuming the issuer doesn't default, and you hold the bonds to maturity, you'll get your original investment back, with one caveat. If you purchase bonds at a premium price (above par), then you will only get "par value" back at maturity, so you could see a loss on the actual bond position.
- **Diversification:** High-quality bonds often retain their value when equities struggle.

Bonds are not risk-free. Primary risks include the following:

- **Interest-rate risk:** Bond prices tend to fall when interest rates rise.
- **Credit risk:** The issuer may default, or there could be a downgrade that negatively impacts the price of the bond.
- **Inflation risk:** Fixed payments lose purchasing power.

Seeing how buffer and barrier income ETFs stack up against bonds

Like bonds, buffer and barrier income ETFs are used primarily to generate income. So, what makes them different? Here are some of the potential advantages buffer and barrier income ETFs have over bonds:

- **Higher income potential:** Buffer and barrier income ETFs can generate higher income than many high-quality bonds, especially in market environments with elevated volatility and interest rates.
- **Partial downside protection:** The fund's buffer or barrier absorbs the first portion of market declines in the reference asset. Bonds have built-in downside protection, too, assuming you hold the bond to maturity, and the issuer doesn't default.
- **No credit risk:** Buffer and barrier income ETFs aren't exposed to potential losses due to a downgrade or default. However, they're not risk-free. The fund's NAV may produce a negative return if the buffer or barrier is breached.

Buffer and barrier income ETFs also have some disadvantages compared to bonds, including the following:

- **No return of principal:** When bonds mature, you get your money back (assuming no default by the lender). With a buffer or barrier income ETF, there is no "return of principal" because you didn't loan your money to anyone (as you would do with a bond). If the buffer is breached, you could lose money if the "breach" is more than the amount of income you received. Barrier income ETFs will provide no protection if the barrier is breached.
- **Higher correlation to equities:** Buffer and barrier income ETF performance is tied to equity markets and can lose value during severe market downturns, whereas high-quality bonds generally (but not always) act as a hedge against stock market losses, retaining their value.
- **Higher expense ratios:** Buffer and barrier income ETF expense ratios are typically higher than those of bond mutual funds and bond ETFs.

REMEMBER

Buffer and barrier income ETFs and bonds are not mutually exclusive. You can hold all in a balanced portfolio, along with equities, capped or uncapped buffer ETFs, traditional ETFs, and other investment vehicles.

Checking Out Available Buffer and Barrier Income ETFs

If buffer or barrier income ETFs seem like a good fit for your portfolio, consider looking into the following ETFs:

- **Innovator Premium Income 15 Buffer ETF:** Innovator has four 15 percent buffer income ETFs that are designed to provide investment performance that is equal to the distribution rate while providing a buffer against the first 15 percent loss of the SPDR S&P 500 ETF Trust (SPY): LJAN (January), LAPR (April), LJUL (July), and LOCT (October), all with an annual expense ratio of 0.79 percent. The funds distribute monthly income and reset annually (12-month outcome period).

- **FT Vest U.S. Equity Buffer & Premium Income ETF:** FT Vest has four 10 percent buffer income ETFs that seek to provide investors with a consistent level of income while providing a buffer (before fees and expenses) against the first 10 percent of SPDR S&P 500 ETF Trust (SPY) losses: XIDE (December), XIMR (March), XIJN (June), and XISE (September), all with an annual expense ratio of 0.85 percent. The funds distribute monthly income and reset annually (12-month outcome period).

Generally, the shallower the buffer, the higher the distribution rate. In other words, you're probably going to receive more income from a buffer or barrier income ETF with a 10 percent buffer than one that has a 15 percent buffer. At the start of 2026, Innovator Premium Income 15 ETF (LJAN), which has a 15 percent buffer, offered a net distribution rate of 4.89 percent. In contrast, FT Vest U.S. Equity Buffer & Premium Income ETF — December (XIDE), which has a 10 percent buffer, offered a net distribution rate of 6.20 percent at the start of its new outcome period in late December 2025. So, if you're confident the reference asset (SPY) will not decline more than 10 percent at the end of the outcome period, you could earn an extra 1.31 percent in annual income by purchasing XIDE. Of course, the extra income comes with a higher risk in the form of a shallower buffer.

REMEMBER

Less downside protection translates into a potentially greater income distribution, but also places the value of your investment at increased risk. With a buffer income ETF, if the buffer is breached at the end of the outcome period, the shareholder will absorb any loss beyond the buffer. And, if the buffer is breached at the end of the outcome period of a barrier income ETF, the shareholder will have no protection whatsoever and will lose principal.

WARNING

Innovator offers Premium Income Barrier ETFs with 20 percent and 30 percent downside protection, but this protection is conditional. If the buffer is breached, the fund is fully exposed to all reference asset losses. I would steer clear of barrier income ETFs unless you fully understand and appreciate the risks involved. If you're interested, check out the following funds:

- **Innovator Premium Income 20 Barrier ETF:** Innovator has four 20 percent barrier income ETFs that track the S&P 500: JANH (January), APRH (April), JULH (July), and OCTH (October), all with an annual expense ratio of 0.79 percent. The funds distribute quarterly income and reset annually (12-month outcome period).

» **Innovator Premium Income 30 Barrier ETF:** Innovator has four 30 percent barrier income ETFs that track the S&P 500: JANJ (January), APRJ (April), JULJ (July), and OCTJ (October), all with an annual expense ratio of 0.79 percent. The funds distribute quarterly income and reset annually (12-month outcome period).

Using Buffer and Barrier Income ETFs to Generate Growth and Income

TIP

The biggest drawback of buffer and barrier income ETFs is that they require you to relinquish upside potential. For example, if the reference asset that tracks the S&P 500 produces a 20 percent return, your fund's return is limited to the distributions you receive minus expenses.

However, you may be able to purchase shares of buffer or barrier income ETFs opportunistically during the intra-outcome period to generate both growth and income. For example, if both the reference asset and fund's NAV decline during the outcome period, you could purchase shares of the ETF at a reduced price, and if the fund's share price subsequently increased and remained elevated until the end of the outcome period, the fund's total return would include the increase in the fund's NAV, in addition to any distributions you received.

However, purchasing buffer or barrier income ETFs during the intra-outcome period has some potential drawbacks, such as the following:

» **Reduced or no downside protection:** The remaining buffer or barrier could be less than the starting buffer or barrier. And, if the buffer or barrier has been breached, and the reference asset drops further, you will experience additional losses.

» **Reduced distributions:** If you buy shares following a distribution date, you will not be entitled to distributions made prior to the distribution date and will therefore not receive the full annual defined distribution rate for the outcome period. Similarly, if you sell shares prior to a distribution date, you will not receive the full defined distribution rate for the outcome period and will not be entitled to distributions after the sale.

See Part 3 for more about buying and selling buffer ETFs during the intra-outcome period.

5

Diving into Advanced Buffer ETF Concepts

IN THIS PART . . .

Understand the factors that influence upside caps and use that deeper knowledge to your advantage.

Decide on an outcome period that fits with your investment time horizon.

Decide whether to cash out at the end of an outcome period or roll your investment into the next period.

Consider the possibility of replacing or complementing a bond allocation with buffer ETFs.

Compare buffer ETF structures and understand how they differ from structured notes.

IN THIS CHAPTER

» Recognizing the forces that drive caps up or down

» Deciding when more protection is worth a lower cap

Chapter 19

Getting the Inside Scoop on Upside Caps

Nearly all buffer ETFs have an *upside cap* — the maximum return the ETF can earn over its full outcome period (usually 3, 6, or 12 months). Understanding the factors that drive caps higher and lower is important for determining whether a given cap is reasonable and when it's appropriate with respect to market conditions.

This chapter examines factors that drive caps higher or lower and provides guidance on how to choose the right balance between downside buffer and upside cap.

Evaluating Factors That Influence Upside Cap Levels

To create a buffer and cap, the ETF buys and sells *options* (contracts that grant the ETF the right, but not the obligation, to buy or sell an asset at a fixed price):

- The ETF buys a *put* to create the downside buffer.
- The ETF sells a *put* to help finance the cost of the protective put. This put sale releases the downside protection at the buffer level. A *put option (put)* gives

the owner the right, but not the obligation, to sell an underlying asset (for example, SPY), at a specified price within a specific timeframe.

- The ETF sells a *call* to also help offset the cost of the downside protection. A *call option (call)* gives the owner the right, but not the obligation, to buy an underlying asset (for example, SPY), at a specified price within a specific timeframe. This sale of a call option creates the upside cap.

The cap level is determined by how much premium the ETF can collect relative to how much it needs to spend for downside protection. So, the more money it can get from selling the call, and the less it has to pay for the protective put, the higher the cap.

The two factors that primarily influence call and put option price changes are volatility and interest rates:

- **Volatility:** *Volatility* is a measure of how much share prices fluctuate over time. Higher volatility results in increased prices for both call and put options.
- **Interest rates:** Higher interest rates increase call prices and reduce put prices, driving caps higher. Lower interest rates reduce call prices and increase put prices, pushing caps lower.

Understanding how volatility affects option pricing

TECHNICAL STUFF

Volatility is one of the biggest factors that affects the price of options. When volatility is high, option premiums tend to rise. When volatility is low, option premiums decline. Options derive value from uncertainty. Higher uncertainty regarding the future price of the underlying asset increases the probability of large price moves, making options more valuable.

The more volatile the reference asset, such as SPDR S&P 500 ETF Trust (SPY), in a buffer ETF, the greater the chance an option on SPY will end up "in the money." (*In the money* describes an option contract with intrinsic value. For example, a call option is "in the money" if the reference asset price is above the strike price; a put option is "in the money" if it is below the strike price.) So, increased price volatility of the reference asset generally results in a higher cap.

Understanding why higher interest rates can make call options more valuable

TECHNICAL STUFF

When interest rates rise, borrowing money to buy stocks directly becomes more expensive. Because call options offer a way to control a stock or stock index without buying it outright, they become more attractive when rates rise. For example, if you buy $100,000 worth of SPY *on margin* (borrow money from a brokerage firm to purchase securities by using your holdings as collateral), this form of leverage allows you to buy more shares, increasing potential gains or losses. The cost to use margin is much higher when interest rates are at 6 percent, for example, than when they are at 3 percent. So, a trader may prefer to buy a call option on SPY to avoid paying increased margin interest. With a long call option, a trader can pursue a potential increase in SPY's price without paying margin interest. Therefore, call buyers are generally willing to pay more when rates increase.

(Note, margin rates are primarily determined by the broker call rate, which is the interest rate banks charge brokerage firms to finance margin loans. The base rate is influenced by the federal funds rate set by the Federal Reserve. Brokerage firms typically add their own percentage markup to the base rate to determine the end rate charged to investors.)

You can see how this plays out in the real world by looking at a brief history of upside caps of a 15 percent buffer ETF relative to one-year U.S. Treasury yields, which reflect interest rates (see Figure 19-1). Less than two years after Innovator's launch of its buffer ETFs in 2018, Treasury yields plummeted, putting downward pressure on cap levels. As rates moved higher in 2022, caps also moved higher. The increased volatility of the 2022 bear market also contributed to the rise in cap levels. Driven by rising interest rates *and* volatility, the cap on Innovator's 15 percent U.S. Equity Power Buffer ETF (POCT) peaked at 20.72 percent on its reset date (September 30, 2022). Since then, cap levels have generally come down as market volatility decreased and interest rates stabilized.

TIP

In an environment of rising interest rates and increased volatility, consider buffer ETFs for attractive risk versus reward opportunities — funds that provide the downside protection you may need to stay comfortably invested.

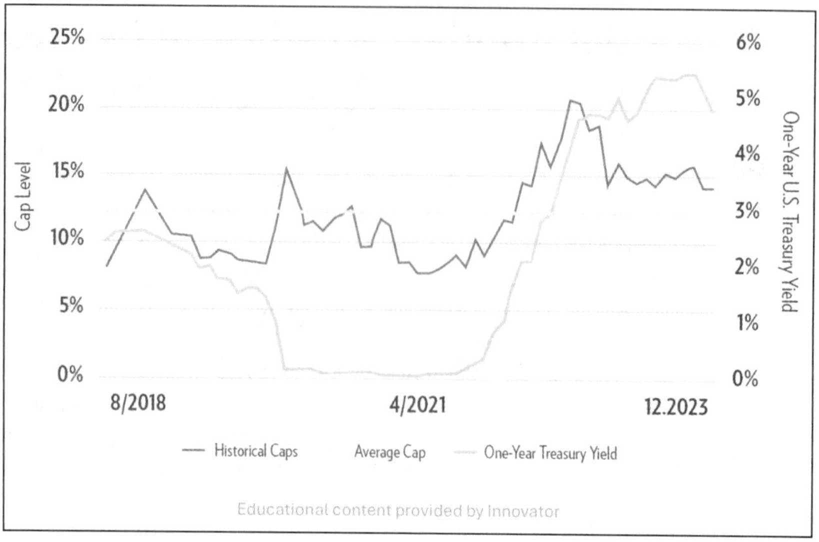

FIGURE 19-1: A 15 percent buffer ETF's caps versus one-year U.S. Treasury yields from 2018 to 2023.

Courtesy of Innovator

Weighing Downside Protection against Upside Caps

One type of ETF you'll never find is one with a 100 percent buffer and no cap. Why? Because with buffer ETFs, the price you pay for the buffer is the cap. All other factors being equal (reference asset, outcome period, and so on), the deeper the buffer, the lower the cap.

When you're shopping for a buffer ETF, you need to decide how much upside potential you're willing to give up for the level of downside protection you want. While a higher cap can be enticing, consider your risk profile and focus on how much downside protection you need to invest comfortably.

Take the following approach to comparison-shop for buffer ETFs that conform to your risk-return profile:

1. **Identify funds that have the level of downside protection you need to remain comfortably invested in the market.** Would you be stressed with only 10 percent downside protection, or would it take 20 to 30 percent or deeper downside protection to calm your nerves? Could you live with potentially suffering an initial 5 percent loss to gain a deeper level of protection? If so, you may want to consider a fund that offers downside protection from –5 to –30 percent, for example.

2. **From the funds that offer the level of downside protection you want, select those that offer the highest upside potential.**

As you compare buffer ETFs, you'll start to notice a close correlation between buffers and caps. For example, FT Vest has two January buffer ETFs — FJAN and GJAN — that differ primarily with respect to their levels of downside protection. In January 2026, they offered the following starting buffers and caps:

- FJAN (10 percent buffer) had a starting cap of 13.68 percent (net of fees).
- GJAN (15 percent buffer) had a starting cap of 10.97 percent (net of fees).

What you would need to decide in this case is whether giving up 5 percent in downside protection would be worth chasing another potential 2.71 percent gain.

How do the caps on minimal and moderate buffer ETFs compare to the caps of deep buffer ETFs? Compare the starting buffers and caps in January 2026 of the following three funds from FT Vest:

- FJAN (10 percent buffer) had a starting cap of 13.68 percent (net of fees).
- GJAN (15 percent buffer) had a starting cap of 10.97 percent (net of fees).
- DJAN (25 percent buffer, downside protection from –5 to –30 percent) had a starting cap of 10.78 percent (net of fees).

As you can see, DJAN offers 10 percent more downside protection than GJAN and nearly the same cap. The reason? The first 5 percent of downside protection is the most expensive. By forfeiting protection on the first 5 percent loss, DJAN can offer nearly the same cap as GJAN while protecting against deeper losses.

DEEPER BUFFER OR HIGHER CAP?

I asked Bruce Bond, co-founder and CEO of Innovator Capital Management LLC, "Are some of your Buffer ETFs more appropriate during bull or bear markets, or sideways, range-bound markets?" Here's what he had to say:

> "The beauty of buffer strategies is that investors don't have to worry about whether the market goes up or down. If the market goes up, a buffer strategy will participate to a predetermined maximum level, and if it goes down, the strategy offers the chosen level of protection. The smaller buffers that have higher caps tend to perform better in positive markets, while the bigger buffers tend to perform better during bear markets."

DON'T OVERLOOK FLOOR ETFS

If you're looking for downside protection beyond what most buffer ETFs offer, consider a floor ETF. With a floor ETF, you give up protection on the first percentage loss in exchange for protection against any loss beyond the floor. For example, AllianzIM U.S. Equity 6 Month Floor5 ETFs provide downside protection from –5 to –100 percent. In July 2025, AllianzIM's U.S. Equity 6 Month Floor5 ETF (FLJJ) had a starting cap of 5.89 percent (net of fees) over the 6-month outcome period.

During my interview with Johan Grahn, former Head ETF Strategist at Allianz Investment Management LLC, I asked how floor ETFs were able to offer deep downside protection along with a respectable upside cap. His response:

> "The most likely losses are just south of 0 percent. So, protecting against those is more expensive. If you wanted to protect from 0 percent down, it gets really expensive. But the further down you want to protect, the less expensive it becomes."

See Chapter 16 for more about floor ETFs.

TIP

Vest Financial has a very helpful tool on its website that shows the estimated caps for different outcome periods, reference assets, and levels of protection, starting on each day, for the prior five business days. Some issuers only provide this information a few days before a reset date (and some issuers don't provide estimated cap levels for the next outcome period), but Vest provides it daily. To access the tool, go to `vestfin.com`, open the Tools menu, and select Target Buffer Strategy Caps.

A more challenging choice may arise when you're considering buffer ETFs that offer nearly the same downside protection with only slightly different caps. For example, compare the buffers and caps of Innovator's 9 percent buffer series to AllianzIM's 10 percent buffer ETF for February 2026:

- AllianzIM U.S. Equity Buffer10 ETF (10 percent buffer) had a starting cap of 15.47 percent (gross).
- Innovator U.S. Equity Buffer ETF (9 percent buffer) had a starting cap of 16.60 percent (gross).

The one percent difference in downside protection resulted in an approximate one percent difference in caps.

By accessing each issuer's website, you can easily compare the starting cap levels between the 12 FT Vest Moderate Buffer ETFs with 15 percent downside protection and the 12 AllianzIM Buffer20 ETFs with 20 percent downside protection. Over the course of 2025, the FT Vest buffer ETFs with the lower 15 percent buffer provided an average gross starting cap approximately 1.43 percent higher (12.37 percent versus 10.94 percent) than AllianzIM's 20 percent buffer ETFs. The ETFs that offered 5 percent more downside protection provided only about 1.43 percent less upside potential.

In my opinion, the cost to increase downside protection by 5 percent (from −15 to −20 percent) is really not that expensive in terms of how much upside cap you're forfeiting.

In a bull market, consider a buffer ETF with less protection and a higher cap, but during a bear market, you may find the extra 5 percent downside protection very comforting.

WARNING

Don't let greed tempt you to choose less protection for a higher upside cap. Your chosen level of downside protection should fit your risk profile.

IN THIS CHAPTER

» Appreciating the importance of the outcome period

» Choosing between a 6- and 12-month buffer ETF

» Deciding when a 3-month buffer ETF is appropriate

Chapter 20

Comparing Outcome Periods: 3, 6, and 12 Months

Buffer ETFs differ not only in their level of downside protection and upside caps but also in the length of their outcome periods — typically 3, 6, or 12 months. But choosing the right outcome period isn't just a matter of picking a time frame; it's about deciding how long you're willing to commit to a specific upside cap, how often you want a fresh buffer, what your outlook is on the short-term return potential of the reference asset, and how actively you're willing to manage your position.

This chapter highlights the pros and cons of different outcome periods and provides guidance to help you decide which is best for your risk profile, investment strategy, and time horizon.

Understanding Why the Length of the Outcome Period Matters

The outcome period is the time frame over which a buffer ETF's downside protection and upside cap are designed to work, and it determines how often the buffer ETF resets with a new buffer and cap. It shapes how the investment behaves and how smooth the ride is relative to movements in the reference asset.

REMEMBER

Here are four important points to keep in mind as you compare buffer ETFs with different outcome periods:

- **The buffer and cap apply fully only over the complete outcome period.** If you buy or sell during the intra-outcome period, you may not receive the full downside protection, and you may not participate fully in the upside of the reference asset to the fund's cap. If you need to pull your money out before the end of the outcome period, you could lose more than you had expected when you invested in the ETF or not gain as much as you had hoped.
- **The cap depends on market conditions at the start of the outcome period.** Interest rates, volatility, and the length of the outcome period all influence the cap level. All other factors being equal, longer outcome periods tend to allow for higher caps, but not always.
- **The length of the outcome period influences how the ETF behaves relative to its reference asset.** Shorter outcome periods reset more frequently, which can make returns feel more responsive to fluctuations in the value of the reference asset. Longer periods may result in ETF performance that diverges more noticeably from the reference asset during the outcome window, especially after large early gains or losses.
- **Your investment time horizon should be at least the duration of the outcome period.** Although you can sell your shares at any time, the defined outcome is designed for investors who plan to hold to the end of the period. Shorter outcome periods allow for more frequent repositioning. Longer periods require greater patience and commitment to the structure.

The length of the outcome period influences not only how often the fund resets but also your experience owning it. For example, a buffer ETF with a longer outcome period may give you a smoother ride in a volatile market; however, it may make you feel "locked in" and frustrated during a strong rally or a deep market decline. On the other hand, a buffer ETF with a shorter outcome period can make you feel more in control, but it may require greater vigilance and management.

Comparing 6-Month to 12-Month Outcome Periods

If you lack the patience to invest in a 12-month buffer ETF or you prefer the flexibility of more frequent resets, you may want to consider a 6-month buffer ETF.

This section explores the pros and cons of having a shorter outcome period and provides guidance to help you choose the right time frame based on your investment objectives and temperament.

Weighing the pros and cons of a 6-month outcome period

Your choice of outcome period depends on whether you think the benefits of more frequent resets outweigh their drawbacks. Here, I present the pros and cons so you can decide for yourself.

Appreciating the potential benefits of a shorter outcome period

Here are the potential benefits of a 6-month buffer ETF over a comparable 12-month fund:

- **More frequent resets:** The fund resets twice per 12-month period, providing a new buffer and upside cap in half the time you'd have to wait for a 12-month reset. In a rising market, the new cap increases your upside potential. In a declining market, a buffer reset provides renewed protection against deeper losses.

  REMEMBER

  With more frequent resets, you won't feel as "locked in."

- **More frequent opportunities to reposition:** The shorter outcome period can be helpful for active investors who seek to reevaluate and possibly reposition over shorter periods.

- **Closer tracking to the reference asset:** A buffer ETF with a 6-month reset typically tracks the reference asset more closely than the comparable 12-month version. You may find this attribute attractive if you want a return that correlates more closely to the reference asset. In a bull market, closer tracking may result in a higher return.

- **Less active monitoring and trading:** With 6-month resets, you may be less inclined to sell shares to protect your gains in a rising market or get a new buffer in a declining market.
- **Improved tax efficiency:** If you don't have to sell shares to protect gains or adjust the buffer level, you don't realize capital gains, which could be subject to taxation. You realize capital gains or losses only when you sell your shares. (This benefit applies only if you're holding your shares in a taxable account.)
- **Potential for improved performance:** Depending on the price changes of the reference asset, a 6-month fund has the potential to outperform a 12-month fund. For example, suppose the reference asset rises 5 percent in the first 6-month outcome period and then declines 5 percent in the next 6-month outcome period. In this scenario, with a 6-month buffer ETF that offers 10 percent protection, you'd have a 5 percent return (before fees) over the full 12-month period because the 5 percent gain in the first 6-month period was protected over the next 6-month period. With a 12-month buffer ETF, your return would be flat, before fees.

REMEMBER

Regardless of the length of the outcome period, your investment in a buffer ETF automatically rolls into the next period (with a new buffer and cap) unless you sell your shares before the start of the next period. So, if desired, you can hold your 6-month buffer ETF for the long term.

Recognizing the potential drawbacks of a shorter outcome period

If you're a more active investor, you may have a strong preference for a buffer ETF with a shorter outcome period. However, you should be aware of the following potential disadvantages compared to a 12-month period:

- **Lower caps:** On an annualized basis, caps for buffer ETFs with a 6-month outcome period have typically been lower than the caps for 12-month funds that have comparable buffers (see Table 20-1). However, cap levels change based on market conditions, so they may not always be lower for 6-month funds.

  WARNING

  Don't underestimate a slightly lower cap. Over several years, a 1 to 1.5 percent difference in the annualized cap can really add up.

- **Less time to recover from a loss:** In a declining market, if the reference asset is trading below its buffer level, a 6-month buffer ETF has less time to recover and finish within the buffer.
- **Higher volatility:** A 6-month buffer ETF typically tracks its reference asset more closely and will therefore show higher volatility than a buffer ETF with the same level of protection but a 12-month reset. The higher volatility may not appeal to conservative or moderate risk investors.
- **Deeper drawdowns:** In a declining market, the ETF with the shorter outcome period is likely to show deeper declines. Although these intra-outcome period drawdowns don't result in a loss unless you sell your shares, or the reference asset finishes the outcome period below the buffer level, they could make your ride feel bumpy.

TABLE 20-1 AllianzIM Buffer10 Cap Comparison (February 28, 2026)

Ticker	Reset Month	Buffer	Outcome Period	Starting Caps (Gross)	Starting Caps Annualized (Gross)
SEPT	September	10%	12 months	14.69%	14.69%
SIXP	March/September	10%	6 months	7.15%	14.30%
JANT	January	10%	12 months	15.60%	15.60%
SIXJ	January/July	10%	6 months	6.99%	13.98%
FEBT	February	10%	12 months	15.47%	15.47%
SIXF	February/August	10%	6 months	7.45%	14.90%
OCTT	October	10%	12 months	14.87%	14.87%
SIXO	April/October	10%	6 months	7.22%	14.44%
NVBT	November	10%	12 months	17.50%	16.76%
SIXZ	May/November	10%	6 months	8.04%	16.08%
DECT	December	10%	12 months	16.61%	16.61%
SIXD	June/December	10%	6 months	7.90%	15.80%

Source: `www.allianzim.com/etfs`

Considering your investment objectives and temperament

If you're torn between a 6-month buffer ETF and a comparable 12-month fund, consider the following factors:

- **Your time frame:** If you have a short-term investment objective, such as using the money for a down payment on a car or to cover living expenses, you may lean toward a fund with a 6-month outcome period. If you can leave your money in the fund for at least a year, a 12-month fund is likely to offer higher upside potential and a smoother ride.
- **Your risk tolerance:** If you're a conservative or moderate risk investor, a buffer ETF with a longer outcome period is likely to be a better fit, especially if it enables you to remain invested. A 12-month fund is likely to encourage you to ride out short-term market volatility.
- **Your need for flexibility:** If you prefer to monitor and manage your investments more actively, a 6-month buffer ETF may offer the flexibility you need.
- **Your desire for simplicity:** If you prefer a "set it and forget it" approach to investing, a fund with a 12-month outcome period is likely to appeal to you.

Checking out some 6-month buffer ETFs

If you're thinking about investing in a 6-month buffer ETF, check out the following offerings:

- **Innovator Equity Defined Protection ETFs** track the return of the SPDR S&P 500 ETF Trust (SPY) to a cap with a 100 percent downside buffer (before fees and expenses). Innovator has two 6-month buffer ETFs, each with an annualized 0.79 percent expense ratio:
  - JAJL (January/July)
  - APOC (April/October)
- **AllianzIM Buffer10 U.S. Equity ETFs** track the return of the SPDR S&P 500 ETF Trust (SPY) to a cap with a 10 percent downside buffer (before fees and expenses). AllianzIM has six 6-month buffer ETFs, each with an annualized 0.74 percent expense ratio:
  - SIXJ (January/July)
  - SIXF (February/August)
  - SIXP (March/September)

* SIXO (April/October)
* SIXZ (May/November)
* SIXD (June/December)

» **AllianzIM Floor5 U.S. Equity ETFs** track the return of the SPDR S&P 500 ETF Trust (SPY) to a cap with a 5 percent floor (investors absorb the first 5 percent loss but are protected against any further loss). AllianzIM has two Floor5 funds, each with an annualized 0.74 percent expense ratio:

  * FLJJ (January/July)
  * FLAO (April/October)

Considering a 3-Month Buffer ETF

A 3-month buffer ETF is not simply a shorter version of one with a longer outcome period — it serves a more tactical role (for example, you might use a 3-month buffer ETF with deep protection in place of short-term bonds). It also behaves differently: buffers and caps adjust more often, performance responds more quickly to current market conditions, and investors face more frequent decision points.

Weighing the pros and cons of a 3-month outcome period

If the concept of a buffer ETF with a 3-month outcome period appeals to you, weigh the pros and cons before you make a final decision. This section outlines the potential benefits and drawbacks of 3-month buffer ETFs compared with similar 6-month and 12-month funds.

Exploring the potential advantages

Quarterly (3-month) buffer ETFs have many of the same advantages as 6-month buffer ETFs, but those advantages are amplified. Due to the shorter outcome period, the fund resets four times every 12-month period, providing a new buffer and cap, and with more frequent resets, you have more opportunities to lock in gains and reposition.

Looking at the potential disadvantages

The potential disadvantages of a 3-month buffer ETF are similar to those of a 6-month buffer ETF — caps tend to be lower on an annualized basis, the ETF has less time to recover from any loss, the ETF tends to track the reference asset more closely, and drawdowns may be deeper in a declining market. While the fund locks in any gains more frequently, it also essentially locks in losses more frequently, if a buffer level is breached at the end of the outcome period.

REMEMBER

Assuming the same level of downside protection, you can expect a smoother ride in volatile markets with a 12-month buffer ETF than with a comparable 3-month or 6-month fund.

Knowing when a 3-month buffer ETF might be a good choice

A 3-month buffer ETF can be a great tool for managing short-term, clearly defined, or tactical risks. Here are some situations in which a 3-month buffer ETF may be useful:

- **You're concerned about the market impact of a specific event, such as a federal election, a geopolitical crisis, or a major central bank decision.** In this situation, a 3-month buffer enables you to obtain downside protection for a specific short-term period instead of committing your investment capital for 6 to 12 months.
- **You're concerned about a sudden increase in market volatility but believe the turbulence will be brief.**
- **You expect a certain reference asset to spike soon, and you want to participate in that potential gain if it does.** However, you want some downside protection in case you're wrong.
- **You want to invest your cash, but only for a very short period.** For example, you may need the money to cover living expenses or a major purchase a few months from now. Instead of sitting in cash, earning next to nothing in a bank checking account, you could buy a quarterly buffer ETF with deep protection that still gives you decent annualized upside potential.
- **You're looking to replace some or all of your bonds with protected equity exposure.** For a bond allocation replacement or complement, consider a quarterly buffer ETF with deep protection.

Checking out some 3-month buffer ETFs

If you're considering a 3-month buffer ETF, check out the following offerings:

- **Innovator Quarterly ETFs:** Innovator has several 3-month ETFs that track different reference assets and offer varying levels of downside protection, including the following:

Fund	Ticker	Reference Asset	Starting Buffer	Expense Ratio
Defined Wealth Shield Buffer ETF	BALT	SPDR S&P 500 ETF Trust (SPY)	20%	0.69%
U.S. Equity 5 to 15 Buffer ETF	EALT	SPDR S&P 500 ETF Trust (SPY)	–5% to –15%	0.69%
U.S. Equity 10 Buffer ETF	ZALT	SPDR S&P 500 ETF Trust (SPY)	10%	0.69%
U.S. Small Cap 10 Buffer ETF	RBUF	iShares Russell 2000 ETF (IWM)	10%	0.69%
Nasdaq-100 10 Buffer ETF	QBUF	Invesco QQQ Trust (QQQ)	10%	0.79%
International Developed 10 Buffer ETF	IBUF	iShares MSCI EAFE ETF (EFA)	10%	0.85%
Emerging Markets 10 Buffer ETF	EBUF	iShares MSCI EM ETF (EEM)	10%	0.89%

- **FT Vest Quarterly Buffer ETFs:** FT Vest offers the following four 3-month buffer ETFs:

Fund	Ticker	Reference Asset	Starting Buffer	Expense Ratio
Gold Strategy Quarterly Buffer ETF	BGLD	SPDR Gold Trust (GLD)	–5% to –15%	0.91%
U.S. Equity Quarterly 2.5 to 15 Buffer ETF	DHDG	SPDR S&P 500 ETF Trust (SPY)	–2.5% to –15%	0.85%
U.S. Equity Quarterly Dynamic Buffer ETF	FHDG	SPDR S&P 500 ETF Trust (SPY)	5% or 7.5%	0.85%
U.S. Equity Quarterly Max Buffer ETF	SQMX	SPDR S&P 500 ETF Trust (SPY)	Approximately 10%	0.85%

» **AllianzIM Quarterly Buffer ETFs:** AllianzIM has two 3-month buffer ETFs:

Fund	Ticker	Reference Asset	Starting Buffer	Expense Ratio
Buffer100 U.S. Equity	AIOO	SPDR S&P 500 ETF Trust (SPY)	100%	0.64%
Buffer15 U.S. Equity	QBSF	SPDR S&P 500 ETF Trust (SPY)	15%	0.64%

REMEMBER

Note, on April 1, 2026, AllianzIM introduced seven new quarterly resetting ETFs that seek buffers of either 5 percent or 15 percent against core equity exposures over each 3-month outcome period:

» 5% buffer against S&P 500 exposure: QBSV
  - 5% or 15% buffer against Nasdaq-100 exposure: QBQV and QBQF
  - 5% or 15% buffer against Russell 2000 exposure: QBKV and QBKF
  - 5% or 15% buffer against MSCI EAFE exposure: QBIV and QBIF

» **iShares Quarterly Laddered Buffer ETFs:** iShares offers the following 3-month laddered buffer ETFs (see Chapter 12 for more about laddered buffer ETFs):

Fund	Ticker	Reference Asset	Starting Buffer	Expense Ratio
iShares Large Cap Moderate Quarterly Laddered ETF	IVVM	iShares Core S&P 500 ETF (IVV)	0% to –5%	0.50%
iShares Large Cap Deep Quarterly Laddered ETF	IVVB	iShares Core S&P 500 ETF (IVV)	–5% to –20%	0.50%

IN THIS CHAPTER

» Knowing what resets on a buffer ETF's reset date and why it matters

» Exploring what happens on a buffer ETF's reset date

» Using your understanding of resets to your advantage

Chapter 21
Understanding How Buffer ETFs Reset

Most buffer ETFs are perpetual products that are designed to rebalance on their *reset date* — the trading day before the start of the ETF's next outcome period. The reset gives the ETF a fresh buffer and upside cap. The starting buffer is determined by the fund's issuer and described in the fund's prospectus. The level of protection is the same at the start of each new outcome period for the life of the ETF; for example, FT Vest U.S. Equity Moderate Buffer ETF series has a 15 percent buffer at the start of each outcome period. The starting cap, however, is calculated at the beginning of each new outcome period and is ever-changing, based on numerous factors, including the fund's buffer percentage, the length of the outcome period, the volatility of the reference asset, and interest rates. The starting cap will vary from one outcome period to the next, sometimes quite significantly.

Understanding what happens when buffer ETFs reset can help you become a more informed investor and may help you buy or sell at an opportune time.

This chapter explains how buffer ETFs rebalance on their reset dates (also sometimes referred to as "roll" dates) and highlights important considerations you need to make on the timing of your buffer ETF trades.

Getting Up To Speed on Reset Basics

As explained in Chapter 2, buffer ETFs are built on the purchase and sale of *options* (contracts that grant the buyer the right but not the obligation to buy or sell an asset at a set price called the *strike price*). A conventional buffer ETF uses one options contract to track the reference asset, two options contracts to establish the buffer, and a fourth options contract to set the cap. These option contracts are all purchased/sold at the same time on the reset date, and the execution prices determine the outcome parameters for the new outcome period.

During a reset, the ETF reinvests the proceeds from the expiring basket of options into a new set of options that track the reference asset and set the new starting buffer and cap for the next outcome period. All the necessary transactions occur simultaneously inside the ETF wrapper, typically without creating a taxable event (such as the distribution of capital gains).

Knowing when buffer ETFs reset

Most buffer ETFs reset on the last trading day of the month at the end of the outcome period. The notable exception is FT Vest, which typically resets its buffer ETFs on the third Friday of the month, which corresponds with options expiration.

REMEMBER

To find a buffer ETF's reset date, visit the issuer's website and look up the ETF you're interested in purchasing. All issuers post the start and reset dates for their ETF offerings.

REMEMBER

The new outcome parameters for an ETF take effect at the close of the last trading day of the outcome period. When the market opens on the first trading day of the new outcome period, the new outcome parameters are already in place.

Recognizing the factors that influence the cap

TECHNICAL STUFF

On its reset date, an ETF's basket of options contracts is auctioned off to market makers. The options are packaged together, and the highest bid from the market makers determines the cap for the next outcome period. The cap is the only outcome parameter that changes on the reset date; the buffer, length of the outcome period, and reference asset remain the same.

Several factors influence the bids from the market makers and, hence, the cap level:

- **Reference asset's market value:** The market value of the reference asset, such as SPDR S&P 500 ETF Trust (SPY) or Invesco QQQ Trust (QQQ).
- **Buffer ETF's net asset value (NAV):** The dollar value of each share of the buffer ETF. The NAV at the end of the outcome period is also the beginning NAV for the new outcome period.
- **Outcome period length:** The longer the outcome period, the higher the cap (typically).
- **Buffer level:** The more downside protection the buffer ETF provides, the higher the cost of the protective put option, which lowers the cap. Keep in mind that protection against the first 5 percent loss is the most expensive.
- **Market volatility:** Volatility has a significant impact on cap levels, with higher volatility typically resulting in higher caps.
- **Interest rates:** The cost of borrowing money affects options pricing. Higher interest rates typically drive caps higher, and lower interest rates typically push them lower.
- **Expense ratio:** The ETF's expense ratio adds to the total cost of ownership of the fund, which can lower the cap.

Taking a Look Inside a Buffer ETF on Reset Day

As an investor, you can approach a buffer ETF as a black box — you don't need to know what's going on inside the box to own buffer ETFs and benefit from the downside protection and upside potential they offer. However, by peeling back the ETF wrapper and looking inside, you can gain a better understanding of how they work and what you're paying for when you purchase shares.

A conventional buffer ETF comprises three layers involving four transactions that enable the ETF to track the reference asset and establish the starting buffer and cap:

- **Layer 1:** Buy a call option to provide synthetic 1:1 exposure to the reference asset (for example, SPY). In a buffer ETF, a synthetic investment is designed to replicate the return of the reference asset, without actually owning it.

REMEMBER

Although Layer 1 provides 1:1 exposure to the reference asset, the share price of your buffer ETF will not track the share price of the reference asset precisely. Thanks to the buffer, your buffer ETF share price will typically experience less volatility.

- **Layer 2:** Buy and sell put options to define the buffer. Buying a put (*long put*) grants the buyer the right to sell shares of the reference asset at a fixed price (the *strike price*). Selling a put (*short put*) grants the buyer of the put the right to sell shares of the reference asset at the strike price. The long put establishes where downside protection starts, and the short put establishes where it ends.
- **Layer 3:** Sell a call option, which grants the buyer the right to buy shares at the strike price. The strike price on the sale of the call option sets the ETF's cap. When the price of the reference asset exceeds the cap, the owner of the call option can exercise the right to purchase the shares at a price lower than their market value.

REMEMBER

Any gain of the reference asset that surpasses the cap will be effectively forfeited by the investor. This is the cost of having a level of protection in place during the outcome period.

On the reset date, the four options contracts from the previous outcome period expire automatically. The assets in the ETF then roll into a new basket of options containing four options contracts for the next outcome period. On the ETF's reset date, a package of the four options contracts is auctioned off to market makers. The options aren't bought or sold separately; they're packaged together. When the highest bid is known, the cap level is determined for the upcoming outcome period. The upside cap level is the only unknown heading into each reset date. The reference asset, outcome period, and buffer remain the same as all prior outcome periods.

Table 21-1 gives you a peek at the transactions inside the ETF wrapper of Innovator U.S. Equity Power Buffer — March Series (PMAR) on its reset date, February 27, 2026. It also provides a snapshot of all PMAR holdings for its new outcome period, which begins on March 1, 2026.

The following sections describe the layers and their associated transactions in greater detail.

Layer 1

On its reset date, PMAR purchased a call option to provide synthetic 1:1 exposure to the reference asset (SPY). The cost of this transaction was $603,878,352, representing 98.84 percent of the cash available in the ETF on its reset date.

TABLE 21-1 Transactions Inside a Buffer ETF on Its Reset Day

Layer	Transaction	Security Name	Shares	Price	Market Value	Weighting	Notes
1	Buy call	SPY February 26, 2027 6.86 C	8,976	$672.77	$603,878,352	98.84%	1:1 S&P 500 ETF
2	Buy put	SPY February 26, 2027 685.99 P	8,976	$41.91	$37,618,416	6.16%	15% Buffer
2	Sell put	SPY February 26, 2027 583.09 P	–8,976	$18.75	($16,830,000)	–2.75%	15% Buffer
3	Sell call	SPY February 26, 2027 773.73 C	–8,976	$16.81	($15,088,656)	–2.47%	12.79% Upside Cap
		Cash & Other		$1.0	$1,257,015.65	0.21%	Cash
		Net Assets			$610,835,127.65		

Layer 2

Layer 2 is a *put spread* created by the purchase and sale of put options:

- PMAR purchased a put option granting it the right to sell shares of SPY at its current price of $685.99. This transaction set the starting level of downside protection (0 percent).
- PMAR sold a put option, granting the purchaser the right to sell shares of SPY at $583.09, which is 15 percent less than its current share price. This transaction set the ending level of downside protection (–15 percent).

REMEMBER

If the buffer is exhausted at the end of the outcome period, any further loss in SPY will see the buffer ETF's value decrease by the same percentage (1:1) as the reference asset's loss. For example, if the reference asset falls 25 percent at the end of the outcome period, a buffer ETF with 15 percent protection would lose 10 percent (before fees).

Together, the two transactions form the put spread that defines the level of downside protection from 0 to −15 percent.

PMAR paid a total of $37,618,416 to purchase the put option. That cost, along with the cost of the call option in Layer 1, would have resulted in a dollar deficit. However, PMAR partially offset the cost of the put option with proceeds from the sale of the put option, raising $16,830,000.

Layer 3

Layer 3 involves the sale of a call option, giving the purchaser the right to buy shares of SPY from PMAR at a share price of $773.73, which is 12.79 percent higher than SPY's share price on PMAR's reset date. This transaction sets PMAR's cap. In addition, the sale generates $15,088,656 in premiums, further offsetting the cost of the protective put.

In Table 21-1 you can see the premiums received from the sales of the put and call options don't fully cover the cost of the protective put. The protective put cost $37,618,416, but the sale of the put and call options raised only $31,918,656 ($16,830,000 + $15,088,656), resulting in a deficit of $5,699,760. How is there enough cash in the ETF to pay for the total cost of the protective put?

Well, the purchase of the call option in Layer 1 was done at a "discounted" price that was basically ex-dividend on the reference asset (SPY). (*Ex-dividend* means the ETF will not receive any SPY dividends over the course of the outcome period.)

Call options don't pay dividends, so the call buyer effectively gets a discounted price on the options by the dollar amount of the dividends that should be paid during the outcome period. The annual dividend yield on SPY was approximately 1.15 percent on the reset date, which adds up to a little over $6 million, effectively covering the deficit in the ETF.

Putting This Deeper Understanding to Good Use

What goes on inside the buffer ETF wrapper may interest you, or it may not, but how buffer ETFs function and what happens when they reset reveal some important takeaways:

- Buffer ETFs automatically reset with a new buffer and cap at the end of their outcome periods, so you can typically hold them as long as you like without generating capital gains or losses.
- Your buffer ETF may fall outside the range of downside protection during the outcome period, but as long as it finishes inside the buffer zone at the end of the period, your investment is protected. Any loss within the buffer is limited to the fund's expenses.
- When a buffer ETF you own is nearing its reset date, pay close attention to the starting cap for the next outcome period. The only outcome parameter that changes at the beginning of the next outcome period is the starting cap. The outcome period, starting buffer, and reference asset are the same as they were at the start of every preceding outcome period.
- If you sell a buffer ETF before the end of its outcome period, you may not get the full benefit of the buffer and cap, and you will lock in any gains, which could be subject to capital gains taxes (unless you're holding the position in a tax-deferred account). Note, if you've held your position less than a year, you could be hit with a taxable short-term capital gain.

IN THIS CHAPTER

» Understanding the case against a heavy bond allocation

» Recognizing the benefits of buffer ETFs over bonds

» Looking into replacing a portion of your bond allocation with buffer ETFs

Chapter 22
Swapping Bonds for Buffer ETFs

Traditionally, investment portfolios have held a mix of stocks and bonds — stocks for growth and dividend income, and bonds for stability, diversification, and interest income. However, during periods of interest rate uncertainty and lower yields, many investors start to rethink how they implement diversification and downside protection.

This chapter explores the differences between bonds and buffer ETFs, challenges conventional thinking on using bonds to protect against downside risk, and explains when buffer ETFs may or may not be an appropriate substitute for bonds in a diversified portfolio.

Rethinking the Traditional 60/40 Equities/Bonds Allocation

If you conduct a Google search for "recommended asset allocation for a retiree or pre-retiree," you'll likely find many articles advising a traditional 60/40 (60 percent stocks, 40 percent bonds) portfolio. I question this advice, particularly in the current low-yielding bond market environment. I think fixed income, which is typically at least 40 percent of the recommended asset allocation for a retiree, provides little value.

Sometimes, the 40 percent allocation in bonds works well, such as during the 2008 Global Financial Crisis. As shown in Figure 22-1, while the S&P 500 fell 55 percent, the U.S. Aggregate Bond Index gained 7 percent, helping reduce losses and smooth volatility.

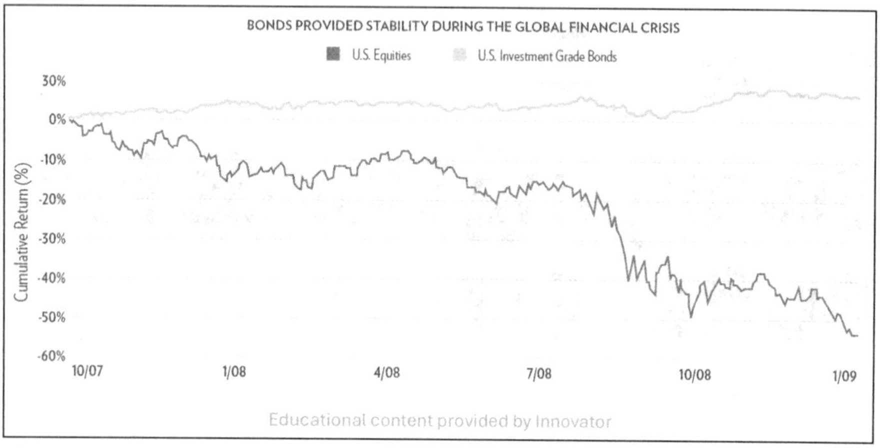

FIGURE 22-1: Bonds vastly outperformed stocks during the 2008 Global Financial Crisis.

Courtesy of Innovator

After the 2008 Global Financial Crisis, the 60/40 portfolio became the go-to investment strategy for both institutional and individual investors. The reason is simple — when stocks fall, bonds help steady the portfolio. At least that's the conventional thinking.

However, just because bonds rose when stocks fell in 2008 doesn't mean they always do. Occasionally, stocks and bonds decline together and are highly correlated. In 2022, for example, U.S. stocks fell about 18 percent. Instead of helping, core U.S. bonds also declined by roughly 13 percent (see Figure 22-2). This decline in stocks *and* bonds surprised many investors who relied on bonds for stability.

WARNING

Many investors continue to place too much confidence in a strategy that benefited from a very specific market environment. The traditional 60/40 allocation can limit long-term growth while leaving portfolios exposed to large losses.

The following sections highlight some of the disadvantages of having a sizable allocation in bonds.

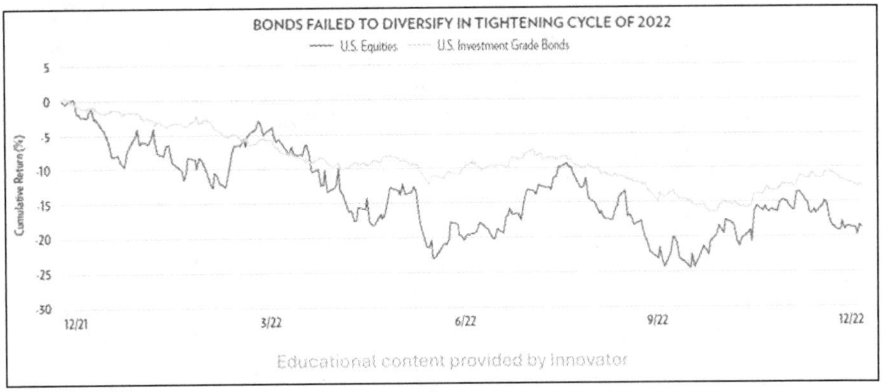

FIGURE 22-2: In 2022, bond prices fell along with stocks.

Courtesy of Innovator

Recognizing the limited upside potential of bonds

Unlike stocks, bonds don't benefit much from strong economic growth or corporate profits. They can't compete with a stock market surge of 20 to 30 percent — not even close. A bond's return is mostly fixed, limited primarily to interest payments and the return of principal when the bond matures. Certainly, bond prices can rise when interest rates fall, potentially providing an opportunity to sell bonds at a higher price, but rates can fall only so far, and when yields are low, future appreciation potential shrinks.

These conditions can make bonds less attractive, because upside potential is limited while exposing your portfolio to downside risk — interest rates can rise, leading to a decline in bond prices. And, if you need to sell your bonds before they mature, you could lose money.

Understanding why bonds don't always protect portfolios

Bonds don't provide reliable downside protection in all market environments, and history proves it. Research from Piper Sandler examined every stock market drop of 10 percent or more since 1960. Out of 27 major declines, 14 were caused by rising interest rates — the same situation investors faced in 2022 (see Figure 22-3). When rates rise, bond prices usually fall, which means bonds often don't provide protection. In fact, more than half the time (53 percent), bonds have failed to effectively offset stock market losses during major corrections.

EVERY 10% MARKET CORRECTION SINCE 1964 ON S&P 500

Start	End	Drawdown	Length (weeks)	Higher Rates	Rising Unemployment	Global
2/9/1966	10/7/1966	-22.2	34	x		
11/29/1986	5/26/1970	-36.1	78	x	x	
4/28/1971	11/23/1971	-13.9	30	x		
1/11/1973	10/3/1971	-48.2	90	x	x	
7/15/1975	9/16/1975	-14.1	9	x		
12/31/1976	3/6/1978	-19.1	61	x		
9/12/1978	11/14/1978	-13.6	9	x		
10/5/1979	11/7/1979	-10.2	5	x		
2/13/1980	3/27/1980	-17.1	6	x	x	
11/28/1980	8/12/1982	-27.1	89	x	x	
10/10/1983	7/24/1984	-14.4	41	x		
8/25/1987	12/4/1987	-33.5	14	x		
1/2/1990	1/30/1990	-10.2	4	x		
7/16/1990	10/11/1990	-19.9	12		x	x
10/7/1997	10/27/1997	-10.8	3			x
7/17/1998	8/31/1998	-19.3	6			x
7/16/1999	10/15/1999	-12.1	13	x		
3/24/2000	10/9/2002	-49.1	133		x	
10/9/2007	3/9/2009	-56.8	74		x	
4/23/2010	7/2/2010	-16.0	10			x
4/29/2011	10/3/2011	-19.4	22			x
7/20/2015	2/11/2016	-14.1	29			x
1/26/2018	2/8/2018	-10.2	2	x		
10/3/2018	12/24/2018	-19.6	12	x		
2/19/2020	3/23/2020	-33.9	5		x	
1/3/2022	10/12/2022	-25.4	40	x		
7/31/2023	10/27/2023	-10.3	13	x		

Educational content provided by Innovator

FIGURE 22-3: More than half the time, bonds have failed to offset stock market losses.

Courtesy of Innovator

Combining this unreliable protection with bonds' limited upside raises an important question: Is the traditional 40 percent bond allocation in a 60/40 portfolio really doing its job? You may want to rethink the fixed-income portion of your portfolio and look for ways to improve its performance.

Recognizing the tax inefficiency of bonds

Bonds don't just have limited upside — they also come with a tax disadvantage. The income they generate is usually taxed at ordinary income tax rates, which are higher than the rates applied to long-term capital gains. For investors holding bonds in taxable accounts, this can significantly reduce what they keep. For example, if a bond earns 6 percent and that income is taxed at a top rate of 40.8 percent, the investor is left with only a 3.55 percent return after taxes. If that same 6 percent return was earned through long-term capital gains, taxed at 23.8 percent, the investor would keep 4.57 percent. That's nearly 29 percent more after taxes, simply because of how bond income is taxed.

Over time, this difference matters. Paying higher taxes every year reduces how much money can compound and grow. For investors focused on building wealth over the long run, investments that allow returns to be taxed later or at lower rates generally have higher overall growth than those that generate returns subject to being taxed as ordinary income.

You might ask, "If I reduce or eliminate bonds, what can I do to replace my bond income if I need it to cover living expenses?" One option to consider is the following:

> "Invest in equity buffer ETFs and sell shares when you need money to cover living expenses. Preferably, sell shares you've owned for longer than one year, so any realized gains are taxed at lower long-term capital gains rates. Consider investors who own shares in Berkshire Hathaway. Berkshire pays no dividends, so if shareholders need money to cover living expenses, they need to sell shares to raise cash. But that's totally fine — the gains will be taxed at the likely lower capital gains tax rate rather than ordinary income tax rates that would apply to bond income."

REMEMBER

Long-term capital gains tax rates are typically lower than ordinary income tax rates. Reducing or completely eliminating bond interest from your portfolio is likely to save you money on taxes.

Understanding How Buffer ETFs Can Improve a Portfolio's Performance

Adding buffered strategies to a traditional 60/40 portfolio can be a smart way to potentially improve its performance. These strategies can be used to complement, supplement, or replace the 40 percent bond allocation to increase upside potential and add downside protection.

Buffer ETFs offer a way to participate in stock market gains, but with limits on upside potential. Like bonds, they have a capped return, meaning gains are limited. However, those caps, historically, have been much higher than the yields offered by traditional core bonds. In fact, from June 30, 1976, to August 30, 2024, the median cap for a hypothetical 30 percent buffer ETF was about 8.9 percent higher than the bond yield, highlighting a buffer ETF's stronger return potential compared to that of U.S. Investment Grade Bonds (see Figure 22-4).

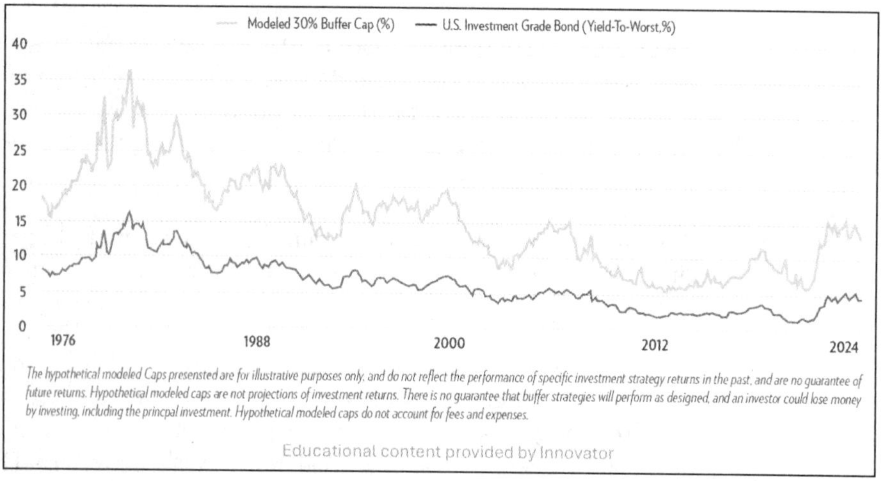

FIGURE 22-4: A 30 percent buffer ETF return versus bond yield 1976–2024.

Courtesy of Innovator

REMEMBER

The stock market is a powerful engine for long-term wealth creation. Buffered strategies enable investors to tap into that growth without taking on the full risk of the market. Although returns are capped, investors gain more exposure to equities while keeping risk in check. This balanced approach blends growth and protection.

WHY NOT MAKE A MORE MEANINGFUL ALLOCATION?

I asked Bruce Bond, co-founder and CEO of Innovator Capital Management LLC, "If Buffer ETFs can serve as a core holding, why not allocate nearly an entire portfolio in Buffer ETFs?" Here's what he had to say:

> Over time, progressive advisors are realizing that this will likely be the way to go in the future. Some have begun to transform their businesses already. The poor performance of 60/40 portfolios over the last few years has made investors and advisors realize that bonds aren't immune from downturns and that relying on historical correlations can be a big mistake.

Considering an Alternative Approach to the Traditional 60/40 Portfolio

As an alternative to the traditional 60/40 portfolio allocation, consider a 60/20/20 allocation — 60 percent stocks, 20 percent bonds, and 20 percent buffer ETFs. A 60/20/20 allocation offers the following potential advantages over a 60/40 allocation:

- **Increased upside potential:** You retain 60 percent uncapped exposure to stocks while adding another 20 percent exposure that's capped but provides some downside protection.
- **Continued downside protection:** With a moderate or deep buffer ETF, you're not sacrificing much of the downside protection offered by bonds.
- **Reduced dependence on bonds:** Traditional bonds can struggle when interest rates rise. By reducing bond exposure from 40 to 20 percent, your portfolio may be less sensitive to rate increases.
- **Potential to profit:** If bond prices rise as stocks fall, your 20 percent bond allocation can still help offset losses in your unhedged equity investments.
- **Increased tax efficiency:** If your investments are held in a taxable account, reducing bond income can help reduce taxes, leaving you with more investment capital to fuel growth. If your positions are held in a tax-deferred account, such as an Individual Retirement Account (IRA), this is a moot point.
- **Smoother ride:** Buffered strategies are designed to limit a portion of market losses in exchange for a cap on gains. This may help reduce volatility and improve consistency of returns.

TIP

When replacing bonds with buffer ETFs, you may want to consider buffer ETFs that have moderate or deep protection to provide adequate downside protection in most market environments. For a bond replacement, I generally wouldn't consider any fund with less than 15 percent protection. You may want to invest in a combination of buffer ETFs with different levels of downside protection, ranging from 15 to 100 percent downside protection. Just remember: The deeper the buffer, the lower the cap.

A 60/20/20 allocation enables investors to enhance their portfolio's upside potential, mitigate some negative characteristics associated with traditional fixed-income investments, and seek more consistent risk management over time.

According to research from Innovator, a hypothetical 60/20/20 allocation (using a blend of 15 percent and 30 percent buffer ETFs) resulted in a 13.4 percent higher ending portfolio value compared to a traditional 60/40 allocation over the same period (January 1, 2019, to August 31, 2024). See Figure 22-5.

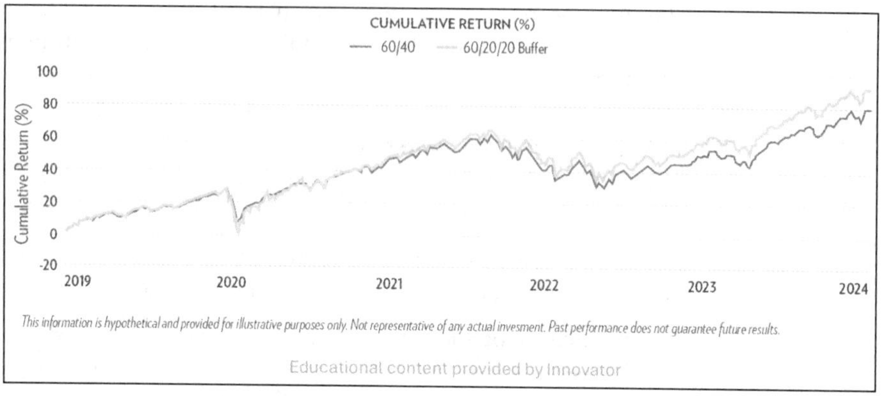

FIGURE 22-5: A 60/40 versus a 60/20/20 portfolio 2019–2024.

Courtesy of Innovator

REMEMBER

Although the 60/40 portfolio still serves as a common starting point for many investors, a 60/20/20 allocation, which incorporates buffered strategies, may be a better approach. If you're looking to strengthen your portfolio without taking on excessive risk, it can be an attractive alternative.

IN THIS CHAPTER

» Understanding how buffer ETFs are structured

» Recognizing the key components of structured notes

» Comparing structured notes to buffer ETFs

Chapter 23
Comparing Defined Outcome Structures

Defined outcome investments are designed to provide a predetermined range of potential returns over a specified period. Instead of offering unlimited upside but full exposure to downside risk, these products are structured to provide the potential for a positive return with some degree of protection against a potential loss, within a defined outcome period. Investors can choose from the following two popular defined outcome investment vehicles:

- **Buffer ETFs:** Exchange-traded funds that use option strategies to track the performance of an underlying reference asset to a cap while providing protection against a specific percentage of losses over a defined outcome period (typically 3, 6, or 12 months).
- **Structured notes:** Debt securities issued by financial institutions that are designed to deliver specific payoff profiles tied to the performance of an underlying index or asset. Unlike buffer ETFs, which trade like stocks, structured notes are typically illiquid and are therefore usually held to maturity.

This chapter explains how these two defined outcome investments are structured and reveals their respective pros and cons, so you can make a well-informed choice when deciding between the two.

Gaining Insight into the Conventional Buffer ETF Structure

Conventional buffer ETFs are structured around four options contracts that shape the return profile over an outcome period (typically 12 months). An *option contract* grants the buyer the right to purchase or sell shares of an asset at a predetermined price called the *strike price*. The following four transactions involving options contracts establish a connection with the reference asset and set the buffer and cap:

- **Purchase a deep-in-the-money call option to replicate reference asset exposure.** *Deep in the money* means the strike price is significantly lower than the current market price of the reference asset. This transaction provides synthetic exposure that mimics the performance of the underlying reference asset.
- **Purchase a put option to create downside protection.** This transaction establishes where downside protection begins (usually at 0 percent, but with some deep buffer ETFs, protection starts at –5 percent, meaning investors absorb the first 5 percent loss of the reference asset).
- **Sell a put option to help finance the cost of the protection.** The sale of a put option removes the downside protection for any loss deeper than the buffer. So, if a buffer ETF protects against the first 0 to –15 percent loss, the put option removes downside protection from any loss deeper than –15 percent. The premium earned from the sale of the put option helps finance the cost of the downside protection.
- **Sell a call option to help fund the cost of the protection.** The sale of a call option creates the upside cap and further offsets the cost of the downside protection.

The following sections dissect three conventional buffer ETF structures (one each from FT Vest, Innovator, and AllianzIM), along with an alternative structure used by BlackRock for its iShares buffer ETFs.

FT Vest U.S. Equity Buffer ETF — December (FDEC)

FT Vest U.S. Equity Buffer ETF — December (FDEC) is a 12-month 10 percent buffer ETF that seeks to provide investors with returns (before fees and expenses) that match the price return of the SPDR S&P 500 ETF Trust (SPY) to a cap, while providing protection on initial losses to –10 percent. Table 23-1 shows the four holdings used to create FDEC's defined outcome.

TABLE 23-1 FDEC Holdings

Transaction	Strike Price	Expiration
Purchase Call Option	$6.81	December 18, 2026
Purchase Put Option	$680.59	December 18, 2026
Sell Put Option	$612.53	December 18, 2026
Sell Call Option	$780.98	December 18, 2026

The purchase of a call option replicates the performance of the reference asset (SPY) over the outcome period.

To better understand how the level of protection is created and released, and how the upside cap level is determined, review the simple math. FDEC purchases a put option at $680.59 and simultaneously sells another put option at $612.53, creating and then releasing the downside protection at a predetermined level. The difference in the strike prices is approximately 10 percent, which is the level of protection in place at the start of the outcome period. The ETF sells a call option at $780.98, which is 14.75 percent above the starting level, $680.59. The difference of 14.75 percent represents the upside cap.

Investors receive protection on the first 10 percent loss and participate in the upside of SPY up to its cap of 14.75 percent (before fees) to the end of the outcome period on December 18, 2026.

Innovator U.S. Equity Power Buffer ETF — January (PJAN)

Innovator U.S. Equity Power Buffer ETF — January (PJAN) is a 12-month 15 percent buffer ETF that seeks to provide investors with returns (before fees and expenses) that match the price return of the SPDR S&P 500 ETF Trust (SPY) to a cap, while providing protection on initial losses to −15 percent. Table 23-2 shows the four holdings used to establish PJAN's defined outcome.

TABLE 23-2 PJAN Holdings

Transaction	Strike Price	Expiration
Purchase Call Option	$6.82	December 31, 2026
Purchase Put Option	$681.92	December 31, 2026
Sell Put Option	$579.63	December 31, 2026
Sell Call Option	$765.86	December 31, 2026

The purchase of a call option replicates the performance of the reference asset (SPY) over the outcome period.

PJAN buys a put option at $681.92 and simultaneously sells another put option at $579.63, creating and then releasing the downside protection at a predetermined level. The price difference is approximately 15 percent, which is the level of protection in place at the start of the outcome period. PJAN sells a call option at $765.86, which is 12.3 percent above the starting level, $681.92. The difference of 12.3 percent represents the upside cap.

Investors receive protection on the first 15 percent loss and participate in the upside of SPY to its cap of 12.3 percent (before fees) to the end of the outcome period on December 31, 2026.

AllianzIM U.S. Equity Buffer20 Jan ETF (JANW)

AllianzIM U.S. Equity Buffer20 Jan ETF (JANW) is a 12-month 20 percent buffer ETF that seeks to provide investors with returns (before fees and expenses) that match the price return of the SPDR S&P 500 ETF Trust (SPY) to a cap, while providing protection on initial losses to −20 percent. Table 23-3 shows the four holdings used to create JANW's defined outcome.

TABLE 23-3 **JANW Holdings**

Transaction	Strike Price	Expiration
Purchase Call Option	$5.11	December 31, 2026
Purchase Put Option	$681.99	December 31, 2026
Sell Put Option	$545.54	December 31, 2026
Sell Call Option	$753.32	December 31, 2026

The purchase of the call option replicates the performance of the reference asset (SPY) over the outcome period.

JANW purchases a put option at $681.99 and simultaneously sells another put option at $545.54, creating and then releasing the downside protection at a predetermined level. The price difference is approximately 20 percent, which is the level of protection in place at the start of the outcome period. JANW sells a call option at $753.32, which is 10.47 percent above the starting level of $681.99. The difference of 10.47 percent represents the upside cap.

Investors receive protection on the first 20 percent loss and participate in the upside of SPY to its cap of 10.47 percent (before fees) to the end of the outcome period on December 31, 2026.

iShares Large Cap 10% Target Buffer Dec ETF (TEND)

iShares Large Cap 10% Target Buffer Dec ETF (TEND) is a 12-month 10 percent buffer ETF that seeks to provide investors with returns (before fees and expenses) that match the price return of the iShares Core S&P 500 ETF (IVV) to a cap, while providing protection on initial losses to −10 percent. Table 23-4 shows the four holdings used to establish TEND's defined outcome.

TABLE 23-4 **TEND Holdings**

Transaction	Strike Price	Expiration
Purchase iShares Core S&P 500 ETF (IVV)	N/A	N/A
Sell Put Option	$616.45	December 31, 2026
Purchase Put Option	$684.94	December 31, 2026
Sell Call Option	$798.98	December 31, 2026

TEND is built on a structure that differs from that of the previous buffer ETFs covered in this section; instead of using a deep-in-the-money call option to replicate the performance of the reference asset, it holds shares of IVV directly and uses three options around the core IVV holding to establish the buffer and the cap.

Table 23-4 shows the four holdings used to establish TEND's defined outcome.

The purchase of iShares Core S&P 500 ETF (IVV) tracks the performance of the S&P 500 over the outcome period.

TEND purchases a put option at $684.94 and simultaneously sells another put option at $616.45, creating and releasing the downside protection at a predetermined level. The price difference is approximately 10 percent, which is the level of protection in place at the start of the outcome period. TEND sells a call option at $798.98, which is 16.6 percent above the starting level, $684.94. The difference of 16.6 percent represents the upside cap.

Investors receive protection on the first 10 percent loss and participate in the upside of IVV to its cap of 16.6 percent (before fees) to the end of the outcome period on December 31, 2026.

TEND uses a three-option structure rather than the four-option approach typically employed by most buffer ETF issuers. By purchasing IVV shares instead of a deep-in-the-money call option, TEND can provide a higher cap to shareholders. However, the higher cap is possible only in specific market environments; the difference in TEND's structure may not always allow it to provide a higher cap.

WARNING

TEND and other iShares buffer ETFs that are structured like TEND may distribute capital gains and/or dividends, which could make these ETFs less tax efficient than their conventional counterparts. Some shareholders may appreciate the distributions, whereas others may not.

Comparing Structured Notes to Buffer ETFs

Structured notes and buffer ETFs both aim to provide a defined investment outcome — offering stock market participation with a level of downside protection. However, they're built and managed very differently. This section explains what structured notes are and how they differ from buffer ETFs.

Understanding what structured notes are

Structured notes are hybrid financial instruments issued by large financial institutions and investment banks that combine the features of debt securities, such as bonds, with derivatives. (A *derivative* investment in a structured note derives its value from an underlying asset, such as a market index like the S&P 500.)

Together, the bonds and derivatives create a customized return profile linked to the underlying asset. Like buffer ETFs, structured notes are often owned by risk-averse investors who want upside participation in the stock market, but with a defined level of downside protection.

REMEMBER

One of the key benefits of buffer ETFs over structured notes is liquidity. You can sell a buffer ETF at any time (although, by doing so, you may forfeit some downside protection or upside potential). Structured notes are designed to be held to maturity. You may be prohibited from selling them before their maturity date or from selling them at all. Note, while most notes have a fixed maturity date, some are "callable," meaning the issuer may redeem them before the maturity date if certain conditions are met.

Exploring the key components of structured notes

Structured notes are typically made up of the following two components:

- **Bond component:** Most of the investment consists of zero-coupon bonds. A *zero-coupon bond* is a debt security that does not pay regular interest (coupons). Instead, it is issued at a deep discount to its face value, and the investor receives the full principal amount at maturity. The return is the difference between the discounted purchase price and the face value received.
- **Derivative component:** The remaining capital is used to purchase call and/or put options, which tie the investment to equities, indexes, commodities, or currencies and determine the level of downside protection and upside potential (cap).

Together, these two components seek to deliver the following defined outcome parameters:

- Fixed maturity date
- Specific payoff formula
- Preset protection and participation levels

Highlighting key differences between structured notes and buffer ETFs

Structured notes and buffer ETFs are both defined outcome investments with similar objectives — to enable investors to participate in the upside potential of an underlying asset with some protection against a potential loss. However, they're quite different. Table 23-5 highlights their key differences.

REMEMBER

In terms of their respective risk/return profiles, both investment vehicles offer a wide range of strategies — from conservative to more aggressive — depending on protection levels and upside caps.

TABLE 23-5 **Structured Notes versus Buffer ETFs**

Characteristic	Structured Notes	Buffer ETFs
Issuer	Large financial institutions and investment banks.	ETF providers.
Customization	Highly customizable — tailored to specific investor preferences.	Standardized, "off-the-shelf" products.
Market presence	Long-established market with over $3 trillion invested globally.	Rapidly growing market with over $80 billion in assets under management.
Liquidity	Limited-liquidity windows. Frequently subject to multi-year lock-ups. Typically held to maturity, but may be callable if certain conditions are met.	Trade intraday like stocks and other ETFs. No lock-up periods. Typically held for the duration of their outcome period.
Cost transparency	Fees can be complex and harder to identify. May include upfront and trailing commissions.	Transparent pricing and clearly disclosed management fees. Expenses prorated based on the holding period. May have a lower total cost of ownership.
Portfolio management flexibility	Generally, they must be held to maturity to realize their intended outcome, limiting flexibility.	Trade intraday like stocks and other ETFs, so you can: • Lock in gains early. • Harvest tax losses. • Adjust exposure during the intra-outcome period. • Swap into a different buffer ETF with a new buffer and cap. • Manage volatility strategically.
Tax efficiency	Limited tax management flexibility due to illiquidity. Typically, they're tax-inefficient — when they mature, a taxable event is automatically triggered.	Generally very tax-efficient. Can be used for tax-loss harvesting. Gains may qualify for long-term capital gains treatment. Appropriate for taxable and tax-deferred accounts.
Counterparty risk and oversight	Subject to the credit risk of the issuing financial institution. Returns depend on the issuer's solvency.	No direct issuer credit risk. Options clearing is guaranteed by the Options Clearing Corporation (OCC).

Choosing between structured notes and buffer ETFs

While both structured notes and buffer ETFs provide defined outcomes with a level of downside protection and upside participation, buffer ETFs are generally better suited for investors who value the following traits:

- Simplicity
- Transparency
- Liquidity
- Tax efficiency
- Portfolio flexibility

Structured notes may appeal to investors seeking highly customized solutions, but they come with trade-offs in liquidity, tax treatment, and issuer credit risk.

Ultimately, determining whether a buffer ETF or a structured note is more appropriate comes down to your personal preference and any differences in cost. Conduct a diligent review and compare your choices closely before making any investment decision.

6

The Part of Tens

IN THIS PART . . .

Gain valuable insights from buffer ETF industry leaders.

Get answers to ten frequently asked questions about buffer ETFs.

IN THIS CHAPTER

» Considering factors commonly overlooked

» Managing your expectations to avoid unpleasant surprises

» Understanding why you can't replicate a buffer ETF on your own

» Comparing underlying buffer ETF structures

» Maximizing your potential upside with an uncapped buffer ETF

Chapter 24

Ten Buffer ETF Takeaways from Industry Leaders

I interviewed ten leading experts in the field of buffer ETFs. This chapter presents valuable insider insights extracted from those interviews.

Choose a Buffer Based on Your Risk Tolerance and the Market Cycle

From Bruce Bond, co-founder and CEO of Innovator Capital Management LLC

"The beauty of buffer strategies is that investors don't have to worry about whether the market goes up or down. If the market goes up, a buffer strategy will participate to a predetermined maximum level, and if it goes down, the strategy offers the chosen level of protection. The smaller buffers that have higher caps tend to perform better in positive markets, while the bigger buffers tend to perform better during bear markets."

"Whether we are in a bull market or a bear market, the preferred buffer level typically boils down to the risk tolerance of the investor and where we are in the market cycle. For example, after an extended bull market, valuations are often stretched. In that kind of scenario, investors begin to believe the market could reverse course, causing them to get out of stocks, or at the very least to stop adding exposure. This approach is beneficial if the market falls, but detrimental if the market continues to climb. We see greater demand for buffer strategies in circumstances like this; if the market does go down, the buffers provide built-in protection, but if it doesn't, the strategy will participate in the continued positive performance."

Use Buffer ETFs to Mitigate Poor Decision-Making in Volatile Markets

From Johan Grahn, former Head ETF Strategist, Allianz Investment Management LLC

"Human nature guides you, and you feel pain points five times more heavily than the positive points. So, when bad events happen, your brain automatically kicks into survival mode, and you try to do something about it because it doesn't feel right. And when things don't feel right, you want to take action. And a lot of times in the investing world, you take the wrong action, and you make a bad decision."

"Did more eyeballs turn to these [buffer] strategies in a year like 2022? Yes, there's no doubt. They turn to anything that looks like a 'risk-off' asset, but one of the benefits of the defined outcome space is that it helps mitigate poor decision-making that, frankly, is somewhat pervasive. If you are invested in these types of products, then you won't feel as much pain, and you will be less inclined to make poor decisions when the sky is falling, so to speak."

Consider Making Buffer ETFs a Core Allocation in Your Portfolio

From Karan Sood, CEO of Vest Financial LLC (Vest)

"If advisors want to manage risk in a portfolio through buffer strategies in a meaningful way, it commonly takes a decent percentage allocation to the strategy to do that. For example, 5 percent of a portfolio in a buffer strategy has tended to not make as meaningful a difference to the overall risk characteristics of the portfolio. So, I have seen advisors migrate their usage of buffer strategies over time from a slice to more of a core holding."

"However, if these products make up a core allocation and require actively managing within intra-outcome periods, it can become a burdensome process. About a year into launching these products, we noticed that advisors were asking for systematic solutions. That's why we developed solutions-oriented strategies that are designed with that sort of operational appeal in mind."

Don't Be Surprised

From Wes Mathews, former Principal, Director of Portfolio Solutions, Milliman Financial Risk Management LLC

"Investors often ask, 'What's the worst-case scenario? How could I be surprised in a negative way by these products?' The most common 'surprise' I hear from investors is that the funds may not fully reflect the buffer they thought they were going to get a month or two into an outcome period. Sometimes I'll get questions from an investor who, for example, invests $1 million, and the market declines a bit, and his account statement shows he's down below $1 million. And he'll ask, 'Why wasn't I buffered against the loss?' Investors might not understand that the interim value fluctuates intra-outcome period and can show losses, even if it's within the buffer range. So, they need to clearly understand that the defined outcome is over the full outcome period beginning on the reset date."

"The other potential area of misunderstanding is that if you don't buy these funds around the reset date, you're taking on some additional upside or downside exposure by buying funds above or below the starting point. Investors need to understand the exact outcome parameters at the time they are buying."

Don't Try This at Home

From Burke Ashenden, Director of Capital Markets, Innovator Capital Management LLC

"Retail investors, advisors, and institutions often ask us, 'Can we do this ourselves?' And the answer is, in most cases, 'No.'"

"Let's dissect this because I think it's really interesting. First, managing options is burdensome and can lead to user error, and most advisors aren't even allowed to trade options. We've seen issues with clients who've come to us after trying to manage option overlays. They had a dedicated trader focused on it and still made costly mistakes. It can be complicated and onerous. Receiving similar exposure through an ETF reduces operational risk. There are also other hurdles. For instance, there's a minimum investment threshold for FLEX options."

"The second key point I'll highlight is the liquidity network. If you're a retail investor, advisor, or smaller institution, you don't have access to Innovator's liquidity network. These are relationships, an ecosystem, that we've developed over many years. We use a competitive process when we trade/reset the buffer funds. We place a group of leading option market makers in competition to give us their single best price on the option basket. Garnering the attention of these top trading firms and banks in the world would be nearly impossible if you tried to execute this yourself on a smaller scale. We've been told by market makers that the ETF liquidity network can add hundreds of basis points of additional upside potential (cap) versus a DIY approach."

"Lastly, tax efficiency is lost when trading outside of the ETF wrapper. Buffer ETFs reset to a new outcome period within the ETF wrapper. This means that at the end of a 12-month outcome period, an investor can hold without a taxable event and receive a new upside cap/downside buffer. The investor only realizes a gain/loss when he sells the ETF. If this same investor held options, he'd be forced to pay any capital gains on expiry for those options."

Understand the Logic Behind the Buffer

From Matthew Collins, Head of ETFs at PGIM

"When we developed our buffer series, we felt that it was important to have significant historical research on typical market drawdowns going back for extended periods of time. First and foremost, we wanted a strategy that protected against the most common market drawdown, which, based on the data we reviewed between 1957 and year-end 2025, we believe is approximately −11.8 percent over rolling monthly annual return streams. Our view is that if you maximize your buffer to the most common drawdown of approximately 12 percent, you are maximizing your overall upside as well. More risk-averse investors looking for full protection down to bear market levels may prefer a 20 percent buffer series, while a 100 percent buffer offering may be attractive to investors seeking a tax-favorable, non-income-producing alternative to cash investing since many offer an attractive spread over typical lower risk rates."

Weigh the Pros and Cons of the Underlying Buffer ETF Structure

From Graham Day, Executive Vice President and Chief Investment Officer, Innovator Capital Management LLC

"A pro for an all-option construction [compared to a fund that holds equities or a conventional ETF] is that it tends to provide the most precision in delivering stated caps or buffers. This is because the funding rate is locked in at the commencement of the outcome period, so any changes in the funding rate after the beginning of the outcome period will not have any impact on the defined outcome."

"Our goal is to always provide our investors with the highest upside caps, while maintaining the defined outcome. What's interesting is the upside potential of these various methods is dynamic based on changes in market conditions like funding rates, perceived risk in the market, capital availability, etc. For example, an all-option approach over a 1-year outcome period currently offers a slightly lower upside cap than a method that would involve owning the individual stocks or ETF and layering the protection and upside cap on top. Over a 3-month outcome period, however, the benefit is currently immaterial. Furthermore, there have been periods where an all-option approach has generated slightly higher upside. In non-US markets, an all-option approach is currently better for upside caps, though this may evolve."

"A con for the individual or stock approach is that funding rates are assumed, and so if not properly managed or considered beforehand, they could adversely impact the defined outcome. Additionally, dividends will be distributed from the underlying ETF or single stocks, but this is where having a holistic approach to determining which method to use is essential. The focus for a firm like Innovator is to maintain flexibility on a go-forward basis to pivot between methods that maximize upside cap while still delivering a defined outcome."

Consider the Three-Option Approach

From Igor Zamkovsky, Senior Strategist, Outcome ETFs — BlackRock

"We chose this [three-option] approach with scale in mind. As this space continues to grow, we heard feedback from our trading and market-making partners that capacity will become an important consideration. We then developed an operating model that we believe to be very efficient from a scale perspective, which has had the added benefit of delivering significant client value."

"We are constantly evaluating all options in the market to ensure that our products deliver the highest quality and value to our clients. We think about this both at a top-down level (other instruments and structures that we should consider) and a bottom-up level (how those coincide with the specific product we are building), keeping the client experience front and center."

Don't Minimize the Importance of the Upside

From Mike Loukas, CEO, TrueMark Investments

"As the pioneer of the 'uncapped' buffer ETF, TrueShares was intent on developing a structure that not only helped mitigate drawdowns (the left tail) but also captured a meaningful amount of the outsized upside moves (the right tail) that are so vital to compounded returns. An examination of historical 12-month rolling returns indicated that these 'outsized' right tail moves happened roughly one third of the time and that trend directly supported our thesis that capturing large upside moves was just as important as mitigating downturns in the context of compounded returns. This was the driving force behind a TrueShares Structured Outcome Series that was engineered to address both tails."

"With our traditional buffer ETFs, TrueShares utilizes a two-option strategy supported by a cash alternative yield portfolio. This approach allows for tighter intra-investment period upside correlation and uncapped growth potential, which dovetails with our belief that capturing outsized upside moves is as important as mitigating drawdown exposure."

Don't Underestimate the Upside of Downside Protection

From Matt Kaufman, SVP & Global Head of ETFs, Calamos Investments

"The defined outcome space is still in its early innings. When the first buffer ETF launched in 2018, it was a novelty. Today, the category approaches $80 billion in assets and has been growing at roughly 40 percent annually. I believe that growth understates where this category is ultimately headed."

"Several forces are converging. Over 11,000 Americans turn 65 every single day through the end of this decade, and every one of those retirees represents a client who needs a better answer than 'just stay invested and hope for the best.' 2022 was a generational wake-up call: stocks and bonds crashed simultaneously, destroying the core logic of the traditional 60/40 portfolio for many investors. When the ballast in a portfolio fails at exactly the moment it's needed most, advisors and their clients become acutely receptive to structures that provide genuine, contractually defined protection."

IN THIS CHAPTER

» Understanding what buffer ETFs are and how they work

» Discovering the benefits of an ETF wrapper

» Comparing expense ratios of buffer ETFs to other popular investment vehicles

» Recognizing that not all buffer ETFs have capped performance

» Knowing what happens at the end of an outcome period

Chapter 25

Ten FAQs about Buffer ETFs

I get a lot of questions from investors about buffer ETFs, and in this chapter, I answered ten of the most frequently asked questions.

What Is a Buffer ETF?

A *buffer ETF* is an exchange-traded fund that's designed to track the return of an underlying reference asset (for example, SPDR S&P 500 ETF Trust) up to a predetermined cap, while buffering against a certain percentage of losses over a specific period, typically 3, 6, or 12 months. It's considered a *defined outcome* investment vehicle because it seeks to deliver a predetermined range of potential gains/losses over a set period.

How Do Buffer ETFs Work?

Buffer ETFs perform their magic by buying and selling *options* (contracts that grant the buyer the right to purchase or sell shares of an asset by a certain date for a predetermined price). A conventional buffer ETF uses four options transactions to create a defined outcome (see Chapter 23 for details):

- **Purchase a call option.** This transaction allows the share price of the buffer ETF to mirror the price changes of the underlying reference asset.
- **Purchase a put option.** This transaction establishes where downside protection begins — typically at 0 percent, but downside protection can start at any level, such as -5 or -10 percent, meaning the investor is exposed to the first 5 or 10 percent loss.
- **Sell a put option.** This transaction establishes where downside protection ends — typically at -9, -10, -12, -15, or -20 percent. (Numerous buffer ETFs provide 100 percent downside protection.)
- **Sell a call option.** This transaction sets the cap.

Buffer ETFs may employ variations of this structure. For example, instead of purchasing a call option, a buffer ETF may purchase shares of stock or an ETF, which can reduce costs and increase the cap. Other ETFs may omit the third transaction, thereby creating a *floor ETF* — for example, exposing the investor to the first 5 percent loss and protecting against any additional loss. Some ETFs omit the fourth transaction, thereby creating an *uncapped buffer ETF*.

What Are the Benefits of an ETF Wrapper?

A buffer ETF consists of options transactions within an ETF wrapper. The ETF wrapper offers the following advantages:

- **Liquidity:** Buffer ETFs trade like stocks and other ETFs. They have their own ticker symbols and are free of any early-redemption penalties. However, buying or selling a buffer ETF during the intra-outcome period may result in less downside protection or upside potential.
- **Transparency:** Buffer ETF issuers post the potential outcome parameters for each fund throughout the outcome period, so you know what to expect before you purchase shares. In addition, expense ratios are clearly indicated on each issuer's website, so you know how much you're paying.

REMEMBER

If you're buying shares during the intra-outcome period, check the fund's remaining buffer and cap and its *downside before buffer* — the percentage of your investment you could lose before it's protected against a loss.

- **Tax efficiency:** Most buffer ETFs use an in-kind creation and redemption process, which can reduce or eliminate taxable capital gains distributions.

Aren't Buffer ETFs Expensive?

Buffer ETFs are actually reasonably priced, given they're actively managed, sophisticated investment vehicles. The expense ratios typically range from 0.50 to 0.95 percent, with most issuers charging 0.79 to 0.89 percent annually. These expense ratios are generally higher than those of traditional ETFs but comparable to many actively managed mutual funds. See Table 25-1 to compare buffer ETF expense ratios to those of traditional ETFs and mutual funds.

TABLE 25-1 ETF and Mutual Fund Expense Ratios

Fund Type	Typical Expense Ratio (percentage)
Buffer ETF	0.50–0.95
Traditional index-based ETF	0.03–0.15
Actively managed ETF	0.50–0.75
Actively managed mutual fund	0.50–1.0

REMEMBER

Fees vary greatly for all investment vehicles, so do your homework and comparison shop before investing.

What If I Buy Shares after the Reset Date?

When you buy shares of a buffer ETF on its reset date, you get the full benefit of the ETF's starting buffer and cap. At any other point in the buffer ETF's outcome period, the remaining buffer and cap may be greater or less than the starting buffer and cap. If the reference asset has declined in value, the buffer ETF will have less protection remaining (and more upside potential), and if the reference asset has increased in value, the buffer ETF will have less upside potential remaining and downside-before-buffer risk.

REMEMBER

Before purchasing a buffer ETF during the intra-outcome period, always check the remaining buffer and cap and the downside-before-buffer risk (how much you could lose before the buffer provides any downside protection).

Does a Buffer ETF Mature?

No. A buffer ETF has an outcome period (a start and end date), but it doesn't mature like a bond. At the end of the outcome period, the ETF automatically resets with the same reference asset, starting buffer, and outcome period. Only the upside cap level is subject to change, typically based on market volatility and interest rates. Because a buffer ETF automatically resets at the conclusion of its outcome period, it may be held indefinitely. If desired, buffer ETFs can be a passive "set-it-and-forget-it" investment for long-term investors.

REMEMBER

Fluctuation in price during a buffer ETF's outcome period doesn't really matter. What matters is the price of the reference asset at the end of the outcome period, at which point the buffer is applied to any loss, and the cap is applied to any gain to calculate the buffer ETF's return (less expenses).

Is My Investment Guaranteed?

No. Unlike certain insurance and structured products, buffer ETFs are not backed by the faith and credit of an issuing institution such as an insurance company or a bank, which also means buffer ETFs are not exposed to credit risk (the risk of the issuer defaulting). The options held by the ETFs are guaranteed for settlement by the Options Clearing Corporation (OCC). In the unlikely event the OCC becomes insolvent or is otherwise unable to meet its settlement obligations, the ETFs could suffer significant losses. However, regulators have heightened their oversight of the OCC due to its designation as a Systemically Important Financial Market Utility (SIFMU).

Can a Buffer ETF Show a Loss during the Intra-Outcome Period?

Yes. If the reference asset has declined during the intra-outcome period, a buffer ETF is also likely to show a loss. For example, if you own a buffer ETF that provides 15 percent protection at the start of a new outcome period, and a few months later the reference asset has dropped 10 percent, your buffer ETF will likely also show a loss, but typically not as deep as the reference asset.

REMEMBER

What's critical to understand is that although your buffer ETF could show a loss during the intra-outcome period, as long as you hold the position, and the reference asset doesn't finish the outcome period (reset day) below the buffer level, then you should not lose money (before fees). This assumes you purchased your buffer ETF at the start of a new outcome period with the full published protection.

Don't All Buffer ETFs Have Capped Performance?

No. Although the defined outcome category started with most issuers pairing downside protection with a cap on gains, TrueShares and AllianzIM have issued many uncapped alternatives. Uncapped buffer ETFs offer a level of downside protection but no cap on gains, so they have unlimited upside.

REMEMBER

With an uncapped buffer ETF, you will forgo a portion of the gains (the spread or a targeted participation rate), but in certain market environments, this could be preferable to capped alternatives.

Given the fact that 41 percent of annual returns of the S&P 500 exceed 15 percent (with a 24 percent average return during those periods), having uncapped performance in very strong markets can be a huge advantage over capped buffer ETFs.

Aren't Buffer ETFs Too Complicated?

No. Buffer ETFs are managed by experienced fund managers with deep expertise in managing options strategies. However, the ETF itself is straightforward and easy to understand. As an investor, you should focus on the following factors:

- Buffer ETF type (conventional, laddered, floor, uncapped, and so on)
- Reference asset (the underlying asset the buffer ETF tracks)
- Level of downside protection (buffer)

- Level of upside participation (cap)
- Term (length of the outcome period)
- Expense ratio

Of course, you need to consider all these factors in the context of your investment objectives and risk tolerance.

Index

A

B

C

D

E

F

G

H

I

K

L

M

N

O

P

Q

R

S

T

U

V

W

Z

About the Author

Stuart Chaussée is a fee-only investment advisor with more than four decades of experience guiding high-net-worth individuals in building, preserving, and managing their wealth. His expertise lies in designing customized, defined-outcome investment strategies that seek to balance growth with disciplined risk management.

He earned his Bachelor of Arts from the University of California, Berkeley, and a Master's degree from Thunderbird School of Global Management. Chaussée began his investment career in 1986 with Prudential-Bache Securities in Brussels, Belgium, and later worked for Merrill Lynch in both Luxembourg and Belgium. He is the founder of Stuart Chaussée & Associates, Inc.

A prolific author, Chaussée has written seven books on investing, including *Advanced Portfolio Management: Strategies for the Affluent* (Palisade Business Press), which was recognized in a *Barron's* feature titled, "The Best Investment Books of 2002." His more recent works — *Understanding Risk, Investor Behavior and Surviving Bubbles* and *Dividend Investing for Income and Growth* — are featured in *Essential Works of Stuart Chaussée.*

His insights have been quoted or cited in leading financial publications and media outlets, including *Barron's, CNBC,* ETF.com, *ETF Express, Financial Times, Investment News, Kiplinger, Reuters,* and *Yahoo Finance.*

He is married with three children and is a long-time resident of Palos Verdes Peninsula, California.

Dedications

To my parents, Dick and Jackie; my sister, Laura; my wife, Linda; and my children, Al, Daisy, and Henry — thank you for your unwavering love and support.

And to my best friend, Bryan Price, thank you for the laughter and friendship over the years.

Author's Acknowledgments

I am grateful to the following individuals for their support in the development of this book and/or my ongoing education in the buffer ETF space: Burke Ashenden, Tracy Boggier, Bruce Bond, Mike Capizzi, Jeff Chang, Graham Day, Johan Grahn, Mike Hickerson, Joe Kraynak, Whitney Kueltzo, Rick Kughen, Sam Moore, Murari Mukundan, Andrew Nelson, Mark Seume, and Igor Zamkovsky.

Publisher's Acknowledgments

Acquisitions Editor: Tracy Boggier
Managing Editor: Murari Mukundan
Development Editor: Rick Kughen
Copy Editor: Rick Kughen

Production Editor: Athiyappan Lalith Kumar
Cover Image: doraclub/stock.adobe.com